H<u>ome</u> S<u>chool</u>:

Taking The First Step

the complete
program planning guide

Also by Borg Hendrickson

How to Write a Low Cost/No Cost Curriculum for Your Home School Child

Mountain Meadow Press

THE AUTHOR

Borg Hendrickson is a former public school teacher — grades K-6 regular and remedial reading classes and grades 7-12 English. She has also served as a librarian, trained teacher aides, and given workshops to both public and home school teachers. During the 1970s and '80s she became inspired to use her knowledge of "official" educational procedures and expectations and her broad teaching experience to help home schoolers function independently as planners of their own educational programs.

Home School:

Taking the First Step

the complete
program planning handbook

by

Borg Hendrickson

Mountain Meadow Press

Home School: Taking the First Step

by Borg Hendrickson

Published by Mountain Meadow Press
P.O. Box 318
Sitka AK 99835-0318

REVISED EDITION
Fourth Printing
Printed in the United States of America

Hendrickson, Borg.
    Home school : taking the first step : a program planning handbook / by Borg Hendrickson. — Rev.
    p. cm.
    Rev ed. of work first published in 1989.
    Includes bibliographical references and index.
    ISBN 0-945519-19-2
    1. Home schooling--United States--Handbooks, manuals, etc. 2. Education--United States--Parent participation--Handbooks, manuals, etc. I. Title.
LC40.H46 1994   649'.68
                                 QB193-22123

Table of Contents

Section 2   Your Home-School Plan

Section 3   Key Components

Section 4   State Regulations and Procedures

Note:
- All names used herein as examples are fictitious.
- Feminine and masculine references are intermixed with no bias intended.
- Interpretations of state statutes are those of a layperson and do not constitute legal advice.

Acknowledgment

Special thanks to the many
home educators throughout
the United States whose
survey and telephone interview
responses provided useful
information for the original and
revised editions of this book.

Dedicated to
the public school children
who called me Ms. Borg
and who taught me
that children do not belong
in public schools.

Choice

an introduction

Tall, hulky, but not athletic. A doughy sort of hulkiness. Andy wore gabardine pants with white tube socs and oxfords in an era of blue jeans and tennis shoes. He wore a brown corduroy jacket with a dingy, simulated fur collar, the hem and sleeves too short. Bulging out of his sleeves, his forearms dangled, exposed. He looked ignorant. His brown eyes hung expressionlessly under droopy lashes, and he stood or sat, silent, still, sometimes leaning slightly as if he might keel over. Yes, he looked ignorant, but his IQ? 140.

Andy was about to graduate from high school, a virtual nobody amongst his peers, his teachers, his community...an unaccomplished boy...his brilliance blackened by lack of notice, lack of individual attention to his talents and needs, lack of academic and emotional nurturing. No one had intended to turn Andy into a nobody; it was simply that he'd been run through the system, the complex, striving but struggling, misshapen system called "public school." While the system hadn't tried to fail Andy, it had failed him. He'd been crushed in the cogs, permanently crippled, endlessly unfulfilled.

Despite the good efforts of many skilled educators and even the meager effort of those not so skilled, the American public school system misses the mark all too often. Andy exists in multiple numbers — some of high intelligence, some (according to the educators) of low, and even some of average intelligence, regardless of public education's egalitarian, middle-of-the-road attempts to teach to the average.

We don't need to lay blame. We don't need to rage with anger. We could attempt systemic reform, join the public school reform movement, but the system is truly not likely to be satisfactorily repaired ...and in the meantime your child is growing, becoming an older and older learner, until his time with "school" will be gone. Yes, you need to deal now with "in the meantime." Doing so requires choice.

How will you educate your child?

I am a former public school educator — a total of eighteen years, kindergarten through college, including teacher and teacher aide training. While I strove diligently to teach well myself, never during those eighteen years did I not question the efficacy of public schools. I continuously grappled with the mammoth, unwieldy system that public education is, became depressed at times with the stranglehold the system often administered to children's curiosity, creativity, thinking, and sense of well-being. I taught alongside many excellent teachers who managed in their own corners of the school building to fashion as many miracles as they could — despite the system. However, I also taught alongside several of the dregs of the teaching vocation. They outstayed me, incidentally, and are still there. Their perpetual presence and the overpowering dominance of the colossus that the education system has become drove me away from the public schools.

During most of my years as a public school educator, home school was a barely mentioned anomaly and the reality of home schooling as remote as a rhodora in an untouched wilderness. I had always home schooled my daughter, I realize now — evenings, weekends, summers — reading, writing, gardening, health, values, and so on, but I had not become aware of home schooling *per se.*

Then one year my brother and his family returned to Idaho to begin a ministry and to establish a Christian school. His small school was in many respects a home school. While I didn't agree with all of his teaching methods, I could see that he, his wife, and his three children supped on academic nourishment within a close and supportive family environment. The family was the educational setting. Because learning was so integral to family life, wherever the family went, along tagged learning.

I was impressed. I began to read about home schooling. Andy roamed through my thoughts as I read. Several Andys. Gradually, home schooling emerged in my mind as the best educational alternative for parents who truly intend to make a wise choice for their children's education. Thus were planted the seeds of this book. Home-school parents, I recognized, need to design educational programs that will provide a fine education for their children and also, when necessary, be acceptable to public school officials. I realized, too, that with my public school background I could help home schoolers design quality programs...without turning their home schools into public school clones. Providing that help is the intention of this book.

Home School: Taking the First Step is a book for parents who have elected to home school for many diverse reasons. My brother's reason was religious, a reason shared by a majority of home educators today. However, thousands of parents teach their children at home for other reasons. These parents also need guidance as they set out to establish effective learning environments at home.

Yes, the reasons are numerous. The benefits and rich rewards experienced by home-schooling families are likewise numerous and are noted throughout this book. But we must admit at the same time that difficulties don't entirely hide from home schoolers. Be forewarned, for example, that home schooling isn't for the lazy. Also, at the beginning, personal uncertainty may tug at you. You may fear causing your children educational harm. Questions about legalities, materials, methods, and programs may fill your mind. You and your children may at first not feel entirely comfortable with each other as learners and teacher(s). Pressure from family and friends who think home schooling constitutes child neglect may nudge at your conscience. Almost inevitably you will have to deal with some of these difficulties. However, I believe the strength of your commitment to home schooling will grow as you read this book and other books about home schooling and as you talk with practicing home schoolers. *Home School: Taking the First Step*, for starters, is chock full of confidence-builders. It shows you explicitly how to proceed. As you do begin, however, there are a few key personal characteristics you should nurture within yourself.

First, naturalness. Home schooling, you'll discover, is a much more natural process than one may expect. Have you taught your toddlers to make a peanut butter sandwich? Have you taught your daughter to sew on a button? Read to your youngsters regularly? Gardened with them? Taught your son to ride a bike? Pointed out sights, sounds, fragrances, textures, and flavors in your children's world? All such interactions with your children just happen naturally, but they are home schooling. To officially home school you needn't propel your family into a lofty world of educational space. That, in fact, is one of the things you'll be avoiding — that other world, that world of school. Instead you can keep your children at home or bring them back home to their world, your world, where you can truly, naturally teach and they learn.

Patience is a second key characteristic. Establishing a home school takes time. Learning takes time. Success takes time. Accumulating results takes time. Improved relationships with your children may take time. Caution yourself not to rush back to public school or point fingers of impatience at yourself before your home school has been carefully rooted, watered, and given ample time to flower.

Third, flexibility. Decisions won't light like butterflies onto your shoulder. You will have to study your options, argue the pros and cons of various possibilities, be open to various routes, be willing to alter your direction, listen to your children, and deal with your daily doses of home-schooling quandaries.

Fourth, participation. Heeding research which shows that parent involvement is vital to student success, public school personnel have lately invited parent participation. This is a positive step. However, in view of the research, we should recognize that to send children into the institution of public education in the first place is counteractive to that research. Parent participation is instantly diminished once the child walks out the front door to board the bus that will take him to school. Home school offers an extraordinary opportunity for parent participation in a child's education. And perhaps nothing could be more supportive of your child's learning efforts than your close and constant participation in those efforts.

Lastly, faith. You *can* home teach. Have faith in yourself. If you're feeling confused or burned out at any point, seek support and counsel — from your spouse, a fellow home schooler, a support group, a friend, God. You can home teach.

May I give you your first measure of support? Section One in this book will answer many of your initial questions and lead you to other resources for further answers. Sections Two and Three, the heart of this book, will show you how to plan your home school in a manner that will provide you with a sound beginning as a home teacher and that should prove acceptable to public school officials. Sections Four, Five and Six offer information about legalities, support groups and services, and resources. The three appendices discuss teaching methods or approaches, effective teaching, and the lesson plan. Finally, a glossary defines a roster of educational terms you may need to understand.

I wish you and your family well as you take your first step towards home schooling and throughout the duration of your joint educational journey.

Borg Hendrickson

Home-Schooling Questions and Answers

Questions and Answers

Like most potential home schoolers, you no doubt have many questions about home schooling. Some of your questions will be answered by your state's laws or established procedures. Others will best be answered by already practicing home schoolers. Many will only be answered via the immersion process once you actually start home schooling. To begin, however, *Home School: Taking the First Step* provides many answers, much in the form of step-by-step procedures you can follow to become a home schooler. First, however, let's address a few broad-view questions, questions frequently asked by parents preparing to take the first step to home school.

1. Is Home Schooling Legal?

A. Courts and state legislatures have warranted the possibility of home schooling in all the individual states. While the states have been granted the legal right and responsibility to see to the education of their citizens, a number of court cases have established that states may not limit school attendance to public schools. Nevertheless, there is no question that the states do have the legal power to reasonably regulate, inspect, and supervise schools. Your home school may be one of those "schools." Your state's education officials flex the muscles of educational authority in their own fashion and to whatever degree your state's legislators have decreed. As you read through Section Four of this book, "State Regulations and Procedures," you will get a sense of the degree of legal rigidity or flexibility your state allows with respect to home schools. Then, once you secure copies of your state's laws, regulations, and procedures and consult with other home schoolers in your area, you'll begin to understand how your state school officials, and even local school officials, operate in their dealings with home-schooling parents. You'll find that home schooling is an option, but that some requirements and/or limitations may exist.

B. All states have compulsory education laws which require parents to see that youngsters of designated ages are schooled. In a few states, laws apply almost no restrictions and requirements to home schoolers, but before you *silently* home school your children, check on your state's laws and confer with practicing home schoolers. Know the consequences of ignoring compulsory education laws. You may decide to take the risk, but at least you will have made an informed choice.

C. As you study your state's home-school requirements and compulsory education laws, beginning with the legal information for your state provided in this book, look for answers to questions such as the following:

- How is *home school* defined by my state?
- Who may home teach in my state?
- How old can my children be before I must submit their names as home-schooled children?
- Who has jurisdiction over home schools in my state? Who supervises home schools in my state and school district?
- How many hours and days must my home school be "in session" each year?
- What courses must I teach?
- Do I need a curriculum of my own? Do I need to write out lesson plans? Do I need a list of materials and resources that I plan to use?
- Must my children take standardized achievement tests?
- What records should I keep?
- Is there a formal home-school approval process that I must follow in order to legally establish my home school? Are there deadlines related to that approval process?

For now, just let these questions serve as food for thought while you read on. Sections Two and Three in this book take you step-by-step through planning processes that enable you to find and use the answers to all the above ten questions and much more. Also, Section Four provides you with basic answers to many of your legal questions, answers to verify through practicing home schoolers in your state.

D. New legislation is enacted and new court cases are processed periodically which result in changes in the legal picture of home schooling in individual states. Home schoolers not only remain alert to these changes, many home schoolers choose to affect the direction and impact of those changes through their own monitoring of legislative activities and lobbying of legislators. In the planning stages, however, you will want to concentrate on accurately informing yourself with up-to-date legal information. Section Two describes means for doing so.

2. Must I deal with my local school board and school administrators? If so, how can I work successfully with them?

A. Although in a few states home schoolers submit documents directly to state boards and state departments of education, in most states home schoolers need to deal in some manner with local school boards and school administrators — in a few cases, even if the home-schooled students have become satellite students of private schools or have enrolled in correspondence schools. In fact, in some states, all home school issues and proceedings are handled locally. But don't be dismayed. Identify with whom you will need to interact; then find out as much as you can about them; ask established home schoolers in your school district for suggestions and support; know the education laws in your state; be exceptionally well prepared as per the procedures outlined in Sections Two and Three of this book; program yourself to be firmly, persistently, but calmly diplomatic; and forge ahead looking forward to your board's approval.

B. The more amicable your relationship with local school officials, the better, for you may wish to *use* your public school in various ways during your home-school year — science lab privileges, sports or other extracurricular activity participation by your children, use of audio visual materials and equipment, academic consultation with school staff, and so on — and you may need "official" approval to do so. Generally, during the late 1980s and early '90s, increasing numbers of school districts have been opening their doors to home schoolers who wish to participate part-time in district programs. Some state legislatures have even revised laws in ways that encourage or mandate that school districts be cooperative with home schoolers. In any case, realize the potential rewards to yourself and your children in maintaining from the outset the best possible relationship with your local school board and school personnel.

C. When dealing with your local school board and staff, remember that they may know little or nothing about home schooling. This means that you may need to provide them with pertinent information. If you follow the planning procedure outlined in Section Two, you should have that information. You should be prepared, for example, to present your state's compulsory education laws and any other laws related to home schooling, plus rules, regulations, and procedures that have been adopted for the "reasonable regulation" of home schools. Then, of course, you need to demonstrate that you are complying with the laws and regulations — as you will be if you complete your planning as outlined in Sections Two and Three with adaptations for your state's requirements.

D. Some school board members and superintendents may not only know little about statutes and procedures related to home schooling, they may harbor negative attitudes towards home schoolers based partly upon their lack of knowledge. You may face school personnel who are initially hostile, or who consider you a threat to the institution they support with much time and energy, or who think you are a crazy person for being radical enough to home school. Realize, too, that school structures vary with respect to decision making. Often the superintendent's recommendations sway all decisions and he, therefore, may be the key person with whom you will deal. During exchanges with school personnel, consistently present yourself diplomatically. Present as thorough a home-school proposal as possible, making sure that it complies fully with your state's requirements. In other words, appear serious, sensible, and non-threatening, yet confident in your knowledge of procedures and in the quality of your proposal — and determined in your intention to home teach. The procedures outlined in this book will help you gain such confidence and determination.

E. You may wish to point out several of the research studies that have been conducted which show that home-schooled children fare very well in comparison with their public school peer group. The following are a few samplings and sources of such findings:

- Hewitt Research Foundation — Stanford and Iowa Achievement Test scores from 75th percentile to 95th percentile achieved by several thousand home-schooled children across the country.

- Weaver, Roy et. al., "Home Tutorials vs. Public Schools in Los Angeles," *Phi Delta Kappan*, December 1980, p. 254-255. — Home-tutored children scored higher on standardized achievement tests than did their peers in the Los Angeles public schools and also made significant gains in maturation and social growth.

- Gordon, Edward, "Home Tutoring Programs Gain Respectability," *Phi Delta Kappan*, February 1983, p. 398-399. — A majority of two thousand home-schooled children from various backgrounds achieved notable academic, attitudinal, and motivational progress.

- Living Heritage Academy — Achievement test scores averaging 72nd percentile (grade-equivalent gains of 1.4) during each home-school year were earned by several hundred home-schooled students in Texas.

- Arizona Department of Education — Home-schooled children scored at above average levels on standardized achievement tests in the mid-1980s.

- Alaska Department of Education — Of fourth grade home students who took the Iowa Tests of Basic Skills in the 1991-'92 school year, 42.9 percent scored in the top quartile in reading, 46.4 percent in the top quartile in math, and 25 percent in language arts. (Nationally, 25 percent of students score in each quartile.) Similarly, of home-schooled sixth graders, 60 percent in reading, 33.3 percent in math, and 20 percent in language arts scored in the top quartile. Of eighth graders, 46.7 percent in reading, 28.6 percent in math, and 28.6 percent in language arts scored in the top quartile.

- Duncan, Verne, Oregon Department of Education — 76.1 percent of Oregon's home-schooled students scored above average on achievement tests in 1986.

- National Home Education Research Institute — In 1990 the institute reported results of a 1416-family survey which showed that home-school students scored at least thirty points higher than national averages on standardized achievement tests in every subject tested.

- Wartes, John, Woodinville, Washington — A 1987 comparison of Western Washington home-schooled students' achievement test scores with national norms showed that, with the exception of grade one math scores at the 49th percentile, the home-schooled students at each grade level scored above the 50th percentile in all subjects.

- Quine, David N. and Edmund A. Marek, *Home School Researcher*, Vol. 4, No. 3. — Home-schooled students demonstrated thinking skills equivalent to those of students given specialized training. In a national comparison the home schoolers were well ahead of national averages and developed higher level skills at an earlier age.

- Tennessee Department of Education — In 1986, home-schooled students in grades 2, 3, 6 and 8 outscored public school students consistently. In national comparisons, the home-schooled students scored in the top 3 percent in math, top 4 percent in spelling, top 1 percent in listening skills, and top 6 percent in environmental knowledge.

- Rakestraw, Jennie F., *Home School Researcher*, Vol. 4, No. 4. SAT results showed Alabama home-schooled children at or above grade level in almost all subject areas.

- South Dakota Department of Education — In 1992, home-school fourth grade students scored at the 81st percentile in their composite scores on the Stanford Achievement Test, and in 1993 at the 76th percentile.

Additional research results are available. If you would like to study them in greater depth, you may wish to send for the following three bibliographies: "The Evidence Continues to Grow, Parent Involvement Improves Student Achievement" from the National Committee for Citizens in Education; Thomas Hughes' "Home Education: A Bibliography" from the University of Colorado; and Brian Ray's "Home Centered Learning Annotated Bibliography" from the National Home Education Research Institute. Also, John Whitehead's book *Home Education Rights and Reasons* summarizes the results of several research studies on home education. (See "Readings" in Section Six for sources of these publications.) If your own state requires home-school children to take achievement tests, your state department of education will have compiled reports of the results which should be available to you. You may further want to begin saving news clippings and reports regarding the many studies and test results that demonstrate the academic failings of public schools. Be cautious, however, of using the latter to launch an attack on public schools in general or on your local school district. Attacks typically do not result in cooperation, but rather in conflict.

F. If your initial investigations into the status of home schooling in your state suggest you may encounter opposition from school officials, you may choose to consult a lawyer before making any contact with school officials.

G. Once you have carefully informed yourself of the home-school laws in your state and made initial contact with school officials, you will want to remain available for communications with them. If their posture appears positive, feel free to openly communicate over the phone, in person, and by mail. If, on the other hand, you discover that their attitude is skeptical or negative, you may want to limit communications as much as possible to mail. Why? First, when you know antagonism exists, comfort comes with fewer face-to-face encounters. Second, offhand remarks are less likely to occur in writing. Third, strong emotional reactions on either side will be given time to mellow before responses are sent. And fourth, you will have written documentation of all exchanges, proposals, agreements, deadlines, and so on. If phone calls come, be unerringly polite, but insist that comments, promises, and requests be committed to writing and sent to you for your careful consideration and response. If face-to-face meetings are unavoidable, and if they take on negative tones, remain objective, rely on your own well-researched information, be *professional*, and amicably leave at a propitious moment. Visibly take notes while there and request just before you leave that the school personnel with whom you've been talking write out their statements and send them to you. If their doing so seems unlikely, summarize their comments by reading aloud to them your notes. Tell them you'll respond soon. Then calmly leave. To confirm your understanding of the exchange, you may wish to type your notes, date them, list persons present, and send a copy to each person who was present.

But do remain thereafter available for communication. Being evasive at this point may arouse suspicion and further ire. Retreat, consult with other home schoolers and a lawyer if need be, restudy the statutes and procedures, recognize the true legal limits of the school officials' authority so you can determine if they have overstepped their bounds, and prepare your response. Avoid responding with more than what is needed if antagonism is present. Just prepare what you are legally obligated to prepare in response. You may even choose to completely ignore other areas for which they request information or action. You want to avoid confrontations over issues that simply muddy the waters, that are not legally issues that school personnel in your district have a right to address. Politely acknowledge their concern over such issues, but avoid commenting in response.

H. Relax. Only a very small percentage of the home schoolers in our country are pushed by local school boards and administrators into court. Most issues can be and are resolved through persistent nonjudicial communication. Further, the national media have in recent years provided the general public with increasing numbers of reports that depict home schooling either in a neutral or positive light and as a fairly common and widespread alternative educational choice. Partly in response to the attitude of acceptance reflected overall in these reports, many school personnel today are becoming more open to, even favorable towards, home schoolers. One aim of *Home School: Taking the First Step* is to enable you to present so impressive a home-school plan that school personnel will not just be favorable, but agreeable, flexible, and even cooperative.

3. What are my options if I'm not legally qualified to home teach?

A. In almost all states certification of home-school teachers is not mandatory, and in all states some option exists for noncertified home teachers. Check the "Basic Information Chart" in Section Four of this book for your state's specifications regarding certification.

B. If you are unable to qualify as a home teacher in your state, consider other alternative schooling options: enrolling your child in a church school or other private school, correspondence school, or community alternative school; attaching your home school as a satellite to a private school; becoming a single-family private or religious school if allowed in your state; arranging for a certified person in your community to do the home teaching (for the most part); enrolling your child as an extension student with a public school; moving to a state which has less restrictive qualification requirements. Please note also that many states are quite liberal with religious-conflict exemptions from adherence to public school regulations, including certification requirements. If you feel particularly energetic, you may want to join with other parents to start your own multi-family private or church school. (Read Robert Love's *How to Start Your Own School*, a couple issues of the *National Coalition News* or a copy of the "National Directory of Alternative Schools" published by the National Coalition of Alternative Community Schools, or portions of Allen Graubard's *Free the Children*) Perhaps you or your spouse works for a company that would be willing to create a quality, private "company school" for the children of its employees. You might try the certified teacher-consultant-supervisor option, if it is allowed in your state. In any case, read carefully through the legal information you obtain from your state department to determine which option will be the most feasible in your state.

C. In every state you will find home-school support groups. Contact them to ask about alternatives for noncertified or legally unqualified parent teachers. See Section Five for a list of home-school groups in your state or region.

D. Consider taking the National Teacher Exam or any teachers' exam given in your state in order to verify your literacy. Fear not… these exams test *basic* skills and knowledge. Also, if you pass, check your state's statistics on the scores of persons in your state who have taken the test. You'll find failures! In some states, many failures. However, regardless of low scores, some of those who failed may be teaching in the public schools. In fact, certification is granted in some states to applicants who score at the 50th percentile. This information could provide good ammunition in a battle to prove your qualifications.

E. If even *you* doubt the effectiveness of home schoolers who are noncertified, consider the impressive results of the studies noted in question *2, e.* About 80 percent of the parents who home taught those children included in the studies were not certified and most did not have college degrees.

F. If yours is a state which maintains restrictive teacher qualification requirements, perhaps you and others would like to challenge those requirements in court. Read *Phi Delta Kappan*, June 1986, "Emergency Certificates, Misassignment of Teachers, and Other 'Dirty Little Secrets'" by Robert A. Roth for a stunning rundown of public school staffing practices that indirectly lends support to noncertified and unqualified home educators. Locate and read home-school studies, such as those noted in answer *2, e* above. You may also wish to contact the Home School Legal Defense Association in Virginia before engaging in any interactions with officials. (Address in Section Five.) Also, from time to time some of the home-school periodicals list lawyers friendly to home schooling.

G. As noted earlier, in response to qualification requirements, some parents opt to *silently* home teach their children. As a last resort — are you one of them?

4. Will my home-schooled children be too isolated? Don't they need socializing?

A. Since you are already concerned about your children's socialization, it is likely that you will see to it that they are not too isolated. And, yes, they do need socializing, but...

B. Who says socializing is the exclusive territory of peers? Children need various kinds of socializing: with relatives — young, old, and in-between; with neighbors and friends — young, old, and inbetween; with your entire immediate family (perhaps most important, yet in many families most neglected); and *sometimes* exclusively with peers. Public school children, who interact almost entirely with peers, become what has been termed "peer dependent," a state of dependency into which I doubt you want your children to sink — unless, of course, you'd like your children's choices of clothing, hairdos, readings, activities, values, behaviors, and more, strongly influenced, if not entirely molded by, their peer group.

C. According to *The Random House College Dictionary* (N.Y.: Random House, 1988), the term *socialize* means "make fit for life in companionship with others." Have you visited a public school playground lately or spent a day eavesdropping on public school children's conversations? My eighteen years of on-the-scene observations confirm that children in public schools learn (every day, every year) that "companionship with others" involves bullying, gossiping, ostracizing, competing, fist-fighting, humiliating...how lengthy a list I could write (and some involve the teachers as well as the children). Then consider a few statistics: As reported by CBS News in October of 1993, during the 1992 school year, 500,000 weapons went to school with students of our public schools. According to *U.S. News and World Report* (November 8, 1993), "Today, more than three million crimes a year are committed in or near the 85,000 U.S. public schools...." Drugs of various degrees of potency are routinely available in virtually every public school in the nation. You can imagine what happens *within* a child as he becomes "fit for life in companionship" with other public school children. How *fit* do you want *your* children to be?

D. Nonetheless, your child does need some socialization with other children. You can arrange for that and yet maintain more control over your child's socialization experiences than public school teachers are able to provide. Conflicts will surely arise even in carefully selected peer situations, and you won't want to overprotect, but for your home-schooled child you can at the least minimize the indoctrination effect. Arrange and/or encourage your child's involvement in youth group activities — and be involved yourself at times too. Sports activities, musical groups, church groups, nature clubs, arts and crafts workshops, Scouts, community drama groups, neighborhood kids' activities, kiddie parades, youth roller-skating or ice skating, children's reading clubs, storytime at the local library, and so on, are often potential socialization opportunities in even the smallest of American towns. If few are available, perhaps you and another parent or two could organize some. Many home-school parents and kids join each other for regular fun days, field trip days, or craft days. Taking your child to a public park at times when other children are typically there is another option. Also, public schools offer special kids' activities in which your child may be able to participate. As noted under question 2 in this section, if your relationship with your local school board and with school administrators is friendly, you may be able to use the local schools in this way. Explore possible participation for your child in school band or choir, science fairs, sports teams, etc., if you and your child are interested in such activities that the public school offers. In some school districts, home students may even enroll in academic classes on a limited by-choice basis. Sometimes special classes, which may fit into a home-school student's schedule and bring him in contact with other learners, are offered by local organizations, such as the YMCA craft associations, city park and recreation departments, or by local alternative schools.

E. Socialization can also take place within your child's learning community. You need not teach your child alone. Instead, develop for him a learning community — an elder who share-teaches a craft with him or shares stories of old with him, community service folks who involve your child in their service work, neighbors with whom he can exchange favors (such as errands or chores), team experiences with other children and with adults, pen pals, a librarian who accepts his volunteer help in a library, a younger child to whom he can read, customers who buy his small business products or services (such as a neighborhood kids' newspaper, vegetables for sale, a neighborhood yard-garbage clean-up service, or a vacation dog-watching service), a music instructor, a dance instructor and fellow dancers, an older person with whom he simply likes to visit a lot, an expert who visits your home to "teach" a day's lesson, a practitioner with whom he could be an apprentice, anyone with whom your child shares learning or from whom your child learns.

F. Read together and discuss together biographies of people who have contributed significantly to or exhibited sensitivity to the welfare of the community, of human society globally, and of the environment.

G. Play *cooperative* games with your children. You can turn many board games and outdoor games into activities in which players help each other reach a common goal. Begin by sending for a copy of the Animal Town Game Company catalog and the Family

Pastimes catalog for good selections of cooperative games. (See addresses in Section Six materials list.) These catalogs may also stimulate your thinking so that you might develop cooperative games of your own. To help yourself along, you may wish to read the *Parents Magazine*, April 1988, article "Everybody Wins" which discusses and gives examples of cooperative games or one of the following books about cooperative games: *The Cooperative Sports and Games Book* or *The Second Cooperative Sports and Games Book* both by Terry Orlick; *The New Games Book* edited by Andrew Fluegelman. (See "Readings" in Section Six.)

H. Create cooperative learning lessons in which your children and any other available children work together towards common learning goals. To plan these lessons, establish your goals and then design activities or help your children identify activities that each child, according to his individual capabilities, can perform and that contribute to the attainment of the common goals. For more ideas, read *Tribes: A Process for Social Development and Cooperative Learning* by Jeanne Gibbs.

I. Contrary to the opinions of many public educators, your child's positive sense of self may actually improve in your home-school social setting. During a 1986 study of 224 home-schooled children, John Wesley Taylor V found that only 10 percent scored below the national average on the Piers-Harris Children's Self-Concept Scale, a measure of self-esteem. According to another study, public school children lose their sense of self-worth dramatically as they progress through the grades — from 80 percent with a strong sense of self-worth at school entrance dropping to 20 percent by fifth grade and to 5 percent at twelfth grade. Several of Raymond Moore's publications elaborate on the significance of home schooling in the development of a sound self-concept, and John Whitehead's *Home Education Rights and Reasons* cites further socialization studies. (See "Readings" in Section Six.)

J. If you are living in a physically remote location, you do have a more unique situation with regards to isolation and socialization. Activity may be the key; i.e., staying active with a wide variety of home projects. And you can be a model for your children as a person who enthusiastically pursues her own interests. Pen pals and phone pals is another possibility, or computer network or ham radio friendships. Also, reading about others who have lived and worked in isolation may provide models for such a lifestyle. You might try stories of the lives of zoological researchers, archaeologists, anthropologists, and adventurers, for example. Lastly, if possible, you could invite visitors, perhaps other children, to stay with you to work on a particular week's project or arrange for a sibling exchange with a family who lives elsewhere. Your children could trade brothers and sisters with children from another family for a few day's time.

K. Finally, consider the results of a study done during the sixties by Dr. Harold G. McCurdy of the University of North Carolina. Dr. McCurdy sought information about the childhood lives of twenty historical geniuses in order to derive common factors in their upbringing. He discovered three such factors: 1) "a high degree of attention focused upon the child by parents and other adults, expressed in intensive educational measures...and usually abundant love;" 2) "isolation from other children, especially outside the family;" and 3) "a rich efflorescence of fantasy, as a reaction to the two preceding conditions." ("The Childhood Pattern of Genius." *Horizons*, May 1960) You need not have genius expectations for your child, and socialization with peers is without doubt beneficial to some extent; nevertheless, isolation or a lack of socialization for your home-schooled child can be dealt with and aspects of isolation combined with abundant attention and love from you may prove beneficial.

5. What if my child is "exceptional?"

A. Take heart. In many states, special exemptions from compulsory education laws are allowed for exceptional children. You may find the route *home* simpler with your exceptional learner. Write your state department for copies of the laws and regulations. Check information from home-school support groups.

B. Be wary of labels that public schools may have placed upon your child. *Learning disabled*, for example, has become greatly overused and unjustifiably used, according to an abundance of research. There are even cases in which students identified as learning disabled were upon further study found to be intellectually gifted! There are, of course, learner labels based upon true individual learner characteristics and there are test results that do indeed establish exceptionality. A child's being severely mentally retarded, for example, may be unquestionable. Generally, however, be skeptical of labels applied to kids by educators. If you have a child labeled "learning disabled," you may wish to read Gerald Cole's *The Learning Mystique: A Critical Look at Learning Disabilities*. The title of the cover story of the December 13, 1993, issue of *U.S. News* conveys the seriousness of this problem: "Separate and Unequal: How Special Education Programs Are Cheating Our Children and Costing Taxpayers Billions Each Year."

C. If your child truly does learn slowly, according to your own observations as well as other information, then home teaching is almost without exception going to be highly beneficial to your child. You will be able to provide him with an approach that suits his pace, with loads of individual attention, with methods that are particularly matched to his learning style, with a noncompetitive setting, with much needed motivational feedback, and with desperately needed love and acceptance. If he has been attending public school, it is possible, even probable, that none of the above have been provided.

Recent efforts to curb the numbers of students who attend special education classes in public schools and to place them instead in regular classrooms may or may not alter this fact.

D. A 1986 study by the Appalachia Educational Laboratory and the Kentucky Education Association, involving public teacher responses to a survey covering methods of teaching marginal learners, resulted in several recommendations. Among the most frequently noted successful methods were 1) a reinforcing atmosphere, 2) wide use of community facilities and resource personnel, and 3) designing instruction for individual students. (From "Tips for Teaching Marginal Learners" published by the AEL and the KEA.) I think you'll agree that these tried and proven methods can much more satisfactorily and easily be practiced at home school than at public school.

E. If you have a special needs child and are interested in learning more about learning handicaps, you may wish to contact the Learning Disabilities Association of America located in Pennsylvania, the Council for Exceptional Children in Virginia, the National Challenged Homeschoolers Associated Network in Washington State, and the National Committee for Citizens in Education in the District of Columbia. (See "Support Services" in Section Five.) You may also want to review copies of *The Exceptional Parent* magazine. (See "Periodicals for Parent Educators" in Section Six.)

F. Studies have demonstrated that exceptional children on the lower end of the academic spectrum fare much better on tests when the administrator of the test is a familiar person. In view of this, do all you can to insist that you, your spouse, or a certified-teacher friend of your child give your child achievement tests or other necessary tests, either before or after your child has been labeled "exceptional."

G. If your child is gifted or talented, sending him to public school may constitute, educationally, the metaphorical kiss of death. Home schooling may indeed save his most precious of assets: his exceptional ability and his love of learning. Home schooling may literally save the *life* of his thinking and creativity. Need I say more? (Also, see the National Association for Gifted Children, located in Minnesota, and the Council for Exceptional Children in Virginia. You may wish to read copies of the *Gifted Children Monthly*, *Gifted Child Quarterly* and *Gifted Child Today*, all listed in in Section Six.)

6. If I decide to home school, how can I find out more about child growth and development and its relationship to education?

A. Observe children. Watch your own children and others; take mental or written notes as you do so. Those older than your child may provide clues to the next stages in your child's growth. Watch for changing styles and attitudes involved in your children's interactions with other people, young and old. Watch for those life processes, endeavors, and topic areas that interest and enthuse your children. You'll be gaining ideas for areas of study to include in future lessons for your children. Equally important clues can be gained from noting the length of your children's attention spans and the level of action in their activities. You'll discover, for example, that attention spans grow with age, and that typically a higher amount of action will be an important element in the lessons of the youngest of your children, or at least alternated periods of active and quiet activity. Using information such as this, you can develop home-school lessons and projects that will involve appropriate time spans and action levels.

B. Go to the public library and to nearby college libraries. You'll find both popular/informal and more technical books on the subject of child growth and development. Read enough to give yourself a feel for your child's upcoming growth stages and to derive ideas for home study methods and subjects that will appeal to your child at his current stage. Several of the available books about home schooling offer descriptions of young learners in action, providing readers with clues to childhood development. You may wish to read Raymond and Dorothy Moore's book *Home Grown Kids*, for example. (Also see "Readings" in Section Six.)

C. Read parents' magazines. *Christian Parenting, Parents Magazine, Parenting, Family Life* and *Mothering* are five possible choices. Likewise, read books on parenting, widely available in libraries and bookstores nationwide.

D. Remember that children develop at individual paces according to organic time clocks and that at home school you'll want not to interrupt or try to reprogram your children's natural paces. Doing so is a serious public school flaw. For the sake of egalitarianism, public schools have traditionally attempted to corral the varying developmental time clocks of children into single, age-mandated learning rates. Studying information about child growth and development will help you understand generally your children's stages, but always rely on your own observations to determine how your children individually fit into your findings.

E. Raymond Moore, a well-known home-school proponent, has written extensively about school readiness and unreadiness, as did John Holt, David Elkind, and several others. Moore points out that many studies, often ignored by public schools, indicate that we place youngsters in formal learning situations far too early and that home is the best environment for learning and socializing until a child is between eight to ten years old. If you are interested in learning more about school readiness, you may want to read Raymond Moore's *School Can Wait* and *Better Late than Early*. David Elkind's

Miseducation: Preschoolers at Risk and *The Hurried Child: Growing Up Too Fast Too Soon* also provide insights regarding child development and school readiness. These writers and others confirm for us what we may have suspected all along — forced learning is unhealthy and can result in deep frustration, lethargy, rebelliousness, and a lifelong aversion to schooling and to learning.

F. Check a college bookstore for books about human growth and development, books which are typically the texts for courses the college offers. Also check other bookstores.

G. If feasible, attend parenting workshops and/or participate in parent support groups. Check regional newspapers for possible announcements listing topics, times, and places. Check area college catalogs for parenting courses. Some home-school support organizations also offer parenting classes and workshops.

H. If you have serious concerns about your child's growth and development, make an appointment to see a pediatrician or youth counselor to discuss your concerns. Public school counselors or school psychologists may be helpful or lead you to other help. And often clergy persons can offer suggestions for professional help. Don't wait. Frequently in public school classrooms serious concerns are dealt with through traditional and ongoing methods of maintaining control rather than through sincere, active attempts to *help* the child *now*. Avoid relying on traditional public school means of dealing with serious behavioral problems. Remember, as you and I know, public school may be the *cause* of a child's developmental problems!

7. If I decide to home teach, how can I find out more about teaching methods that are supported by current research?

A. Go to a university library to find journals for educators in the specific fields of your interest. Although the presumption is that the readers of most of these journals are public school classroom teachers, usually the methods can easily be applied to teaching just one or two or three children at home. Also you can usually trust that the methods offered in these journals are based on up-to-date educational practices.

You'll find many, such as *The Reading Teacher* for elementary grade teachers of reading, *School Arts* and *Arts and Activities* for art and craft instruction, *Learning* and *Instructor* which include teaching ideas in varied subject areas, *The Computing Teacher* for computer activities and software reviews, *Journal of Reading* for secondary reading methods, and several others.

B. At university libraries and bookstores you'll also find dozens of books — many easily used by nonprofessionals — about teaching methods for virtually every subject. Look for the most comprehensive ones. You may find, for example, James Moffett and Betty Jane Wagner's book *Student-Centered Language Arts and Reading, K-13: A Handbook for Teachers*, a guide to the design of a language arts and reading curriculum.

C. Write to organizations, such as The National Wildlife Federation (address in Section Six), your local fish and game department, arts councils, health and safety organizations, literary groups, and so on, many of which frequently publish materials for use in teaching — materials typically more than sound with respect to teaching methodology.

D. Search for other books about home schooling; you'll find several revealing and wonderful depictions of fine teaching methods. For a beginning, try these:

- Nancy Wallace's books, *Better than School: One Family's Declaration of Independence*, an insightful record of a family's home-schooling experiences beginning with their initial decision to home school and their proposal to the local school board; and *Child's Work: Taking Children's Choices Seriously*, about how well education happens when you support your children's own learning choices and routes.

- John Holt's *Teach Your Own* - home-school philosophies and how-tos; and *What Do I Do Monday?* - philosophies, how-tos and math and reading sections.

- Howard S. Rowland's *No More School*, an account of an American family's year of home schooling in Spain.

- Theodore E. Wade's *The Home School Manual* includes subject area teaching suggestions.

- Mario Pagnoni's *The Complete Home Educator*, on computer education methods.

- Raymond and Dorothy Moore's *Home-Style Teaching*, depicting home education in action.

- Paul Copperman's *Taking Books to Heart; How to Develop a Love of Reading in Your Child*, a guide to reading sessions at home for parents of children two to nine.

- Micki and David Colfax's *Homeschooling for Excellence* - home-schooling philosophies, experiences and methods of the Colfaxes whose sons were accepted by Harvard, Yale, and Princeton after being almost exclusively schooled at home.

- Peter R. Stillman's *Families Writing*, on families writing together.

E. Confer with experienced home schoolers regarding methods they have found successful. Those with whom I've spoken give foremost emphasis to the need for flexibility and to the importance of not copying public schools. You'll find many suggestions for teaching methods from other home schoolers in *Home Education Magazine*, *Growing Without Schooling*, *The Teaching Home*, *Homeschooling Today*, and other home-school publications. (Addresses in Section Six.)

F. Make friends with a public school instructor who is an excellent teacher. (Avoid consulting other public school teachers.) The excellent teacher probably reads current teaching literature, takes courses in the application of new teaching methods, and practices applying them in his classroom. Ask him for recommended readings or even a course you might take and perhaps for permission to observe him in action. One caution: watch and draw from the subject matter teaching methods, not from the public school system in action. Inculcating yourself with public school classroom processes will likely lead to stifled teaching and learning at home. You won't want to duplicate public school methods *en masse*, just borrow a few subject area methods that work.

G. Read Appendix A, "Teaching Methods/Approaches" and Appendix B, "Effective Teaching" at the end of this book.

H. Do not ignore what your children themselves silently or verbally tell you about effective teaching methods. *Teaching methods* should not imply *imposition*. Children often know for themselves their own effective learning methods, and teaching methods should primarily be means by which parent teachers encourage and stimulate learning methods that work for children. Listen to your children's *methods*.

8. How can I be sure my children will be motivated to learn at home?

A. If your children have already attended public school, they may need a period of weaning from forced learning. Children are sometimes unmotivated to learn (or to be in any way productive) *because of* the methods used in public schools to make them learn and produce. While many attempts to motivate public school students involve enthusiasm and the genuine interests of children, others are negative in nature. Think about some of those negative methods: surveillance, coercion, regimentation, forced conformity, competitive pressure, punishments, and extrinsic rewards (letter grades, stickers, awards, privileges, parties, etc., external to the act of learning itself). Children, first of all, can become stressed by such methods. Also, they'll likely conclude that learning is supposed to be done, not because of their fascination with the world of knowledge nor because of their innate love of learning, but because some other person pressures them to learn and threatens punishments otherwise or because a reward is offered as the result of carrying out the act of learning. Pressures, punishments and extrinsic rewards — for something one just naturally loved to do as a toddler — often results in sadness, in a sense that something is askew, and in a lack of genuine self-motivation, even amongst the brightest of children. Many children just tolerate school while following their deepest learning passions outside of the classroom. Or they learn to vegetate. To tune out. Or to rebel. Education researchers estimate that between 10 and 20 percent of all high school dropouts are intellectually gifted. (For further explanation of the long-term negative effects of extrinsic reinforcement, read Alfie Kohn's book, *Punished by Rewards*. See Section Six.)

Research demonstrates that if the rewards are removed, the *extrinsic* ones, motivation will begin to emerge. Deep within, your children already naturally, organically love to learn. Let them *intrinsically* — inside themselves — feel the joy and excitement, because therein lay the true, natural, most highly motivating reward — and the most highly effective learning. Once you and they are able to rekindle that joy they were born with, motivation and learning for them will never cease. And you will have given them an exquisite lifelong gift.

B. You can in fact urge and feed that inner joy. Your children do seek your acknowledgement and approval of their learning efforts, and you can provide it in several ways. The most important way perhaps is offering your companionship in their efforts. Be close, be supportive, be facilitative, be physically and mentally involved with them as they learn. Take them and their efforts seriously. Respect those efforts. Encourage them to freely question. Help them find answers. Your involvement will demonstrate that learning is one of your values and joys. You will be modeling. You will be nurturing. And you will have given them an exquisite lifelong gift.

C. There are also verbal means to encourage motivation. Acknowledgement, for example, can be extended verbally. For instance, you should frequently comment on specifically what it is you like in the work your children do. Not, "That's a nice story," but "I love that funny, clever clown in your story! His antics are described in such fine detail." Or more objectively, "You were trying to draw a pattern for your new toy box. But you fear the pieces still don't fit quite right. Do you want to remeasure and adjust them?" Such acknowledgement statements confirm the learner's efforts. They don't steal away the learner's intrinsic motivation to continue. Train yourself to use them.

Also, let your child own his achievements. Not, "I'm so proud of how colorful your picture is." Instead, "You must feel mighty proud of how colorful your picture is." Or, "You sure can feel satisfied with the towers on your sand castle." Or, "I'll bet your tummy's growling for those vegies you're growing so well in your garden." Comments like these let the pride rest where it belongs, inside your child. And there it will lead to self-evaluation, self-motivation, and trust in himself as a learner-doer.

D. Again, I urge you to read books like those already noted above that depict and describe home schooling. You'll see learner motivation at work. Also, confer with experienced home schoolers. This is always possible at least by telephone if you get in touch with a support organization. (See Section Five.)

E. Finally, have faith in and patience with both you and your children. Especially if your children have previously attended public school, the motivation issue may be a problem during the days of transition to home schooling. Struggle with it, work with it, trust your intuitions. Read and reread items b, c, and d above until they become ingrained aspects of your involvement in your children's learning. And look for ways of enmeshing more home and environment into your children's schooling, and less of *school* into their schooling.

9. Where will I find the materials I will need to teach my children at home?

A. All around you! One major deficiency of public school is that the environment in which we live and the *real* world of the child are most often left out. At home the world around you can provide a plethora of educational material. Life itself can become your children's educational medium. In public school the system is the medium and, as we well know, problems result.

How can you bring the real world into your home-school lessons? A few examples: To introduce a unit of study on simple machines to a group of fourth graders, I once hung on the wall for visual and tactile exploration common household and woodworking tools — a nail clipper, a curling iron (fulcrums and levers), a screw, a door wedge (inclined plane), etc. In this case real-life objects that were just lying about the house and garage were used to stir interest and lead into structured lessons. To enhance a unit of study on the life cycle of plants, you might help your children dig up and plant seedlings from your lilac hedge, or let your children plant your tulip bulbs, or root cuttings from a houseplant in a glass of water, or grow sprouts, or take *learning* tours through a local park or forest, or press and dry plants harvested from the outdoors at different stages in their growth. To study rural life versus town or city life, take *learning* trips to a farm, to a small town, to a metropolis. Work these items and places into your plans for each unit of study, so you have clearly in mind your children's learning goals as you guide them into and through the world around them. Each time you plan a unit of study, ask yourself how many real objects and places you can work into your plans.

B. There are hundreds of materials suppliers throughout the U.S. Their names and addresses are listed in various home-schooling books and in the many home-school newsletters and periodicals. You'll discover many that supply materials for general use, others for specific subject areas only, others for particular educational philosophies or approaches, such as Bible-based education. Hundreds are both listed and annotated in several of the books listed in the "Readings" portion of Section Six. Among them, for example, you'll find Mary Pride's 4-volume set *The Big Books of Home Learning,* Donn Reed's *The Home School Source Book*, and Rebecca Rupp's *Good Stuff: Learning Tools for All Ages.* In addition, resources are often noted or reviewed in the major home-school magazines and in support group newsletters large and small. To get started, however, look through the teaching materials portion of Section Six in this book where numerous and varied suppliers are listed.

Remember, too, that you needn't look at all available materials to get started; that would take weeks. But don't accept the first batch of materials that comes to your attention. Do look through enough to find those that suit your children's learning levels and learning styles, that offer potential for learning in gradually greater degrees of difficulty, that allow for multilevel activities if you have children of various ages and stages, that will help you make learning fun and stimulating for your children, and, very importantly, that suit your teaching style. You want to find materials that not only include information you want to teach (your curriculum) but that feel right to you as a teacher. This will get easier once you've taught a bit and know how you like to teach. Be adventuresome; be flexible. If, for example, you are more comfortable with and more stimulated by teaching with manipulatives, realia, environmental items, etc., then look for manuals and texts that allow for the inclusion of lots of those items. A couple of good examples of teaching aids along these lines are the *Naturescope* teacher's manuals for science (National Wildlife Federation), and a couple of books with self-explanatory titles, *EcoArt: Earth Friendly Art and Craft Experiences* by Laurie Carlson and *The Backyard Scientist* by Jane Hoffman. See Section Six for several other titles. Also, consider journal writing based on outdoor experiences, teaching math with manipulatives (try Mary Baratta-Lorton's *Math Their Way*), creating real-life historical dramas, or building the Mayflower from a textbook picture (instead of just looking at the picture). If you are a teacher who feels most comfortable teaching with aids and texts such as these, you will feel stymied, frustrated, trapped, and bored with a prepackaged full-curriculum program that follows a similar method in all subject areas and/or that keeps you and your children sitting in your learning chairs all day. On the other hand, perhaps a blend of methods and materials is best for you.

At any rate, as you begin to look for teaching texts and manuals and aids, listen to your intuitions about those you could comfortably and enthusiastically use to teach and those that, in turn, would make learning most interesting to your children. Among the many teachers whom I have observed throughout the years, those who have been the most creative in selecting and inventing materials that suit their teaching styles and the most creative in designing lessons that use those materials to meet students' needs and interests have without exception been the best teachers. You can be creative too.

C. Many Christian, alternative and other private schools offer materials to home schoolers, as do other cooperative services. Several such schools are listed in Section Six.

D. Your local school is also a potential source of materials. If you've established a friendly relationship with a local principal, ask him about the possibility of borrowing materials. Many of the public school teachers' manuals allow for flexibility, even encourage using the accompanying texts only as supplements. However, despite recent educational reform attempts to free teachers from the constraints of being locked in to textbooks, too many public school teachers don't use texts selectively nor go much beyond the texts. Instead, the texts dominate and control classroom activities. At home, you're in control and you can go beyond textbooks. In other words, public school texts aren't to be feared, just used selectively and creatively. So your local public school may be a source of free materials.

E. In several states curriculum guides (or frameworks of learning goals) and materials lists are available (usually for a fee) from the state department of education. Curriculum guides and frameworks are skeletons of the knowledge, skills, or competencies a student will attempt to gain as he works through any course of study. Check the summary for your state in Section Four for the availability of guides and other materials. Teaching methods and materials are sometimes recommended or suggested in guides, but usually not mandated. You can use some, reject some or all, add some, alter some. But, you may find a state curriculum guide or framework helpful as a reference, especially if you feel unsure about designing an entire curriculum yourself in a particular subject area and in selecting materials all on your own.

Tackling the task of writing parts of or an entire curriculum is not actually as daunting as you may think and can save you all the dollars you may otherwise spend on purchased curriculums. Read *How to Write a Low Cost/No Cost Curriculum for your Home-School Child* to find out, step-by-step, how to write a curriculum custom-tailored to meet your child's educational needs and interests. (See Section Six.)

F. University bookstores often stock teaching materials useful to home schoolers, and Christian and other bookstores not only may have teaching materials and books full of teaching ideas, but may be able to order many for you if you supply the names of the titles you want. In large towns and cities you may be able to find a school supply store where all sorts of teaching supplies, from glue to text-books, are available. And if you're looking for computer software, most towns and cities have computer stores. As you browse through the software offered by those stores, you might jot down names and addresses of the companies who make the software and write to ask for catalogs. In the company catalogs you are likely to find numerous programs not stocked locally but that you can order. Also, software distributors from whom you can order at reduced prices advertise in computer magazines. These magazines also aid consumers by review-ing new software. These reviews can be very helpful when you're try-ing to sift through and select from the thousands of educational soft-ware programs available today.

G. For materials in special interest areas, such as art, music, rock collecting, wildlife biology, bird-watching, dancing, etc., ask local adults involved in those fields for recommendations and check with organizations related to those subjects. Some of the organiza-tions included in the support list in Section Five of this book offer instructional materials, and there are many other organizations that do so as well. If you enroll your children as home-school satellite stu-dents of a Christian or other private school, you will probably be pro-vided materials as well as full curriculums. Look them over carefully ahead of time to be sure they project your educational philosophies and suit your teaching style and your child's learning style. Also, be sure they allow the degree of flexibility you seek.

10. Having been home schooled for a period of months or years, will my child, if he wishes, be able to enter or return smoothly to public education?

A. As previously noted, studies have shown that home-schooled children typically perform above national averages on achievement tests. In view of these studies, you probably needn't fear that your child won't compare well academically with public school children.

B. Your child may be required to take subject-related placement exams and her coursework may be reviewed for course verification by public school personnel as part of her admission into an accredited public school. If school personnel hesitate to acknowledge your child's home-school achievement and attempt to place your child below her academic level in public school, you may need to insist that placement exams be given. In any case, you will want to oversee this process yourself and give input regarding her placement. Have faith that you can have an influence in this matter. In fact, be deter-mined to have an influence. Dr. Linwood Laughy's *Getting the Best Bite of the Apple* provides step-by-step guidance on how to remain in control of your child's education in a public school by understanding and then effectively interacting *within* the public school scene. You may also wish to read the article "A,B,C, or F; Test Your Child's School," which appeared in *Parents Magazine*, November 1987 issue and focused on how parents can introduce themselves to their child's school and *Parenting's* February, 1993, cover story "Your Public School: How to Make It Better. Now." You may further wish to contact the National Committee for Citizens in Education and the Alliance for Parent Involvement in Education for information regarding parental rights and involvement in public schools. (See Section Five.)

C. If you keep full and accurate records of your child's home-school attendance, work, materials, tests, etc., as delineated in Section Three, these records will provide evidence to a public school staff of the sequence and levels of your child's lessons and of her achievement.

D. Be aware that in public school your home-schooled child may stand out as unique in some ways from other children, perhaps especially in learning style and thinking skills. Support these uniquenesses. They are the stuff of which true learners are made. They are exactly those assets your home-schooling efforts can lovingly set out to nurture.

E. If you have socialized your child according to the suggestions given under question 4 above and in other ways you and she devise, she will likely socialize herself comfortably when she returns to public school. She will already have acquaintances among public school children and perhaps teachers, and may already be involved in activities with them. She will probably have interacted frequently with a variety of adults and will have gained skills that enable smooth, rewarding relationships with teachers as persons and as new members of her learning community. In addition, she will have acquired at home a strong set of values and views that will enable her to socialize at public school without loosing the *self* you have so lovingly helped her develop.

However, do keep tabs on this issue. As earlier acknowledged, public schools are not typically pleasant or particularly healthy places with regards to socialization. During your home-school years with your child, the two of you will have developed a close, trusting relationship; maintain that relationship when she enrolls in public school. You can learn to periodically check in with her emotional/psychological/social frame of mind and discuss with her any problems that evolve out of her public school social interactions.

F. Do be prepared for initial change anxiety. As anyone might, your child could experience a period of anxiety due to the process of change. The pace, regimen, crowding, and other organizational factors at public school may cause the greatest anxiety and stress for your child when she enrolls. To ease her into the routine, explain and discuss with her ahead of time the pattern of public school days, the numbers of students in classrooms, the lessening of freedom and friendliness she may experience, and other such factors that you are aware of that are peculiar to the public school she will attend. Let her vent her frustrations with any of this and express her views and thoughts about how she can deal with these factors. A visit to the classroom and with the new teacher may help. Ask the teacher to describe the daily routine and to provide a small tour of the facility explaining how various locations in the building will relate to your child's daily life at public school. When she starts attending classes, you can attempt to provide some continuity by becoming an observer or volunteer in her classroom. Frequently be a presence there, at least for the first few weeks and use Dr. Laughy's *Getting the Best Bite of the Apple* as a guide to effective public school parent interaction.

G. Continue to provide opportunities for your child to interact with her home-school learning community even after she returns to public school. In this way, she will be comforted by the integration of the old into the new and not be as likely to develop a sense of estrangement. At this time, remember, too, that you, as her home-school teacher, should continue to be a part of her expanded learning community. Find hours to spend with her in the fashion that you and she shared in home school.

11. If my child completes twelfth grade at our home school, will he be issued a diploma by the local school board or by the state board of education?

A. No. In a few states, *maybe.*

B. Before your child's senior year, encourage him to think about college choices if he is planning to attend college. Most colleges don't require a high school diploma; they are more concerned with SAT* or ACT* scores. However, if his college choice is one of those that does require a diploma, you probably will want to contact the college about obtaining a waiver to that entrance requirement, particularly if his SAT and/or ACT scores are high. A slight trend away from the use of SAT and ACT scores seems to be underway in some of the nation's colleges. However, those schools do look for hard evidence of other sorts — high school records, achievement test results, extracurricular projects and endeavors, and the like. With deliberateness, you can maintain and provide such written

---

*SAT and ACT are the Scholastic Assessment Tests and the American College Testing Service aptitude test, which are taken by many high school students nationwide as a prerequisite to college entrance. The tests measure verbal and mathematical skills and are considered predictive of college academic success. The SAT has recently been redesigned and now assesses a wider variety of subject areas.

evidence of your child's home-school years. You might consider enrolling him as a satellite or correspondence student for his senior year with an accredited school. In this way he could earn a diploma but remain at home for school. Another option for him at eighteen years, or earlier upon local school recommendation, is the GED* exam. Check your state's regulations regarding when and under what circumstances the GED test can be taken. Enrolling in a community college would be another option since community colleges typically have only one entrance requirement: that the student be eighteen years of age. Then his community college credits could be transferred to a four-year institution should he elect to transfer, and the effects of no high school diploma would be eliminated. Yet another high school option is being offered now by a few large home-school organizations — home-school diplomas and graduation ceremonies. Sometimes these organizations do impose academic requirements for those who want to earn diplomas. Finally, do check your state's home-schooling procedures; yours may be one of the few states that makes a diploma available.

C. You may have the same concerns regarding job applications if your child does not plan to attend college. Again, check your state's home-school diploma position. Please realize, too, that on job applications he may state that yes he did "graduate" *after twelve years of schooling* — his school? — home school. He would want to be prepared to explain the depth of his home schooling and the skills he possesses, particularly those applicable to the job for which he is applying. Many employers, in fact, distrust the credibility of a public school diploma and look for actual *evidence* of academic ability. On the other hand, your child may wish to consider the GED exam. Be aware, however, that some employers will hesitate to hire a GED graduate, because the employer may suspect that the graduate was a high school dropout, and "dropout" has uncomplimentary associations for many employers. A small job experience record from your child's teen years and an impressive academic record will help. In any case, having no diploma is not an insurmountable obstacle and may turn out to be no obstacle at all. There are many, many highly successful adults in our nation who entered the world of occupations and careers, as well as college, with no public school diploma.

D. When applying for college or a job, your young adult should be coached to interview well. Often, just letting the interviewer know who he is, what he has accomplished, what his goals are, how he feels about work, and so on, will open avenues. He can also have

---

*The GED exam is the General Education Development exam taken by nonmatriculated secondary students or adults who hope to earn a high enough score on the exam to be awarded a high school diploma by the state department of education.

available to hand to the interviewer an outline of courses completed (a "transcript") and projects undertaken during his secondary level home-school years; perhaps portfolios of polished home-school project samples; and letters of recommendation from former employers, customers (if he's run a small business), resource people with whom he's studied or worked. The problem, you see, for an employer or a college admissions officer is not that an applicant has been home schooled, but that the routine school documents aren't available. So what then should the officer or employer ask to see? Upon what evidence of competence should he base his decision about the applicant? The home-schooled job or college applicant needs to supply the answer to these questions — without being asked.

12. I wonder what my friends and relatives will say about our home schooling. How can I deal with pressure from people who disapprove?

A. Smile. Yes, smile; then back up that smile with knowledge about the accomplishments and the frame of mind of home-schooled kids. Your own home-schooled children will eventually be your live evidence, but, as cited earlier, documented research results are available, too. Know those results. Use them. Shying away from doubters and doomsayers may only prolong the home-school mystery for them. Help them hear about home schooling and become acquainted with you as a home schooler.

B. Read regional and national home-school newsletters and magazines. Many times readers write in to share their responses to the nay-sayers in their lives, responses that may work for you too. Home schoolers have learned to be ready to point out that their children choose home education; that their children like having a loving parent helping with math, reading, science, and other subjects; that their children benefit from not having to wait their turn in a class of twenty-five. These parents also help their children learn to respond to questions about home schooling.

C. Be convinced before you start home schooling that it is the best route to learning for your children. Make a list of your own complaints about your children's experiences in public schools, their reactions emotionally to public schools, and just about public schools in general. Read about the flaws of public schools, teachers, and administrators. You can read about them in dozens of books, magazine articles, and daily newspapers. Explain to those who disapprove that despite three decades of attempts to improve public school results, the U. S. Department of Education reported in the fall of 1993 that 47 percent of the nation's 191 million adults can not read and write at a level considered *functional* in the workplace. Then look again to confirmation of home-schooling successes — in books noted earlier and in the research studies noted in question *2, e.* By the time you've read just a few items, the deep seeds of becoming convinced will be planted. Once convinced, you will feel so sure about the fact that you are doing the best thing for your children by home schooling them that comments from other adults won't deter you. In fact, you may feel guilty at the thought of not home schooling them. You can convey that feeling to friends and relatives who question you, and you can tell them what you've read about public schools.

D. Establish your statement of reasons and rights as explained in Section Two ("Statement of Intent" item 5) and your educational philosophies and learning goals for your children as explained in Section Three ("Curriculum and Materials"). Recalling the great importance of your reasons, rights, philosophies, and goals may help you convey your convictions to others with calm confidence.

13. OK, I do want to take the first step towards home schooling — I want to plan my home school. But how do I truly know if I have what it takes to be a home-school teacher for my children?

A. Do you thoroughly enjoy being with your children, engaging in a variety of activities with them, working with them, teaching them crafts or hobbies or how to do household jobs, discussing many topics of interest to them? Do you value your children's ideas? Are you generally patient with your children? Can you let your children find their own way without too much interference from you? Do your children enjoy being with you? Are you and your children friends — or would you like to be friends? Do you have a desire to help your children grow in a truly supportive, friendly, peaceful atmosphere? Do you like the idea of one-on-one teaching (or one-on-two or three) for your children? If you can answer *yes* to most of these questions, you have reached first base in your assets for home teaching.

B. Are you a literate person? (A college degree is definitely not a necessity.) Do you enjoy learning? Do you like to think, question, analyze, and function independently? Are you able to take hold of new projects and follow them through persistently to completion? Do you enjoy books? Do you pursue knowledge in those areas that interest you? Do you enjoy sharing knowledge? Do you like hands-on and explorative learning as well as book learning? Mostly *yes* responses to this set of questions tell you you've reached second base.

C. Are you willing to learn more about home schooling by researching your state's school laws (not as difficult as you may think); reading a few books about home schooling; talking with established home schoolers; searching for home teaching/learning materials (fear not, as noted above, lots of help is available); and by planning well and yet allowing for flexibility for your home school? Yeses? Base three!

D. Are you determined? Are you willing to prepare your home-schooling plan or proposal well enough to feel confident when you approach school officials and/or when you start home teaching? (Preparing the proposal and facing school officials, if required, will probably be the most trying and the least joyful part of your entire home-schooling experience. After that, work, but joy!) Ask yourself, "How deep is my sadness about what has been or will be happening to my children in public school? How much do I value them and their education?" Are you determined to take them home for school? Have you reached *home* base?!

Congratulations if you did reach home base! Take a break, smile to yourself over the wonderful educational freedom you and your children will experience, read sections Two through Six ahead, and then begin work on your plan. *Bon voyage*!

If you didn't reach home base, read through the sets of questions again. Not every question needs a *yes* response, just most. (Home-school parents are fallible.) Look carefully at the questions to which you answered *no*. Have you underrated yourself? Or are there ways of reversing the answers through effort or endeavor on your part? Should you investigate the world of home schooling a bit further and then try the questions again? Perhaps, for example, by contacting a home-school support group in your area you could discuss issues that concern you with someone who is already home schooling. Maybe you could even visit a family during the act of home schooling. Locate books or magazine and news stories concerning home schooling, read them, and let them give you more of a feel for the experience. If you find yourself simply *yearning* to home teach your children, I suspect you do have what it takes. I suspect you just need to explore the matter further in order to discover that you can do it.

The above sets of questions and answers may make home teaching sound formidable. However, it truly is not. **Hundreds of thousands** of parents across our nation are happily home teaching, and news reports tell us the numbers are both increasing and broadening to include a much wider spectrum of American families and social, religious, and ethnic segments of our nation's population. Such figures suggest an obvious conclusion: home schooling can be effective and pleasurable. Nevertheless, home schooling is not always easy. Effort and determination are required, and you do need the basics of your own literacy and the ability and willingness to learn.

Once you feel fairly convinced that home schooling is best for your children and you, read Section Two, "Your Home School Plan." There you'll find examples of the kinds of plans you *may* be required to complete. It includes most of the various requirements that are found in the fifty sets of state regulations and procedures for home schoolers throughout our country. Section Two could be subtitled "Choices and Requirements" because you may be required to complete almost all, just some, or almost none of the included possible plan ingredients. The other ingredients are presented for your choice — yay or nay. Each type of planning procedure is included in at least a few states' requirements and some in most states. The intent of Section Two is not to inundate you with a multitude of plans to complete, but to enable you to complete those you wish to complete. Section Two is a handbook for parents who want to plan a home school, and should first be read entirely through and then be used as a menu from which to select and as a practical guide to your home-school planning process. Following your reading of Section Two, you will want to read Section Three for in-detail coverage of four important components of your home-school preparation — evaluation, curriculum, lesson plans, and records.

Now that you have a general map of our upcoming route, let's embark on your home-school journey. Take along all of your concerns for your children's education. Wear comfortable, sturdy walking shoes for our trek through the planning stages. And remember to pack a suitcase full of anticipation for the freedom and the control that you and your children have the capacity to achieve when you arrive at your destination: home school.

✳✳

Section **2**

Your Home-School Plan

Why Plan?

Are you interested in bringing your child's school home or are you interested in integrating home into your child's schooling? True home education results from the latter. Were you to attempt the former, to bring school home, the process would be relatively mechanical. You could copy! Copy school, that is. Public school. But what we're interested in here is home education, and that process may not be quite so easy. Worth it? Emphatically, yes! — according to tens of thousands of home-schooling families throughout the United States today. Why? Because those family members enjoy close, reciprocal relationships; because social and values guidance evolves from within rather than from without those families; because learning for them is commensurate with patience and love; because their lessons are as explorative, creative, and flexible as family members wish; because home-school time is their friend, not their constraint; because their school building is comfortable and intimate; and because their school doors can be freely opened to the larger world. Yes, home schooling is worth it and wonderful, but in action, not as routine as copying. However, some planning steps, especially those resulting in written documents and records, may best be "copied."

As you will see, some of the documents described in this and the next section may in fact appear annoyingly schoolish to you. Rest assured that such appearance is purposeful and intentional. A major aim of these two segments is to enable you to create paperwork whose appearance is unquestionably schoolish. While you'll want to avoid duplicating public schooling as an overall process, you can advance your progress towards the establishment of a home school by designing plans and paperwork that imitate those of public schools. Public school officials, who may have the power to accept or challenge your home-school program or proposal, would be hard-pressed to question documents that appear in all or most respects similar to the public school documents they have accepted for years. These paper landscapes will provide the official picture of your home school, for school officials will seldom if ever see your home school in action. There will not likely ever be an approval or denial of the *actual*, only of the paper work you present. Therefore, let's make your paperwork as *schoolish* as we can in order to free your children from a *schoolish* education.

In the interest of supplying all the information and explanation you may need and of enabling thoroughness in your planning, many possibilities and much detail are included in this section and also the next. Please take a moment now to look briefly at the samples at the end of this section (pp.76-86). Referring to them frequently as you read this section will help you recognize that none of the tasks described here is formidable. Nevertheless, each is required in at least some states.

Now you may be one of those who bristles upon reading *states require* and other regulatory-sounding terms you will encounter as you begin planning your home school — such as *officials, official procedures, case law, regulations, statutes, codes, laws, mandates, state's rights, state's responsibilities, education department requirements*, or the simple phrase *you must*. If such a heavy dose of these words all at once here leaves you feeling as if you've been riddled by bullets, I suggest that you may need to desensitize yourself to their effects in order to remain rational, to plan efficiently and fully, and to face (let's state it gently) the folks you may need to depend upon for approval of your home-school plan if you live in an "approval state." In truth, they're not all bad folks imposing oppressive regulations. In many school districts, they're quite open, receptive, and helpful — and yet do need to carry out their responsibilities. Remember, too, you may find them and their school facilities useful in any variety of ways once you begin home schooling. In other words, good relationships with these folks could prove beneficial in the long run. More importantly, though, remember why you want to home school and for whom. Try to remember that following the required procedures is not a squelching of your need for freedom, but rather is a route to freedom. Biting your tongue, remaining calm, and trying to follow the expected procedures may be the only way you will be able to bring your children *home* for school.

We need to recognize, too, that in order to begin and carry out your child's home education effectively, *you may need* a solid plan. In fact, having a solid plan can actually provide you with the flexibility you no doubt are seeking for your home school. How can a solid plan provide flexibility? First, once you have the legal path properly laid and the mechanics of a record-keeping system ready to use, you and your children will be freer to concentrate on designing creative, stimulating lessons. Then, having also planned well enough to know your youngster's learning goals and tasks, and your teaching materials and resources, you will have on paper and in your mind, as you teach, the core direction of your child's lessons. You can then encourage your child to move, to explore, to expand, and to achieve within and around and branching out from that core direction. Yet there should be a basic body of knowledge that he aims to acquire. A kind of age-appropriate literacy embellished with philosophies and passions of your own and his own. Thorough planning will ensure that your home-school lessons encompass that basic body of knowledge, plus plenty of self-initiated embellishments, and that your lessons are delivered within what is for you a comfortable, workable balance somewhere between structure and disorder.

To begin the home-school planning process, we will look first at the legalities — a pocketful of indisputables if you wish to legally home school, and another pocketful of guidelines telling you how states expect home schoolers to proceed. Then, we'll look at the design of a home-school program proposal in eleven workable segments. In Section Three we'll take a closer look at four of those segments. When we're done, you'll be ready to prepare your proposal for presentation to school officials for approval and/or to begin home schooling. But first, let's consider one final note.

State requirements for setting up and/or continuing home schools obviously vary, although every state permits home schooling in some form. Your state may have few guidelines, few regulations, few requirements, or it may have many. If it has many, they may be flexible, open-ended, and cooperative, or they may be rigid and restrictive. In the "Basic Information Chart" and in the "Summary of State Requirements and Procedures" in Section Four of this book you will find, in overview, the requirements for your state. Common denominators do exist among most of the fifty states' home-school requirements, and it is to those typically stated requirements that the following procedure is addressed. Although the form for presentation to officials may need to be altered in some cases, were you to follow this entire procedure it would allow you to initially approach, or to responsively present an argument to, the education officials of any of the fifty states with an exceptionally complete home-school proposal.

Learning Your State's
Home-Schooling Guidelines

Begin with whatever statutes, regulations, requirements, procedures — in general, the guidelines — that your state has adopted
with respect to home schools. If home-school program approval is
required in your state, you should consider yourself responsible for
informing local school officials of those guidelines as necessary.
Although these officials may be generally cognizant of state compulsory school attendance statutes, they may know little or nothing
about the statutes' application to home schooling (according to the
law, the courts, or accepted practice) or about other adopted procedures for approving home schools in your state. They may be completely unaware of the scope of their own role in a home-school
approval process and, likewise, of your rights as a potential home-
school parent. However, at the outset, *before* you have contacted the
local officials in any way, you'll need to inform yourself.

To begin that self-informing process, look to Section Four of this
book. There, in quick-reference format, the "Basic Information Chart"
tells you your state's compulsory attendance ages, whether or not
you need to be certified to home teach, whether or not you must
teach a state-required core curriculum, and the minimum number of
hours and days per year that your home school must be in session.
Following the chart, in narrative format, the "Summary of State
Regulations and Procedures" advises you of numerous, specific
guidelines that are particular to your state. In some cases, for example, you'll discover that forms must be completed, deadlines must be
met, meetings must be held, or that you will need to declare your
home a private school, or that you must allow for official supervision
of your home school, or that you will need to arrange for the administration of achievement tests for your children, and so on.

After reading your state's summary in Section Four, you should
compose a brief letter to your state's department of education
requesting a copy of all laws, regulations, and other procedural information related to home schooling in your state. Ask for compulsory
education and truancy laws; regulations relating to religious and
other private schools and home schools; and other requirements or
procedures related to home-school approval and programs. (See state

department addresses at the end of Section Four.) As an alternative, you may find your state's education laws in a law library, public library, or possibly in an information packet offered by a home-school organization in your state. You may still need to request any special procedures or regulations that have been adopted by your state department of education in response to state statutes or to public need. In many states, guidelines exist that stem from the statutes or go beyond the statutes, and you will be expected to know those guidelines and to follow them. However, you'll want to discuss any such extraneous procedures, since they extend beyond laws, with practicing home schoolers in your state. You'll need to determine whether or not they are indeed mandatory or might instead be safely bypassed by you. You may at this point be thinking you'll need a lawyer. But, at least for now, you truly aren't likely to need one. Reading the statutes and other published guidelines is not an overwhelming task. Typically, the applicable laws are not lengthy. Besides, *you* need to know what you are doing...and why, and how the law backs up what you are doing. You need to be knowledgeable enough about the law yourself to proceed wisely and knowingly and to respond to questions that are asked of you throughout any approval process or program review.

Local, regional or state home-school support groups should be able to provide you with additional state or local procedural information and further hints about how to begin. As you gather information from them, your state department of education, and your readings, establish a file of legal and procedural information to which you can refer as you develop your home-school plan, deal with school officials, and implement your plan.

In an article in the January/February 1984 issue of the *Mother Earth News*, home-school proponent John Holt recommended that potential home-school parents contact their elected legislators in order to secure pertinent information. Holt's contention here was that the state department of education will be impressed with and attentive to the fact that national or state legislators have taken an interest in your requests and needs and, therefore, state officials will respond fully and quickly to you. Holt further suggested that talking personally with state department officials could benefit you, especially if you suspect that local officials might be uncooperative. In other words, the assistance of state officials may bring to bear either silent or vocal pressure upon your local school board — in your favor, if such is necessary. As I requested, during the research stages of this book, education statutes and home-school guidelines from the fifty state departments, I received full and quick response from forty of them. Another six responded slowly, a few not too fully. Only four needed further prodding. In view of the good response I received, I suggest that *if* your first attempt to secure information from your state department of education fails, consider contacting a state legislator. Also, *if* your first impressions of your local school board's attitude uncovers negativity, consider personally contacting one or two top state education officials. Support group home schoolers may be able to suggest the names of cooperative or sympathetic officials. In such situations, Holt's recommendations may prove useful. I hesitate to endorse them wholesale, however, because several of the comments I've received from home schoolers throughout the nation indicate, first, that cuing in or stirring up influential folks before you have fully informed yourself can backfire on you, and second, that functioning beyond the level of a whisper during the planning stages can be risky in some states. You may eventually even decide to continue at a whisper — to silently home school. However, a simple letter requesting compulsory attendance laws and other information from your state department is probably not too risky. I suggest that you make other contacts with officials only as elapsed time or unsatisfactory response makes such contacts appropriate, wise, or necessary.

As noted, most of my queries to the state departments provided plenty of information, willingly given. It is less likely today than ever, considering growing public awareness of the home schooling alternative, that the individual who receives your query will ignore it or attempt to brush you off with a preemptive remark regarding your state's practice of not recognizing home schooling as a legitimate alternative to public education. His remarks may, however, indicate that your state maintains a hands-off policy. While such a remark can sound negative; it can actually be positive. Perhaps "hands-off" means that your state doesn't regulate home schoolers at all! It is, on the other hand, possible that your state department of education discourages home schooling, and your contact may make the department's first attempt at discouraging you. In some cases, too, the laws' terminology can at first confuse you. Your state's laws, for example, may not address "home schools" *per se*, but only address "private schools." However, upon second reading, you may discover that the laws actually indicate that a home school can operate as a private school. Finally, the individual who responds to your query may appear to comment cooperatively in her written response to you, but only attach your state's teacher certification requirements to that response — as a not-so-subtle hint or delay. At any rate, don't let negative remarks and responses stand unquestioned as truths or guidelines. Remember, every state allows for home schooling in some fashion. Call upon your determination, continue your independent search for information, write again asking for more detailed information (specify: compulsory attendance laws, etc.), consider trying John Holt's recommendations, contact a support group for guidance, and, as outlined below, continue working on your plans to home school.

Then, once your have secured the pertinent legal information, read it carefully, take notes, check dates to determine if one document (or clause within a document) supersedes another (home-school procedures in your state may be undergoing change), compare documents if obtained from various sources, and ask for a knowledgeable support group member's interpretation. Make special note of items that apply to unique situations, such as home schooling a handicapped child or a child living in a remote location, or a conscientious/religious objection to public schooling. Then using the documents and Section Four of this book, write out your own checklist of items that will apply directly to you as you work through the approval process — procedures you should follow, forms for which you should send, records you should set up, curriculum specifications you'll need to consider, deadline dates, and so on. Let the Procedural Worksheet which follows here help you get started.

This sounds like a lengthy process, but, in fact, the "documents" may consist of a single page and list very few procedures to follow. In any case, after studying your legal information, you will have a fairly full picture of where you stand as a potential home schooler in your state. For instance, you will know if you are legally qualified to home teach, how many and what kinds of requirements you will have to fulfill in order to legally home school, and how much local school district involvement in your home school you may have to tolerate. As mentioned earlier, you should set up a file in which to keep the legal information, your checklist, and from here on any further information and all communications regarding legal matters.

At this point, you will have accomplished one of the two tasks we set out to accomplish at the beginning of this portion of this book: You will have informed yourself. Now, if you anticipate any encounters with local school officials, you can use the above checklist to prepare a written *legalities* overview that you can later use to inform those officials. Again, you needn't be a lawyer to write a basic overview. Write your overview in a fashion you feel comfortable writing and that you feel is appropriate for your circumstance — for example, a list, a chart, a narrative, a letter, notes for oral presentation — including quotations from the statutes as appropriate. Then, particularly if your overview will eventually be submitted on paper to local school officials, be sure to edit and revise and polish your writing. Keep in mind as you write that school officials are your likely audience and your purpose is to inform — objectively, accurately. Also remember that you want your overview, and every other written or oral item you submit, to represent you as a literate, competent person — literate and competent enough to home teach.

The comfort that comes with knowledge should by now be settling into your mind. You have informed yourself of the legal basis of your home-schooling effort and, if needed, you have fully prepared yourself to inform others (even to inform a lawyer, if you should at any time later need a lawyer). If you have written one, tuck your written overview safely into your file. It will wait for you there while you proceed, as outlined below, with your home-school plan.

Procedural Worksheet

My state _____
Ages of compulsory education _____
Daily/weekly hours home schools must be in session _____
_____

Number of days required for a home-school year _____

yes / no   School officials can legally inspect my home school.
              How often? _____

yes / no   My children must take standardized achievement
              tests. Which children? _____
              Who can give the tests? _____
              Where can they be given? _____
              To whom must the results be provided?
              _____

yes / no   I must have my home-school plan/proposal officially
              approved by the following school officials:
              _____

Deadline dates I must meet and documents I must provide in writing before my school year begins:

_____ _____
_____ _____
_____ _____
_____ _____

Other documents I must provide during my school year:

_____ _____
_____ _____
_____ _____

The above documents must be submitted to:

_____
_____

Deadlines school officials must meet and actions they must take in response to my submittals:

_____ _____
_____ _____
_____ _____

Home-teacher qualifications in my state:

yes / no   I must be certified as a teacher.
yes / no   I must work with a certified consultant.
yes / no   I must have a college degree.
yes / no   I must have a high school diploma or GED.

Other home teacher qualification requirements or options:

_____
_____
_____

My children's:

Names	Age/Grade	Courses I must teach
_____	___/___	_____
		_____
		_____
		_____
_____	___/___	_____
		_____
		_____
		_____
_____	___/___	_____
		_____
		_____
		_____

My home school can be operated as a (circle all that apply):
    home school   private school   satellite school
    other: _____

Records I must maintain:

_____
_____
_____
_____
_____
_____

Other legal/procedural items I should note:

_____
_____
_____
_____
_____
_____
_____
_____
_____
_____
_____
_____
_____
_____
_____

Things I have learned from other home schoolers about procedures/laws in my state:

_____
_____
_____
_____
_____
_____
_____
_____
_____
_____
_____
_____
_____
_____
_____
_____

Statement of Intent

Some states require that you prepare what is commonly called a "statement of intent" or "notice of intent" — in other words, a home-school program proposal. Statement of intent requirements vary in form from state to state. The statement typically includes items such as basic personal information about your enrollees, identification of their home teacher, confirmation and often explanation or demonstration of your compliance with all regulations and required procedures, and a thorough description of your home-school education program including a curriculum outline. In your state the statement of intent requirements may be more complicated, simpler, or nonexistent. Some states specify formats for the statement of intent, some supply standard forms to be used, and others ask for both form completion and a description of all aspects of your program. In any case, preparing your statement of intent in full is your next task. Later, you can adapt the statement to the exact format required by your state for submittal to school officials. For the time being, you should think of the statement of intent as a document you are preparing for yourself, because you are the one who will benefit most from having completed it. You will have begun thinking through your home-school design well enough to convince yourself of its efficacy, well enough to feel secure as you begin to implement your program with your children, and, if necessary, well enough to effectively argue for your program. Your statement of intent, along with subsequent planning, will provide you with the concrete foundation of your home school. And concrete is hard to crack.

While studying the fifty sets of state home-school laws and procedures, I found that from the statement-of-intent requirements we could distill eleven possible statement segments:

1. Basic Personal Information — Enrollees

2. Basic Home-School Building Information

3. Evidence of Home-Teacher Qualifications

4. Certificated Home-School Consultant

5. Statement of Positive Reasons and Rights

6. Plans for an Annual Evaluation

7. Curriculums and Materials

8. Lesson Plan Samples

9. Plans for Ongoing Student Progress Assessment

10. Schedules and Calendars

11. Plans for Keeping Records

Although you don't want to become so bogged down in paperwork that you lose your enthusiasm for home teaching, you should study the statement of intent segments outlined below and then complete those you find essential. An effort has been made to present them simply and graphically for ease of completion, and, as noted earlier, you'll find a sample of each segment at the end of this section. Keep in mind as you work that in almost all states you will only need to complete these items, as earlier noted, once at the beginning of each home-school year. In some states this information is submitted in full only the first year and followed by notices of continuation each subsequent year. You would, of course, continue the record keeping and lesson planning and some scheduling throughout the year, but once you have developed a system for carrying out these tasks, they will not be too time-consuming.

Let's examine in detail, then, the eleven possible segments of a statement of intent or home-school proposal and the samples. Then you will be in a position to select those you will complete. Incidentally, when you begin to actually work through the following segments and accumulating papers-in-progress, establish a second home-school file, a statement of intent file, in which to store these papers. When (or if) you eventually submit them to school officials, be sure to keep copies of all documents in your file.

1. Basic Personal Information — Enrollees

In an effort to exercise their responsibility to see that the citizenry is educated, the states gather certain kinds of data on students within each school district. Typically this data is submitted by the parents to the local school office where it is kept as "permanent records," updated throughout the students' schooling years, and stored thereafter for reference purposes. Usually the information is quite basic and innocuous, with grades and achievement test scores added along the way. If a child has special needs, is an "exceptional" child, or such, information relating to testing and services provided with respect to those needs will be kept in separate files, usually in the special education department. In any case, the records provide documentation that your child, one of your state's citizens, is being educated.

If your children currently are or were previously enrolled in a public school, their permanent records already exist. If you have recently moved to the school district within which you now reside, you will need to give permission for the records to be sent to the new district from the district previously attended by your children.

Now, as you plan to *enroll* your children in home school, in almost all states you will be expected to supply the school district in which you reside with personal information regarding your children. The district will file this information in your children's permanent record files as continued documentation that your children are being educated. Check your state's summary in Section Four and the information from your state department of education to determine if and when the personal information must be submitted. The basic personal information requested of you may include any combination of the following:

- Your children's names, ages, sex, race, birthdates, address. Birth certificates may be requested.

- Their parents'/guardians' names, address(es), phone number(s).

- Your children's current grade levels, and names and addresses of the last public, parochial, or private school they attended, if any.

- Notation of any identified special needs of any of your children, such as physical therapy, speech therapy, education for the hearing-impaired or the blind, gifted/talented education, or other forms of special education.

- Complete immunization records and special health information (diabetes, asthma, epilepsy, etc.) for each of your children. If their immunizations are not up-to-date, you may be asked to update them.

Write out this information accurately and simply; then file it in your second, newly created file. (See Sample One, a Home-School Enrollment Sheet, on page 76 at the end of this section.) Later you will either submit your enrollment sheet as written or transfer the information to a standard form if your state supplies one. By checking your state's summary in Section Four of this book, you can quickly find out if a form is available. If so, you will need to obtain that form. If not, you may eventually submit your own original (and keep a copy for yourself). Again, remember, each written document you submit represents you; each is a demonstration of your literacy and competence.

2. Basic Home-School Building Information

States claim the right to reasonably regulate, inspect, and supervise all schools. That right may extend beyond the academic aspects of the schools and may include the physical nature of school buildings. As a home school, your home is a school building and perhaps subject to regulation, inspection, and supervision by public school officials. However, in most states actual physical inspections aren't carried out. Instead, you may be asked to provide information regarding your "school building" as a part of your statement of intent. In a very few states, you will have to demonstrate compliance with local fire, safety, and health ordinances that apply to all school buildings. In several states, a once-a-year visit is scheduled by a local school administrator to review your entire home-school program, and he will probably note your physical school setup during his visit.

If your home school is visited, the official will note some or all of the following factors, which are also those items you may be asked about or may just wish to include in the building information segment of your statement of intent:

- Your building's address/location.

- Names of all persons who reside in your home; i.e., if your home is going to be your home-school building.

- The degree of physical safety and health your children will work under as you home school them. Consider fire escape routes and practices, smoke alarms, overall cleanliness, wash and waste facilities, etc. Check your state's regulations to see if you need formal compliance with ordinances.

- The safety of your student records. Are they being kept in a moisture-free and fireproof area or are duplicates kept in a separate area so the records will not be lost?

- The degree to which your home schoolroom is conducive to learning. Is it quiet enough, spacious enough, neat enough? Is it nondistractive? Does it include study desks or tables, chairs, lamps, project work surfaces, and so on? This may apply to your kitchen, if it is your "schoolroom," or perhaps you'll use more than one room for "school."

- The overall atmosphere of your schoolroom. Is it pleasant, comfortable, cheery, peaceful, stimulating?

- The presence of textbooks and other materials, such as children's magazines, a globe or other maps, art supplies, science supplies, an atlas, an encyclopedia set, musical equipment and materials, etc. You won't need all of these items immediately, but should consider gradually accumulating those you can afford, first because they are useful additions to your children's learning environment, and second, because they will be noted should a school official inspect your school.

- The inclusion of a family-size library or at least the beginnings of one.

- The availability of special equipment or environments. For example, do you have a computer and software, a tree arbor or nursery, a garden, a spotting scope, a microscope, a piano, bee hives, or other potentially educational items? These items are not essential, of course, but if you have them, do mention them on your home-school building report.

Compile a descriptive list of all of the above items that apply in your case. Then fashion your list into a written report, if required, for later presentation to officials or transference to a form if one is provided for this purpose by your state department of education or local school district. (See Sample Two, Home-School Building Report, on page 77.)

You may also take this opportunity to itemize potential educational facilities within walking or driving distance of your home-school building that are available to you and your children. You might list such places as a museum, art gallery, fish hatchery, print shop, gymnasium, science center, stage theatre, wildlife refuge, zoo, community education center, craft workshop, marina, and others. Also consider facilities that may be particularly related to subjects you will cover during your home-school year. Examples might be a post office, fire station, police station, and public library for primary grade studies of cities; local grocery markets and area farms for an intermediate grade unit on human food production; a factory, mechanical shop, or woodshop for secondary vocational studies. After working through the segment on curriculum below, you will develop more ideas to include here. Feel free to note briefly how these places will relate to your children's studies; then you can reemphasize and expand upon them later in the curriculum segment.

File your home-school building report with your enrollment sheet as the first two completed segments of your statement of intent. At this stage you'll probably find yourself buoyed by the generation of ideas for facilities that you can include in your children's educational activities. You can smile in the knowledge that were your children public school students they would not visit and experience many, if any, of those real life places which can so easily enliven lessons. Feel confident, too, in the fact that educational research has demonstrated the tremendous effectiveness of the hands-on, multi-sensory activities that such places can offer to your children as they learn.

3. Evidence of Home-Teacher Qualifications

Having completed the first two segments of your statement of intent in a literate and competent fashion, you will have already begun to establish evidence of your qualifications to home teach. Of course, if yours is one of the few states that mandates that you be a certified teacher, and you're not certified, you'll have to consider other alternatives regardless of your literacy and competence. (See question 3 in Section One for alternatives and check your state summary in Section Four for other qualification options.) If you are certified in your state for the grade levels and subjects you will teach, your qualifications shouldn't be questioned. You will simply need to attach a copy of your certificate to your statement of intent and skip to the next segment here. But in most states and most cases, your qualifications will be judged in part on your ability to present a coherent, polished home-school plan. In other words, the impression you first give to school officials is likely to be a paper impression. This book will help you make it a good one.

Among the pieces of paper you may need to submit is one that accounts for your actual qualifications to teach your children. First of all, however, you may need to convince yourself of your qualifications. Let me help: You may be interested to know that most private schools in the United States, even (or especially) the exclusive, exemplary ones, hire noncertified teachers. Other alternative schools, too, may hire some certified teachers, but do not hesitate to also hire noncertified experts or experienced practitioners in a particular field of study. Even public schools, at least the better ones, bring in resource persons in various fields, such as craftsmanship, health science, or environmental science, to teach a lesson or two, a course or two, from time to time. Further, the number of full-time, regular teachers —without certification— teaching in our public schools each year is in the 80,000+ range. And yet another segment of our public school teaching population holds only emergency certificates, granted due to local teacher shortages and for which there may be few qualifications. I might add, too, that a significant percentage of the more than 230,000 certified teachers in our nation's public high schools are teaching some courses not in the fields for which they are certified and in many cases not even in which they are knowledgeable. The resource persons brought in intermittently to teach in public schools are typically competent in the specific subjects they teach. However, as for the thousands of uncertified, emergency, or out-of-their-teaching-field teachers in our public schools, it is difficult to estimate their degrees of competence or their success rates.

Potential home teachers need recognize that a high school diploma or equivalency, a college education or part of one, vocational education and occupational experience beyond high school, and special talents in any area are useful to one's teaching. Any background experiences along these lines that you can list for yourself will be given consideration as school officials attempt to determine your qualifications to home teach. However, we should all understand that a teaching certificate is not, in and of itself, a qualification that would ensure anyone's ability to teach.

In other words, aside from regulations, most parents are able to teach without certification. In fact, having discovered through the results of home teaching over the years that parents can successfully teach, all states now maintain at least some provisions for home teaching by noncertified parents. Indeed, you may not only be an effective teacher for your children, you may be the best teacher for them. So let's take a look at your qualifications:

- First, what are your children's grade levels in the various subject areas, especially the core areas of reading and math? Now what's your hypothetical grade or skill level in those areas? Make a comparison. How far ahead of your children are you? Herein, we hope, is your first item of qualification to teach your children.

- Next, jot down your educational experiences, K-12, vocational, college, community courses...all of them. Now you have your second set of items that qualify you to teach. You will want to secure copies of applicable diplomas, degrees, and transcripts to attach to your statement of intent if required or if you think doing so would be beneficial and appropriate.

- Go on to your job experiences. Have you become particularly talented in a job-related area that could apply to your teaching? Write out a description of those experiences and you'll have set three of your qualification statements. If you feel a job-related recommendation from an employer would attest to your competence, obtain one and attach it to your qualifications sheet.

- How about hobbies or avocations or other skills and talents? Are you a pianist? That talent would be especially useful in teaching elementary grade children. Are you a naturalist or environmentalist? Useful in science instruction. Are you a seamstress? Useful in home economics instruction. Are you versatile in a foreign language that you plan to teach to your children? List those skills and talents that relate to the grade levels and subjects you will be teaching. Stretch your imagination; look for all the ways that your special talents could be useful as you teach your children. Then list those talents.

- Have you been involved in educational or service groups, particularly any through which you have demonstrated competence and/or leadership ability? Have you been a toastmistress? A Chamber of Commerce officer? A scout leader? A Sunday School teacher? Have you earned special recognition through your involvement in such groups? Add these to your list and you have your fifth set of qualification items.

- Do you have abilities to meet your children's individual learning needs that public school teachers don't have or that teachers aren't able to exercise in the public school classroom setting?

- Have you considered taking the National Teacher Exam or a state teachers' exam if available in your state? A good score could add to your qualifications to home teach.

When you have completed this segment, you should have the makings of written evidence of your home-teacher qualifications that you can use to prepare a written statement, if necessary, or to fill in a required form on your qualifications. (See Sample Three on page 78.) The date for submitting your qualifications information is probably the same as the date for your enrollee and building information. Check your regulations.

You may wish to include a list, too, of other persons, such as your spouse, who will play roles in your children's education, along with the other persons' special qualifications and a brief explanation of how they will fit in with your children's lessons. See question *4, e* in Section One of this book for the kinds of individuals who might make up your child's learning community. Educational research emphatically supports bringing such resource persons into the schoolroom; i.e., into the learning lives of your children.

In addition, throughout your home-school year, keep written records of any home-teacher education and improvement efforts that you undertake. If you take courses, attend workshops, seminars, or conferences in order to improve your skills as a home-school teacher, keep a record of those activities. Include transcripts when available. Further include any studies you've engaged in independently on teaching methods. Even a list of books or journals you've read about teaching could be included.

Any accumulation of educational experiences that will enhance your home teaching will benefit you and your children. But, in addition to that, you may at some time be able to use a record of those experiences to impress upon school officials your seriousness, earnestness, and knowledge as a home teacher.

4. Certificated Home-School Consultant

A few states exercise their right to supervise schools within their jurisdiction by requiring or offering an option for noncertificated home-school teachers to secure the assistance of a certificated educator. For example, the regulations or guidelines might indicate that you need to demonstrate that you have a certificated supervisor available to you. Or you may be requested more specifically to provide evidence that you have available to you a certified teacher consultant for planning, development of your curriculum, program implementation, or for consultation related to your child's learning exceptionality. In addition, the certified consultant may be required for monthly, quarterly, semester, or yearly progress evaluations. Progress evaluations might include actual testing by the consultant, a review of tests you've given, a review of your child's home-school work, a discussion with your child, or other means of determining progress. In any case, certified consultants or supervisors may be involved in a variety of ways. The terms *consultant* and *supervisor* as used here, incidentally, are not necessarily formal labels, but more or less descriptors of a role a certificated teacher would be asked to fulfill intermittently. By checking the summary for your state in Section Four of this book, you can quickly see whether or not you are required to have such a consultant. If one is required in your state, the summary will suggest the extent to which you will need to utilize the services of a consultant. You should also check for further details in the information you request from your state department of education.

Perhaps you find yourself resisting the idea of working with a certificated consultant. You may, for example, feel so negative about public education that you do not want a public educator involved in any aspect of your home school. Or you may fear that a lack of freedom might result from having a *supervisor.* Or you may presume such a consultant would attempt to dictate your curriculum. Perhaps you're just adamant about your right to function independently.

May I interject here, however, a statement made early in this section: "...home schooling is worth it and wonderful, but not...routine...." Now those legislators and state education officials who designed their respective statutes and other regulations to include a consultant requirement may have had any number of reasons for doing so. But the quote noted above implies a potential reason of your own for locating a consultant: You may simply need help.

In view of this possibility, especially when you are first getting started, you may find it worthwhile, even necessary, to make use of a local educator's knowledge. As a means of suggesting areas in which you might benefit from help, let's look at the kinds of knowledge a certified educator may be able to share with you:

- Knowledge of formats that schools typically use for records, curriculum designs, lesson plans, schedules, and calendars, and that are the expected formats for most information that you might submit. Also, the educator would know the appropriate formats for any records that you'll keep at home while your home-school program is in progress.

- Familiarity with curriculums and course syllabi, particularly those used locally and which you may be expected or required to emulate as you design your curriculum.

- Knowledge of the many means of routine student progress assessments.

- Experience with achievement tests and their contents — especially useful if the consultant you choose has taught in your school district for a few years and has administered the locally given test at your child's grade level.

- Acquaintances with and connections to public school staff members whose assistance also may be needed or desired by you, such as a physical therapist, speech therapist, school psychologist, school librarian, art instructor, drama coach and others.

- Knowledge of the uses of your child's permanent records kept at the local school and access to them. (You have legal access to those records, too, but there may be times when you would rather personally avoid the public school scene and yet obtain information from your child's permanent file.)

- Awareness of special and extracurricular public school activities in which your child may wish to participate.

- Familiarity with materials and resources appropriate for various age/grade/ability levels and subjects and means of securing them.

- Awareness of audio visual and other equipment on hand at your local school that might be available for your use.

- Perceptions regarding the personalities and philosophies of school administrators and school board members with whom you may have to deal.

- Awareness of upcoming workshops and courses available to teachers that may be open to enrollment by home teachers in your area.

No doubt a local certified educator will have other knowledge as well that could be of use to you. Very likely the issue for you is maintaining full control of your home-school program yourself, even while seeking the assistance of a certified educator. If you work through much of your statement of intent on your own so that you have your ideas down on paper and then decide precisely what it is you want from a certified consultant, you are likely to get just what you want from that person. In other words, by looking at your own information, you can come up with questions and areas needing further input, areas where state requirements indicate you must consult a certificated educator, or areas in which you just may want additional ideas. Then, when you meet with the educator whom you've chosen and who has agreed to cooperate, you can steer the discussion and control this outsider's input, handle the consultation sessions in a friendly, compatible fashion, and gain needed benefits.

If your state is one that requires a consultant, don't feel that you must ask your local school superintendent or another official for a recommended or assigned educator. Instead, feel free to investigate the possible candidates yourself. Look for a topnotch teacher who works with the grade level range and the subject areas with which you will work as a home teacher. Then, seeking cooperation, approach that person. Once her assistance is assured, add your consultant's name, address, degree held, certificate held, the teaching endorsements for which she is certified, transcripts if required, her current teaching assignment and school, if employed, and perhaps the reasons you chose her, to your proposal, to your statement of intent, or to any forms that require your consultant's name.

If yours is a state that does not require a consultant, your independent inclusion of one in your proposal is likely to impress positively the local officials responsible for reviewing and/or approving your proposal. Be sure to note the ways in which the consultant will be helpful to you, the ways in which your program may benefit from this assistance, and how your consultant's experiences as an educator relate to your home-school situation — grade levels, subjects to be taught, appropriate materials recommendations, and so on.

We don't want to ignore the possibility that you won't find a satisfactory local certificated educator to serve as your consultant or that you simply resist working with one, but still do want a consultant. In that case, you'll need to look elsewhere. You may, for instance, establish affiliations with a Christian or other private school that would result in the services of a consultant. There are numerous so-called "umbrella schools" in operation throughout the United States to which you might look for assistance. I should warn, however, that sometimes these schools delineate their own consultative role, which means that you may have less control over their input. There may be a certified teacher in your area who is not currently employed by a school district or is on a leave of absence and would agree to help you, or even a home teacher who happens to be certified. Thousands of teachers leave the field of education each year (often the brightest of our teachers), to work for higher pay and greater prestige in other jobs or because they became disillusioned with public education. You could attempt to locate one who might provide evening or weekend consultations intermittently. Some home teachers have placed want ads in newspapers, newsletters, and magazines in search of a certified consultant. Should you take this route, be sure you ask for proof of valid certification and for references. In some states the state department of education may be a source of recommendations for potential consultants. Also, if your state requires every home-school educator to have a consultant, other home schoolers that you locate are probably in contact with at least one consultant and may be able to suggest someone for you. In some areas home schoolers can call upon an identified cadre of certified teachers who are willing to help them. You and a local or regional support group may be able to organize such a group of certified helpers. In addition, if you have acquaintances among parents of other school districts in your area, one of those parents may be able to offer a name or two of good teachers in his district who might be willing to be your consultant.

Whichever process you use, take your time. Also, explore as much as possible the teaching background and talents of your candidates. To find out about them, ask others who know them or who have had children in their classes. As noted above, before contacting the person you choose, outline carefully for yourself the services you seek so you'll be able to present them in an organized manner for him. When you meet, he will probably be more inclined towards working with you if he sees that you are prepared, competent, and fully aware of what your home-school program is all about and of exactly what help you're seeking. Be specific and objective, but also pleasant and undemanding. If you're married, I suggest that you and your spouse together visit with him, at least for this initial meeting. I also recommend that you not take any of your children to this first meeting. You're asking initially for programmatic assistance, not, typically, for help in dealing with or working directly with your children.

Once you've reached an agreement with a certificated consultant, cooperatively itemize the consultant's responsibilities. Will there be reports to complete? Will he work in conjunction with a local school official as well as with you? Will he be responsible for reviewing test results or for arranging and administering achievement tests? When should he meet your children? Try to set dates for further meetings and for consultative or supervisory activities for which he will need specific times. Take notes which can later be turned into a written report of your agreement. Attach a copy to the consultant information sheet in your file and deliver one to him. Then, when and if appropriate, submit one along with your other proposal segments to school officials.

Usually a consultant's involvement with a home school is not too time-consuming in the scope of an entire school year, but you may wish or need to offer some form of remuneration for the consultant's assistance. Finding a volunteer is possible, and in some cases the local school district is obligated to provide a teacher to work with you.

We might note here also that once you begin working with your curriculum you may wish to establish a working relationship with more than one consultant, certified or noncertified. Perhaps you'd like to confer with a local science instructor regarding your home-school science lessons, and likewise a teacher of literature regarding creative reading lists and activities, and yet a third teacher who helps you with lesson planning and scheduling. Perhaps, too, you will find persons active or employed in specific fields, such as biology or music, who are not certified teachers, but who could serve as consultants as you develop curriculums in science and music. Also, don't ignore your fellow home schoolers. An experienced and successful home teacher, already established in your area, could be a beneficial consultant too. Remember, of course, the names of noncertificated consultants should not be used to indicate fulfillment of a requirement that you obtain the assistance of a certificated educator.

To complete, then, this fourth segment of your statement of intent, you will file for later reference or submission a personal and qualifications information sheet on your certified consultant with any appropriate attachments and a written report describing the extent of your agreement with the consultant. (See Sample Four on page 79.) Double check to make sure the latter reflects any and all state requirements related to your use of a consultant.

5. Statement of Positive Reasons and Rights

You may wish, or in a few cases be required, to preface or supplement your statement of intent with the reasons and rights you feel justify your decision to home school your children. Parenting responsibilities that stem from religious convictions are the most commonly expressed reasons and rights of home schoolers in the United States, and religious exemptions from compulsory education are the most commonly granted exemptions. As numbers of home-schooled children have risen from a U.S. Department of Education reported 90,000 in 1983 to upwards of 500,000 in 1993, a concomitant broadening of reasons has also occurred. While religious motives remain predominant, today many home school out of concerns for a child's sense of individual identity. These parents dislike the *sameness* of public education and want to allow their children to follow self-identified interests. Some parents have picked up the values banner, but not necessarily from a religious base. These parents abhor the negative influences —drugs, intolerance, violence, self-centeredness— that surround children in public schools. Many others, as our society becomes more and more multicultural, reject the white-oriented curriculums, textbooks, and teachers of our public schools. These parents want to infuse their children's learning with a strong sense of their own ancestral values and ethnic contributions to the global community. Still others parents, dismayed by continuing reports of the academic deficiencies of our public school "products," especially in comparison with those of other industrialized nations, home school in order to achieve better academic results for their children. In other words, varied justifications for home schooling may be offered. Here are a few possibilities:

Special problems and/or needs of your children:

- physical or learning handicaps
- severe hyperactivity or lethargy
- rebellious behavior

- intellectual giftedness
- unusual talent in a specific area
- maladjustment to school
- academic failure
- a fading joy in learning
- a withering curiosity

Special issues of your own:

- values conflicts with public schools
- convictions of the conscience
- dismay over the public school social milieu
- unavailability of a good, local public school teacher at your child's grade level
- knowledge of studies that show that home schools produce academically able students
- knowledge of the studies that show that public schools produce large numbers of illiterates and students who compare poorly on international levels
- knowledge of research that shows that children are sent to school too early
- a burning desire to offer your children an excellent and exciting education
- a desire to feed your children's natural love of learning (and to avoid standing by while public schools squelch it)

Please recognize that I'm not making a wholesale recommendation here that you submit to officials a formal statement of your reasons and rights regarding home schooling, nor that officials would unquestioningly accept your reasons if you did submit them. I am suggesting, however, that you may want to create such a statement for one or more of several possible purposes:

- Perhaps a statement of reasons and rights is required by your state in order for you to win approval for your home school. Check your state's summary in Section Four and your state laws and procedures.

- You'll probably feel more focused as a home schooler if you write out your reasons **for yourself**. You may think of the statement of reasons as a means of confirming your child-related goals as a home-school parent. As time passes, you may use the statement as a guide and reminder of why you and your children became home schoolers.

- You and **your spouse** as joint parents of your children may wish to compare and clarify together your reasons — as a means of screening their validity while you consider the serious issue of whether or not to home school.

- You, your spouse, and **your children**, as a team, may benefit from bringing together your individual thoughts and feelings about why you'd like to home school. From such teamwork you may derive a strong sense of unity and purpose to bolster you during the approval process, initial implementation process, and the weeks beyond.

- You may feel that your reasons and rights are your most convincing pieces of evidence that you and your children should, or must, home school. Perhaps nothing would be more persuasive as you seek official approval.

- Writing your statement of reasons and rights may be the most meaningful way to declare the strength of your convictions regarding the tremendous importance to you of your children and their learning.

- Your statement of rights may afford you an opportunity to crystallize in your own mind your true, exact, legal rights as a home schooler.

- You'll have worked out solid answers for friends and neighbors who frown as they ask, "Why are your children not going to school?"

- Your statement of intent may appear incomplete without a statement of your reasons. Your plans may lack the force that a clear statement of purpose can give them.

Whatever the basis of your statement or list of reasons and rights, when you compose it, avoid vagueness. Your focus will become clearer with increasing specificity. Also, if you plan to submit your statement of reasons and rights as part of your statement of intent to school officials, you will want it to be explicit enough to not offer bait for debate. Offering officials what they may perceive to be a can of worms will only invite their opening it. So hone your wording and your ideas down to their most specific form. (See Sample Five on page 80.) Also, make no statement that would suggest that your purpose is to counter compulsory school attendance statutes. Doing so would be the equivalent of publicly stating, "My purpose is to break the law."

Begin at this point to use your statement of reasons and rights as your declaration of conviction, of determination, as well as of focus. File it, but refer to it frequently, particularly if your determination wavers, and keep it in mind as you plan your curriculum and lessons. In other words, know why you are doing what you are doing. Let the why of your home-schooling effort sink deep within you and become an integral part of your program.

6. Plans for Annual Evaluation

Most states require home schoolers to undergo some form of end-of-the-year evaluation of the home-school students' progress and also, in some cases, of the home-school program. Achievement tests are an evaluative requirement in several states, but other forms of progress assessment are allowed for in other states. Several states also require an overall review of the home-school program, including all files and records kept throughout the home-school year. This, of course, is one good reason for developing and keeping all plans, documents, and daily school records as you home school.

Your state guidelines may indicate that you can carry out the evaluative process yourself or that it must be carried out by a certificated consultant or a school official. By checking the summary for your state in Section Four of this book you can find out if an annual evaluation is required, who should conduct your evaluation if required, and in what form it will need to be completed. Then you should **carefully read "Annual Evaluation" in Section Three** for a detailed discussion of evaluation procedures. Following that reading, you should write out a simple plan for how you will carry out any required annual evaluation. At this point the plan's purpose is to let school officials know that you are aware of the requirement and that you have a plan to complete it. This plan should be filed in you statement of intent file for later submittal to officials and, of course, for implementation at the end of your home-school year. (See Sample Six on page 81.)

In a few states the evaluation will occur not only at the year's end but also quarterly or at the end of each semester. If yours is one of these states, be sure your plan reflects the quarterly or semester evaluation requirement.

7. Curriculums and Materials

Many states require home schoolers to provide curriculums similar to those of public schools for children the same ages as the home-schooled children. Usually this requirement is stated as "equivalent curriculum," suggesting that no less than the public school curriculum should be provided. Typically, however, "equivalent curriculum" actually refers to a basic or core curriculum rather than to the entire scope of a public school curriculum. Also, embellishments of your own and your children's are allowed. In other words, you can alter or create your own course syllabi for any particular course as long as the basics are covered, and you can add subject areas or courses to the required curriculum.

Broadly, a curriculum is an aggregate of courses of study that a school offers to children at any one grade level. For a primary grade student, for example, the basic curriculum would include reading and math. It may also include science, social studies, language arts, music, art, physical education, and so on. The concept of a curriculum is simple: courses of study. The writing out of a curriculum is less simple: a list of learning goals and objectives to be achieved within each course of study.

You needn't feel as if your curriculum design needs to come out of thin air. Help is available in various forms. First, to write out your home-school curriculum you will need to find out which courses of study are required by your state. Check Section Four. Then **read "Curriculum and Materials" in Section Three** where you will find a step-by-step process by which you can design your curriculum. Following that process, you can arrive at a satisfactory written curriculum for submittal to school officials, if required, or for maintenance in your files as evidence that you are providing required courses of study or simply that you are providing a sound curriculum. (Also see Sample Seven on page 82 at the end of this section.)

Once you have established your curriculum, you will need to decide which materials to use to teach that curriculum. Sometimes your materials as well as your curriculum will need official approval. Whether they require approval or not, you will need to undergo an initial search for materials to use and to note how they correlate with your curriculum. To understand the materials search procedure read the materials portion of "Curriculum and Materials" in Section Three. Then write out a basic list of materials you plan to use to teach your curriculum. Please realize that this will be a basic list only, one from which you may deviate as the year progresses and one to which you may add other materials as you become aware of them. Your materials list may be integrated into your written curriculum as in Sample Seven.

After reading Section Three, complete and file your curriculum and materials list, perhaps bound in a notebook, in your statement of intent file to await submittal or later use. Even if you are never required to submit a curriculum or materials list, you will probably find yourself secure in the knowledge that you do have a solid, well-planned curriculum from which to work. Also, of course, if ever challenged in later months or years, you'll have proof of the quality of your children's home-school curriculum.

8. Lesson Plan Samples

Lesson plan samples are required during the approval process in only a few states. Some require lesson plans not during the approval process, but throughout the home-school year. In several states, in fact, lesson plans must be maintained for inspection by school officials. If your state upholds lesson plan requirements, please **read "Lesson Planning" in Section Three.** If yours does not require plans, you may wish to read "Lesson Planning" anyway and to consider regularly writing brief lesson plans. Again, maintaining lesson plans is another opportunity to accumulate evidence that you are providing your children with a sound education.

To find out if lesson plans are required, check your state's summary in Section Four and check information received from your state's department of education. In Section Three I have provided you with a lesson-planning procedure that should be acceptable to school officials. You may wish to plan in some other fashion, but if you need approval of your plans, I urge you to follow the procedure described in Section Three, "Lesson Planning."

If your state or local education officials request that sample plans be included in your statement of intent or home-school proposal, select a portion of each child's curriculum for which you can write out plans. If you select portions from the beginning of a course of study for each child, you'll be able to use the plans you design right away as you begin home teaching. Perhaps plans for one week, the first week of home school, would be sufficient to satisfy the officials that you are able and willing to plan your children's lessons. When completed, file those plans in your statement of intent file, but also keep copies in a notebook in which you will continue writing lesson plans, week-by-week, as you home teach. (See Sample Eight on page 83.)

9. Plans for Ongoing Student Progress Assessment

Assessing the results of your teaching in an ongoing fashion, if required or desired, means that you will utilize either activities or tests to measure your children's academic growth and you will do so frequently throughout your home-school year. Ongoing assessment can enable you to keep tabs on what your children have learned during any one lesson, what reteaching is needed, and which learning experiences to provide next.

Assessments take many forms. If you need written assessments, for example, and you and your children have just finished a lesson on the body parts of reptiles, you might ask your children to complete a worksheet on which they must label the body parts of a turtle pictured on the worksheet. By independently completing the identification and labeling of the turtle body parts and their functions your students would be, in effect, undergoing an assessment. You and they would find out what they had learned and had not yet learned. The written assessment might have taken other forms. For instance, you might have constructed a matching quiz in which your children would have to match the names of the turtle body parts with their functions. You might have used a test that appears in the science textbook teacher's manual. At the primary level the student might have been asked to respond orally rather than on paper. He may even have been asked to pretend he was a turtle and to tell you about himself as a turtle. He could respond manipulatively, like shifting the pieces of a puzzle. Or you could take your child of any grade level into the field to respond orally with a live turtle in view. You could ask him to create a turtle in clay and label the body parts with tiny flags glued to toothpicks poked into the clay. Another possibility is asking him to write a letter to a friend explaining all he has learned about turtles and to let you read the letter before it is mailed. You could design a culminating project that would allow assessment. With your help, for example, your child might obtain, set up a home for, and care for a turtle. His ability to include an appropriate environment, suitable food, water, and so on, will demonstrate a knowledge of turtles. To accompany this project you might urge your child to keep a daily observation diary of the turtle's behaviors, daily patterns, food preferences, mode of locomotion, eye movement, and numerous other such observations.

Simple, routine parent-teacher observations of a child at work can serve as assessments, too. Sometimes progress is evident in a child's daily learning behavior and response. If someone asks you, for example, if and how well your toddler has learned to walk, you can easily respond based upon your observations. A test or culminating demonstration of your toddler's walking ability is certainly not necessary.

You may want to maintain a portfolio of your child's work; i.e., a collection of dated, written student work, project descriptions, learning logs, observation logs, tests, and so on, completed during lessons and available for later review as a means of progress assessment. The key factors to remember regarding ongoing assessment are first, that you as teacher see some demonstration of your student's knowledge and skills, and secondly, that you assess frequently enough to adjust your instruction in order to help your child fill in any gaps and move ahead to greater knowledge and more advanced skills. You can be as creative as you wish in designing your assessments. Formal tests are not always required nor are they necessarily desirable.

Sometimes assessments are built into a particular teaching approach. Mastery learning, for example, includes an itemized accounting of the achievement of each learning objective, as per test results, before a student goes on to the next objective or set of objectives. In other words, objectives for a series of learning activities would be established, the student would carry out the activities, then take a test. If a high score (not necessarily a perfect score) indicates that the student has mastered the objectives, he moves ahead to the next group of objectives and activities. If he does not achieve a sufficient score to indicate mastery, he repeats the activities or completes alternate activities and then tries the test again (or alternate test). Ongoing assessment is obviously built into this approach.

Another approach with built in assessments is known as "diagnostic/prescriptive" teaching. This approach involves assessing or testing first; i.e., diagnosing. Then based upon deficiencies in the student's demonstrated knowledge or skills, activities are assigned; i.e., prescribed. The activities will, if successful, help the student fill in the gaps. Then he is retested.

You can check Appendix A, "Teaching Approaches," at the end of this book for other teaching approaches into which assessment procedures might be built. Whichever methods you use, for the sake of your statement of intent or home-school proposal, you may be required to account for the means by which you plan to assess student progress in an ongoing fashion and by which you plan to keep records of ongoing assessments. For the sake of maintaining evidence of your child's achievement, you will need to design means of recording the results of your assessments. Please refer to "Keeping Records" in Section Three for ideas about how to record those results. Once you have planned a procedure for assessment and for recording assessments, perhaps even several procedures for varying subject areas, write a brief description of your plans and insert it into your statement of intent file. There it will wait for submittal to officials and/or for you to implement once you begin home teaching. (See Sample Nine on page 84.)

Just as lesson planning and ongoing assessment are correlated with your curriculums, our next segment is also based loosely upon your curriculums. We'll look now at schedules and calendars.

10. Schedules and Calendars

Many home schoolers are required to submit schedules and/or calendars as segments of their statement of intent or home-school program proposal. School officials want to be sure that your schedules and calendars show that you are planning for all required subjects, that you will proceed in an organized fashion, that you include the number of required hours per day (if minimums have been set), and that your children will be "in school" the required number of days in the home-school year.

If required in your state, you should design a daily/weekly schedule for each child's home schooling. The schedules should reflect your lesson plans. In other words, the schedules should show the days of the week and the hours of each day during which home-school subjects will be taught. Although lesson plans and schedules are typically written for a week at a time, a traditional schedule for one day in a public school might look like the sample below:

Monday

9:00	science	12:00	recess
9:30	math	12:45	story telling
10:00	English	1:15	social studies
10:30	recess	2:00	recess
10:45	reading	2:15	music
11:30	creative writing	3:00	physical education

Your schedule may be more loosely drawn than this one and be less traditional by not including isolated subject areas but instead allowing for integrated curricular activity blocks. Do remember that in part you are trying to achieve a paper impression that will, if necessary, satisfy school officials who want to see that you are in compliance with requirements, while the schedule may be considered by you as only a basic framework for home-school sessions. Stick to your schedule relatively consistently if you wish, but manipulate it freely as often as you need to in order to allow for field trips, academic presentations by resource persons, library trips, activity days with other home schoolers, lessons away from home (e.g.: music), learning projects, the diverse academic interests of your children, and also to allow for changes to a better routine that you later find useful.

Quite possibly you will find that a condensed version works fine, one in which less time is needed and therefore less time is allotted for some subject areas. During the typical public school day (from which required home-school hours are derived), much time is wasted on nonacademic time. At home, you can make concentrated use of the instructional hours and engage in enrichment activities the remainder of the day, if you wish. On the other hand, you could easily take advantage of the *extra* hours by moving ahead at an accelerated pace as the weeks go by.

A schedule change may be needed once you get started if you discover that your home-schooling schedule doesn't mesh well with your family-life schedule. Also, if you teach more than one child at more than one academic level, schedules may need shuffling before you settle on timing arrangements that work best.

If you alter the schedule significantly, sketch out a new one to keep on file. You may wish to create an official schedule for the file and separately maintain your own schedule. The official schedule should demonstrate that you are meeting state requirements regarding the number of schooling hours and subjects to be taught and look similar to the above sample. Your unofficial schedule may be more flexible while you and your children in actuality still meet the hours requirement, but less formally and less rigidly.

While schedules show each day's routine, calendars for home schools (and public schools) show the entire school year and demonstrate that the required minimum number of days is included. You should either write out a calendar showing all the days your home school will officially be in session or buy a one-page, year's calendar and simply circle the days you'll be in session. School officials should be content to see that you are in compliance, and again, you can deviate from your calendar as long as you *officially* make up days missed. (See Sample Ten on page 85.)

If your state does not require you to submit schedules and calendars, you may want to rough them out anyway so you can assure yourself that you will meet hourly and daily requirements. Also, if you keep your schedules and calendars on hand, you'll have ready evidence that you are in compliance with required time frames.

11. Plans for Keeping Records

Maintaining complete records consistently could be vital to the continued existence of your home school. They may be necessary initially for approval of your home school, necessary later for proof of compliance with requirements or as evidence that you are providing your children with a sound and *equivalent* education. In the planning stages, however, you first need to become aware of the kinds of records you may choose to keep and of the forms in which to keep them. Some we have already mentioned:

- A file of legal information.
- A statement of intent (program proposal) file, including all pertinent documents for each of the eleven segments of the statement that you choose to complete.
- Records of home-teacher education and improvement efforts undertaken by you.
- A log of certificated home-school consultant activities.
- Ongoing lesson plans.
- Progress assessment records.

In the "Keeping Records" portion of Section Three of this book you will learn about other home-school records that you may want or need to keep. At this point, however, you should design a plan for keeping whatever records are required or desirable. School officials will probably be most interested in records related to certain segments of your statement of intent, such as curriculum and annual evaluation, assessment records and attendance records, schedules and calendars. Check the summary for your state in Section Four and the other legal information you obtain for specifications regarding records to keep. **Then read Section Three before completing your written plan for keeping records.** Following that reading, briefly write out a description of how you plan to maintain records that are required or that seem important to you. (See Sample Eleven on page 86.) Place that description in your statement of intent file for later submission to officials. If you are not responsible for explaining your record keeping procedures to officials, you will not need to write such a description. You should, nevertheless, design methods for convenient record keeping and then use them as you begin to plan and to teach.

✳✳✳

With this we complete our walk through the components of a home-school plan or proposal, called here a "statement of intent." Samples of each of the eleven segments of the statement of intent follow in this section. To further help you get started with your home-school plan, I offer the checklist on the next page. After reviewing each segment of the statement of intent in this section, consider whether or not each segment is required, is important to you, or is neither required nor important to you. Then check those that you will want to complete because they are required or important.

Still in the offing, now, is working through each of the components of the statement of intent that you elect to complete, preparing those you must for presentation to officials, and then seeking approval if needed. The upcoming sections of this book will help you carry out each of these tasks. First, Section Three takes you in greater detail into four home-school plan components: annual evaluation, curriculum and materials, lesson planning, and keeping records. You will need to read Section Three carefully before completing the related segments of your statement of intent.

Then, as you work on your statement or proposal, refer to Sections Four through Six of this book as necessary. In Section Four you'll find a chart and summaries delineating all fifty state and District of Columbia regulations and procedures and state department of education addresses. Home-school support organizations are listed in Section Five. In Section Six you'll find reading, resource, and curriculum source lists and finally a glossary of terms used in this book and/or used by the public school officials with whom you may interact.

Let's take a look now at the statement of intent segment samples and then move on to Section Three. You may feel you're in the midst of much information that is new to you and, therefore, a bit overwhelming. Please realize, however, that although there may be several components to your home-school plan, not any one of those components is too difficult for you to complete — whether you are a certified teacher, a college graduate, or neither. You can successfully complete each component. Your planning will take time, but the samples, explanations and aids in this book should carry you successfully through the process.

❋❋❋

Statement of Intent Checklist

I am required to complete this segment.	I feel this segment is important enough to complete.	Statement of Intent Segments
		1. Basic Personal Info – Enrollees
		2. Basic Building Info
		3. Home-Teacher Qualifications
		4. Certificated Consultant Info
		5. Statement of Reasons & Rights
		6. Plans for Annual Evaluation
		7. Curriculum and Materials
		8. Lesson Plan Samples
		9. Plans for Assessment
		10. Schedules and Calendars
		11. Plans for Keeping Records

Deadlines and other information related to the above checked segments of my Statement of Intent:

_____

_____

_____

_____

_____

_____

_____

_____

_____

_____

_____

Statement of Intent Segment Samples

The following samples include suggested formats and content of the statement of intent or program proposal documents. If forms are provided by your state's department of education or by the local school district, use those forms as you plan or transfer information to those forms later. The required content should be similar to that already described in this section or included in the samples. Adjust content as necessary. Of course, there will be as many variations in the actual wording of these documents as there are people who read this book. All samples are only samples.

Note that in brackets [ ] on the sample pages are comments directed at you. The items within brackets are to be read by you, but are not included as part of the sample format.

For Quick Reference

Explanations for the samples which follow here begin on the pages listed.

Sample One: Basic Personal Information - Enrollees

Home-School Enrollment Sheet

Mary   Miller   F   born 8/1/81   (13)   Box 171, Lee Lane, Sky, OK
Suzie   Miller   F   born 6/6/84   (10)   Box 171, Lee Lane, Sky, OK
Tom   Miller   M   born 7/3/86   (8)   Box 171, Lee Lane, Sky, OK
Billy   Miller   M   born 4/2/87   (7)   Box 171, Lee Lane, Sky, OK

[Note: Attach copies of birth certificates if required.]

Parents: Mark and Mazie Miller
Box 171 Lee Lane, Sky, OK 00001
phone: 111-2233

Students' current grade levels and previous schools attended:

Mary   grade seven   Fiddle Middle School, Sky, OK

Suzie   grade five   Intermediate Grade School, Sky, OK

Tom   grade three   Little People's School, Sky, OK

Billy   grade one   (not previously enrolled in school)

Immunization records: A copy of the immunization records for each child is attached. All are up-to-date.

Previously identified special needs:

Mary   – none

Suzie   – none At Intermediate Grade School in Sky, OK, Suzie participated twice weekly in a speech therapy program. At year's end she was exited from the program.
[Note: If Suzie still needs speech therapy, you may need to secure the services of a speech therapist, preferably the local school's speech therapist.]

Tom   – none

Billy   – Arrangements have been made for Billy to complete the usual school entrance screening procedures administered to all incoming kindergartners and first graders in Oklahoma School District #4444.

date _____ signed: _____
(parent)

date _____ signed: _____
(parent)

Sample Two: Home-School Building Information

Home-School Building Report

<u>Address of home school</u>: Box 24, Pine, Idaho 50009;
located three miles NW of Pine
via Highway 12

<u>Condition of home-school</u>: Our home-school building meets county building codes and has established fire escape routes from all rooms. Our children have participated in building safety discussions and in fire escape practices. [Note: If required, attached a statement from fire and safety inspectors attesting to the quality of your home-school building.]

<u>Safety of student records</u>: [Include this item if required.] Student records will be kept in a moisture-proof area in a cardboard file box. Duplicates of attendance records and ongoing assessment records will be kept in a separate building. Records of annual evaluations will be kept by School District #555 as well as in our file box.[Note: The school district may require that you submit other records as well. If so, make note here of the safekeeping of those records.]

<u>Home-school "classroom" environment</u>: We have designated a small room in our home as our home-school library and work-room. Our kitchen table will serve as a desk during sit-down lessons. Thus far, we have a collection of children's books, text-books, a dictionary and an atlas, totaling forty-four volumes, that constitute our home library. We also have access to our local public library's collection of 15,000 volumes, including encyclopedia sets appropriate for children. In our workroom, we also have a globe; United States, Idaho and Pine maps; a small aquarium; a terrarium; a piano; a work table; and miscellaneous math, music, art, and science supplies and equipment. We have access to a computer and educational software at the local public library. Our home school is surrounded by a natural world of creek, meadow, bushes, trees, and animal life which will allow in-the-field science studies. A mile-and-a-half down the road, within walking or driving or biking distance, is the Pine Historical Museum, the Pine Regional Bird Preserve, and the town of Pine, all of which will aid us in science and social studies.

[Note: If required, list names of all persons who reside in your home.]

Sample Three: Evidence of Home-Teacher Qualifications

Home-Teacher Qualifications

Home teacher: Mitzi Peters, mother

Educational background:

      grades K-8   — East Elementary School
                     Salisbury, OR
      grades 9-12 — East High School
                     Salisbury, OR
      high school graduation — 1980
      college   — two years at City Community College,
                     Salisbury, OR
      music   — four years of private piano instruction
      art   — participation in various, intermittent,
                     community education oil painting
                     and pottery workshops

Occupational experience:

      1977   — youth host, Salisbury Historical
                     Museum
      1980 —'82 — teacher's aide, Lincoln Primary School,
                     Stone, OR
      1983 —'89 — assistant librarian, Stone Public Library
      1990 —'94 — home-preschool teacher for two of our
                     children and three other children

Talents:

      piano; pottery; oil painting; storytelling; natural foods
      cooking; and wild plant identification, collection,
      preservation

[Note: If your spouse or other adults will assist you as a
home teacher, write a similar account of their education,
occupations, and talents, particularly those that pertain to
your children's home-school curriculum.]

Sample Four: Certificated Home-School Consultant

Certificated Home-School Consultant

We have secured the assistance of a certificated consultant.

<u>Certificated consultant</u>: Mason Sellers

    address: 1410 Doddridge Avenue, Blueville, KS 00001
    phone: 111- 4455

<u>Degree</u>:   Bachelor of Science
           1985, University of Oregon
           Elementary Education Major
           Library Science Minor

<u>Certificate</u>: Kansas Standard Elementary Certificate
           endorsements: elementary education & K-6
           librarian

<u>Current employment</u>: Sigwald Grade School, Blueville, KS

<u>Current teaching assignment</u>: fifth grade teacher

<u>Agreement:</u> Mr. Mason Sellers has agreed to assist in the development of our home-school curriculum and the selection of appropriate teaching materials. He has also agreed to meet with us twice each semester to informally evaluate our home-school program and to offer recommendations. Since three of our home-school children will be elementary level students and one a seventh grader, Mr. Seller's experience as an educator at the elementary level should prove most helpful.

[Since a certificated consultant is not required in Kansas and you would simply be volunteering this information, you would not need to attach copies of Mr. Seller's university transcripts and certificate.]

Sample Five: Statement of Positive Reasons and Rights

Statement of Positive Reasons and Rights

We the parents of Henry, Lisa, Corey, and Carlene Cellers wish to educate our children at home for the following reasons:

[List your reasons in clear, specific sentences. If appropriate, your compliance with the home-schooling statutes of your state should be noted.]

_____

George Cellers

_____

Tillie Cellers

Sample Six: Plans for Annual Evaluation

<u>Annual Evaluation</u>

We have arranged with Arizona School District #1000 for the purchase of copies of the Comprehensive Test of Basic Skills at appropriate levels for our two children, Tad and Jeff. The tests will be given to Tad and Jeff in our home by the certified head teacher of the Good Samaritan Private School here in Mars, Arizona, on April 14th. We will file copies of the achievement test results with the county superintendent and also maintain copies at our home school.

———————————————
Marvin Jones

———————————————
Mary Jones

Sample Seven: Curriculums and Materials

Grade One Language Arts Curriculum and Materials
for home student Janice Stone

PHONICS: The student will be able to
   -name the 26 upper and lower case alphabet letters on sight
   -associate consonant letters with beginning word sounds
   -distinguish between beginning consonant sounds
   -associate vowel letters with long and short vowel sounds
   -decode (read) words in context by using beginning
      consonant sounds, short and long vowel sounds, and
      consonant ending sounds
   Materials: [You would list one or more titles of textbooks and
      workbooks you plan to use. You may also or otherwise
      list resources, methods, and aids that you plan to use but
      which are not actual textbooks or workbooks.]

READING COMPREHENSION: The student will be able to
   -listen to or read one or more paragraphs and
      note aloud and remember important details
   -follow oral or printed one- to three-step directions
   -listen to or read a story and recall events in sequential order
   -listen to or read a paragraph and identify its main idea
   -listen to or read a story and answer cause/effect questions
   -use oral or written information to predict outcomes
   -group words according to categories of meaning
   Materials: [textbooks, workbooks, resources...]

CHILDREN'S LITERATURE: The student will be able to
   -listen to a complete children's story with pleasure
   -listen to children's poetry with pleasure
   -discuss elements of a children's story that interest him
   -identify story characters, using the term "character"
   -name favorite story titles and authors, using the terms
      "title" and "author"
   -recognize a poem when heard and when seen on a page
   -name favorite children's poems and poets, using the
      terms "poem" and "poet"
   -name favorite children's book illustrators, using the
      terms "illustrator" and "illustration"
   -tell brief, informal stories
   Materials: children's books in our home library and from the
      Mar's Public Library

   [You will need to continue the curriculum in a similar
   fashion for other subject areas.]

Sample Eight: Lesson Plans

Brief Lesson Plan

Subject Area: SCIENCE   Dates _____

Focus: turtles as representative of reptiles

Learning Objective: Students will be able to identify body parts of the turtle and their functions, explain the turtle life cycle and needs, food, dangers, reptilian characteristics, and habitat.

Monday

Observe turtle. Open-ended questions.
Record observations on chart.
Build terrarium.

Tuesday

Biologist Kelly Green
Observe turtle.
Review, summarize, and add items to chart.
Organize chart items.
Determine what information we still need.

Wednesday

Further observations and library research.
Students begin a mural showing turtle habitat, food,
     etc., and identify and label turtle body parts
     and their functions.

Thursday

Orally quiz individual students.
Finish mural.
Develop a feeding and care plan for our pet turtle,
     based upon the information we've learned.

Friday

Individually complete turtle worksheets.
Give immediate feedback with butcher paper drawing.

[Note: In Appendix C, an explanation is given of each of the five lesson steps — anticipatory set, instruction, guided practice, closure, and independent practice.]

Sample Nine: Plans for Ongoing Progress Assessment

Home-School Student Progress Assessment

For both of our sons, Henry and James Sultan, we plan to engage in various, ongoing progress-assessment procedures and to maintain permanent portfolios of their work and of any written tests or quizzes for all subject areas.

Means of Assessment

phonics	**math**	**social studies**
assignments	assignments	assignments
checktests	checktests	unit tests
oral reading	unit tests	projects
	applications	oral discussion

science	**reading/lit.**	**language**
assignments	oral discussion	assignments
unit projects	read-alouds	unit tests
field work and journals	comprehension activities	oral & written use of language
field work		
field journals		

piano	**computer**
daily observation of practice	daily observations of use
recitals	application projects

Sample Ten: Schedules and Calendars

Weekly Home-School Schedule

for Susie & Tim Bayson, grades 1 and 2 respectively

Time	Monday	Tuesday	Wednesday	Thursday	Friday
8:00	phonics/reading/literature – – – – – – – – – – – – –				
8:45	math	computer	math	math	computer
9:15	social studies– – – – – – – – – – – – – – – – –				
9:40	language skills – – –	piano		language skills - - -	
10-12	science & field work	piano		science & field work	
12:00	lunch– – – – – – – – – – – – – – – – – – – –				
1:00	art & special interest activities– – – – – –– library work				

[Note that the above lesson schedule includes a required core curriculum plus piano lessons, art, and library. Other curricular or extracurricular activities may be included in your schedule. There is a possibility that you and your children are among the many home schoolers who gather with other home schoolers one day each week for field trips or activity days. Such days can also be included in your schedule. Just make sure that your schedule includes the mandatory curricular areas and the number of hours required by law in your state. Also, you may decide to arrange your schedule in integrated curricular blocks of time, rather than, as shown above, in isolated-subject time segments.]

Monthly Home-school Calendar

November 1994						
		①	②	③	④	5
6	⑦	⑧	⑨	⑩	⑪	12
13	⑭	⑮	⑯	⑰	⑱	19
20	㉑	㉒	㉓	24	25	26
27	㉘	㉙	㉚			

Sample Eleven: Plans for Keeping Records

Home-School Records

<u>Means of keeping records</u> for Shane & Kay Tuttle:

  portfolios of papers, projects, samples, etc.,
       in all subject areas
  portfolios of actual assessments or reports of
       assessment results
  observation log to be kept by home teacher
  social activities log
  permanent files — report card
       test and quiz score records
       achievement test results
       previous grade report cards
       immunization records
       other health & dental records
  attendance register
  speech therapy records for Kay

[You may be expected to secure the permanent files in as fire-proof and moisture-proof a fashion as possible.]

<u>Teacher-related records that will be kept:</u>

  lesson plan book
  consultant activity file
  weekly lesson schedule
  yearly calendar

[You may not need to include all of the above items in your record-keeping plans. On the other hand, you may wish to add others. See "Keeping Records" in Section Three for a complete list of possibilities.]

Section **3**

Key Components

Why Some Segments Become Key Components

As we walked through the eleven possible segments of your statement of intent in Section Two, it became clear that not all eleven segments are necessarily required by your state, or desired by you, or even essential to home schooling. But for reasons pertinent to your home-schooling situation and your state's procedures and laws, some segments will emerge as key components of your program plan. The four components covered in this section are among those that often surface as most important or most necessary, and they require more than the introductory explanations offered in Section Two. Therefore, in this section you'll find detailed discussions of **annual evaluation**, **curriculum and materials**, **lesson planning**, and **record keeping**.

Many home schoolers consider annual evaluations to be unnecessary and annoying. Nevertheless, in several states evaluation procedures are required for *legal* home schooling. Curriculums and accompanying materials lists are also often required. Whether required or not, a written curriculum can serve as a critical map and compass for your children's academic journeys. Like evaluations, lesson planning is considered by many to be nonessential, but in some instances is required and may be useful, particularly for the beginning home teacher. Lesson plans serve as a daily and weekly mini-map — a cutout, as it were, from the larger curriculum map. Perhaps most important of all components of your home-school plan and ongoing program is record keeping. As you'll see in the "Keeping Records" portion of this section, certain types of records are almost always required — attendance, immunizations, schedules and calendars, for example. Others may be required. However, you'll need to consider not just requirements when you decide which records are essential for you to keep. You may find that maintaining permanent *evidence* of the soundness of your children's home-school program is a key factor necessitating thorough record keeping.

Planning for and completing annual evaluations, curriculum outlines, and lesson plans, as well as maintaining good records, involves more thought and time than some of the other home-school program components. Read slowly and carefully through this section. Study each element, use the worksheets that are provided, get assistance when needed...and have faith in your ability to successfully complete each component.

Annual Evaluation

Potentially useful and required by many states is some form of end-of-the-year evaluation of each home-schooled child's progress and/or learning program. You may be asked to account for your plans regarding annual evaluation in your statement of intent and to have those plans officially approved along with the other segments of your home-school program proposal. At the appropriate time, of course, you would then need to conduct your proposed evaluation. If not required, you may want to conduct a personal evaluation of your children's home-schooling accomplishments and of your teaching program in order to make decisions about your children's next school year.

The process and composition of annual home-school evaluations vary widely. The person responsible for the evaluation may be you or a certificated educator, and sometimes on-site reviews are carried out by school officials. In some states evaluation items must be submitted and "accepted" following their completion. Any of the following annual evaluation elements, singly or in combination, may be required in your state.

- Standardized achievement tests
- Local or state-designed competency tests
- Review of and/or submittal of student portfolios
- Review of and/or submittal of curriculums, lesson plans, report cards
- Narrative reports on student progress in each subject
- Narrative reports on student social progress
- Schedules and calendars
- A summary of quarterly evaluations
- A discussion between your child and a consultant
- Diaries, journals, or logs
- An inspection/supervision visit by public school officials
- Evaluation elements selected by you or by you and a consultant

Official reasons for requiring an annual evaluation may be three-fold: (1) to ensure that each of your children is indeed being educated; (2) to initiate means by which to improve student progress should it be lagging; and (3) to actuate improvement efforts for you as a home teacher if appropriate.

Standardized Achievement Tests

The most commonly required form of evaluation is the standard-ized achievement test. It is also one of the most controversial, even among non-home schoolers. Racial or religious bias, misuse or dis-use of results, lack of correlation with local curriculum content, misinterpretation of results, inflated scores due to invalid or inaccu-rate norms, and similar issues are often cited as problems with the tests. Also, of course, for many home schoolers the *imposition* of tests is an issue.

Usually, however, if standardized achievement tests are a legal requirement, there is no way to escape that imposition. Sometimes participation in a satellite or correspondence program is used as a means to evade the tests. Usually, however, home educators who are required to arrange for the administration of achievement tests simply do their best to prepare their children for them. We should recognize, too, that the results of these tests have offered, and we hope will continue to offer, important and impressive statistical information for use in increasing public awareness of the benefits of home schooling. Your children's scores can be entered into those statistics, indirectly enabling you and them to further the home-school cause in our nation.

There may be requirements you must follow pertaining to your children's testing circumstances. Perhaps, for example, your children must appear at the local school at a specific time on a specific day to take the test with public school children of the same grade levels. You may try to have the circumstances altered, but often your control over those circumstances is limited.

Try to ease your children into the tests with explanatory discus-sions ahead of time. Usually standardized test teacher's manuals include practice tests which all teachers may use to prepare their students for taking the tests. You should be able to get a copy of the practice test and the teacher's directions for giving the practice test from a local school principal or superintendent. There is no official reason the practice test cannot be shared with you. Typically, too, school principals have copies of a test management guide or manual, sometimes called "class management guide." In such a guide may be found suggestions for student activities that would prepare students for the test content and item-by-item formats that appear in the test, as well as actual samples of test item formats. A principal is free to share this information with any or all teachers, including you. Therefore, along with a request for a practice test, you may wish to ask about the availability of test management guide information of the sort noted here. Resistance locally to supplying you with any test information might be followed up by you with a call to your state department of education. You can explain your problem, request assistance, or request a copy of the practice test and other information from your state department.

Another source of test information is your certificated consultant, if you have one, or another teacher who has given the locally used achievement test at the grade levels of your children. The teacher will probably have taken mental or written notes of the content areas covered in the test and can also explain formats that appear in the test. She may even supply you with a copy of the practice test and directions. Although teachers do try to include test content within their year's instruction, oftentimes it is not the content but the formats in the tests that confuse students. Because the formats are not usually used at any other time during a school year, they can be totally new on the day of the test. The major reason for giving practice tests is to acquaint students with a test's format. Noteworthy, too, is the fact that teachers are free to use the formats for regular assignments and activities throughout the school year and would certainly be wise to do so, as would you.

If you are able to secure a practice test, try to set up a mock test environment similar to the upcoming actual test situation. Follow the practice instructions carefully so your child can rehearse listening to and following them. After the practice test has been completed, correct it and then discuss with your child her answers and her reasons for her answers — in other words, her thinking process. Her thinking may fully explain the logic of a wrong answer. Then tell her *what the test expected*, even though her answer was logical. Try to help her realize, too, that although the test experience is somewhat strange, it is just another learning activity. Help her understand that it is in part an exercise in how well she can take a test or play the test game, if you will, rather than simply in how knowledgeable she is. Also, try not to add pressure by elaborating on the possible danger of a low score to your home-schooling status. In addition, discussing typical testing time frames may be useful. You can explain that some parts of the test may be timed and that this means she shouldn't dawdle with those portions of the test game. Tell her to relax, to enjoy the test items, but to move along. Incidentally, if a child finishes a test section before the time is up, she will have to silently wait. She might take a book along to read during the waiting periods. Before the testing begins, let the test administrator know your child has a book to read during spare time.

If you have not been able to secure information on formats or content before your children take their first achievement test, ask your children to tell you immediately afterwards about the content and formats. Take notes and save them for the following year. The specific content will change from year to year but be generally similar. For example, word attack sections in primary grade tests will cover similar content — phonics, deriving meaning from context, etc. — but the specific items will be different and slightly more advanced with each test level. However, the formats will be pretty much the same. So once your children describe to you the formats, you can use those formats for test preparation each year. You can also use them on activities during the year and even type your own practice tests using those formats.

Also, no doubt your fellow home schoolers will be able to tell you about the achievement test used in the local school. They may offer ideas about how to make the test-taking experience as comfortable as possible for your children. They may mention, for example, that if you can choose the person who will give the test, choose a person familiar to your child or acquaint your child with the person well before test day. Studies show that non-anxious test-takers score higher and that positive familiarization between test-taker and test-giver also results in higher scores. Furthermore, a stranger who gives your child the test has no means of adapting his behavior and presentation in any manner that is sensitive to your child's personality, fears, or background. In other words, it is helpful for the test administrator to know your child. You may also want to familiarize your child with the room where she will take the test. You might even volunteer to be a test monitor in the testing room during the time your child takes the test. When public school teachers give achievement tests, they often welcome help with pencils, erasers, papers, and student questions. If you can't be a monitor, you might ask to sit at the back of the room as a silent observer at least the first day of the test. Be certain first, however, that your presence will not in this case distract your child.

When considering steps you might take towards improving testing conditions for your child, it may help to keep in mind what happens when public schools plan for and administer standardized achievement tests. Typically the test company designates a two week testing period throughout the nation, and schools often elect to reserve the second week for make-up tests. During the first week, test subsections are administered in varying blocks of time over a three-to-five day period depending on the test levels and lengths. While public school teaching staffs may agree generally upon testing hours, teachers are usually free to schedule their individual class test sessions as they see fit and they are encouraged to schedule the sessions when testing conditions are optimal for good student performance. Almost universally those conditions include hours when the teachers know students are most alert and yet most able to remain composed and quiet, when the classroom is cool and comfortable, when testing time blocks and breaks can be flexibly arranged, when any potentially disruptive students can be removed from the regular classroom, and when no outside interruptions will occur. The teacher administering the test is almost always the one who has worked throughout the year with the group of students he tests and is therefore the in-school adult with whom the students are most familiar. In many elementary schools, teachers' aides, office workers, or parent volunteers are on hand in each classroom to provide assistance with pencils and test papers, questions, unexpected disruptions, opening a window, offering whispered reassurances to nervous or weary students, and so on. Special-needs students may be given their tests in individual or small group situations away from regular classrooms and by familiar adults. In general, in other words, public school personnel proffer the position that any child who takes a standardized achievement test has a right to optimal conditions. And so does any teacher. (One key reason good test conditions are important to public school personnel is that they facilitate better results, which in turn reflect well upon the teachers and administrators.)

To arrange reasonable achievement test conditions for your children, I recommend that you visit with the principal or other person in charge of scheduling and/or conducting the achievement tests. Ask about the test site. If not a regular classroom, is it well ventilated and roomy enough for the number of students who will be present? Will your children have comfortable chairs and desks or tables on which to work? If your child will take the test in a regular classroom with public school students, has the teacher been made aware that your child will attend the test session? Will he have an extra desk and chair brought in ahead of time? Is lighting adequate? Ask to see the site. Ask to meet the person who will administer the test. Then discuss timing. Sometimes public school administrators will schedule home schoolers' test sessions all in one day in order to make driving to the test convenient for the home-school parents. However, in the case of tests, the children's needs must take precedence if you hope for good results. Completing an entire achievement test in one day would be a tremendous strain, particularly for elementary-age children. I suggest that you do all that you can to arrange for a three-to-five day testing period and also to ensure that adequate breaks will be taken between subtests. Also, you as the teacher of your children know those times of the day when your children are best able to do sit-down work. Recommend to the test arranger that the test be administered during those times if in any way possible.

If the test arranger is reluctant to improve the proposed test situation, question him regarding the conditions under which the students in his school take the test. Ask him to describe those conditions in detail. If he is truthful, you and he will recognize that he is describing optimal conditions. Then suggest that the home-schooled children be given the same considerations. If a number of home-schooled children are being scheduled for the same test, you might offer the assistance of a committee of home-school parents to arrange the test sessions and situation and even to function as volunteer test monitors. Do realize that requesting the same optimal test conditions that the teachers in the local public school maintain is certainly reasonable.

Test Selection

What of the tests themselves? In many states or school districts one test is specified as the one home-school children, as well as public school children, must take. Some states, on the other hand, require home schoolers to select their own standardized achievement tests and to then arrange for the administration of those tests. You may be specifically required, as part of your statement of intent, to complete and submit what is known as a "notice of test selection." This means the state or local school district will not mandate that you utilize the standardized test that they use, but that your children are required to take such a test and that you must submit a form or statement indicating that you are in compliance with the requirement.

In this situation, you'll need to shop for a test. The information you have received from your state department may suggest certain tests or provide you with a list of tests which have already been approved and from which you can choose. Otherwise, you will need to locate possible tests and select one on your own. If you have established a good working relationship with a local public school principal or superintendent, she may be able and willing to supply you with the locally used test. If you are affiliated with private or correspondence school administrators, one of them may be able to supply a test that meets required criteria. You could also contact the state testing division of your state department of education, as mentioned above, or an area university's educational testing, research, or public instruction department. Then too, of course, state or national public education or home-school service organizations may be able to help you obtain test information and/or tests. (See Section Five.)

If you are totally on your own, remember that in order for the test you select to be approved or acceptable to school officials, it must be a standardized, normed achievement test. To be standardized, uniform testing procedures must be used throughout the country. To be normed a test must have undergone a norming procedure during which a representative sample of students was given the test. Then those students' scores become the norm to which all other scores are compared until a subsequent norming procedure is undertaken. Incidentally, you will most likely want to secure the most recent edition of the test you select. Also, realize that no two tests cover exactly the same content. For instance, one may include participles in the language usage segment of the test and others not. One may include coins in the primary math segment and others not. Take advantage of any opportunities to preview test content — firsthand, or secondhand by visiting with others who have used the tests you are considering. This information can help you select a test that is well correlated with the academic areas your children have covered in their home-school lessons. Here are some generally accepted tests from which you might choose:

- California Achievement Test (CAT)
- Comprehensive Test of Basic Skills (CTBS)
- Essential High School Content Battery
- Iowa Tests of Achievement and Proficiency
- Iowa Tests of Basic Skills (ITBS)
- Metropolitan Achievement Battery
- Sequential Tests of Educational Progress
- SRA Achievement Battery
- Stanford Achievement Test Battery

Test Interpretation

Although local school officials (and even teachers) seldom give great attention to individual student achievement test results, and in some cases don't thoroughly understand the results, they will probably use your home-schooled children's test results to determine indeed if your children are being properly schooled. In actuality the test results for any one year are not highly significant. Only when you compile an ongoing chart of year-by-year achievement test results can you begin to see trends in your children's areas of academic strengths and weaknesses. This ongoing information can be significant. However, the officials may use single-year test results for your children to evaluate your children's progress and the effectiveness of your teaching.

In view of this, I provide here a brief explanation of test interpretation. Interpreting achievement test scores can be confusing and complicated, and it is essential that you have a basic understanding of the scores yourself. Equipped with such understanding, you will be able to exercise some control over the possible application of the standardized achievement test results to your home-school evaluation and to spot any misinterpretations by school personnel.

Let's look at some of the types of scores provided on achievement test score reports:

> Raw Score. This score tells you the total number of items in any one category of an achievement test that your child answered correctly. All of the below-noted types of scores are derived from it.

The raw score is not typically accorded much importance. In fact, you may notice what appears to be little relationship between raw scores and other scores. Their relationship to the percentile scores in subtest categories, for example, will vary from subtest to subtest. To explain this variability, let's consider the percentile score.

>Percentile Rank. This score tells you how your child fared in comparison to all other children in the norm group who took the same test. That is, the percentile figure tells you what percentage of those children scored below your child. For example, if your child's percentile rank is 70, then you know that 69 out of every 100 children in the norm group who took the test achieved a score below that of your child.

A perfect, all-answers-correct raw score does not necessarily result in a percentile score of 100. Since the percentile rank reflects how many students scored lower than your child, perhaps a perfect raw score in one category will yield a percentile score in the mid-nineties. In another category it may produce a percentile in the high-nineties, depending on the number of students who answered every item correctly. Thus, the percentile rank allows comparison among students, whereas the raw score does not.

When interpreting the percentile rank, remember this important factor: If the percentile rank for one year in one test category is approximately the same as that score on the past year's test, your child has gained one full year's academic growth in that category. In other words, if your child scores at the 70th percentile in mathematics this year and he scored at the 70th percentile (or thereabouts) last year, he has gained one full year's growth in mathematics. The level of the test he has taken, you see, increased in difficulty by one year.

Therefore, if your child maintains a percentile rank of 70 (or any other single rank) from year-to-year, he is gaining a year's academic growth each year. If his score dips about ten or more percentile points during a single year or over a period of a few years, he may not be maintaining that rate of academic growth. If his score increases about ten or more percentile points, he is making progress greater than one year's academic growth. Further, note that if your child's score dips or rises dramatically just one year while the scores for all years before and after remain relatively the same, you can conclude that the off-year scores are probably invalid.

>Grade Equivalent. This score identifies the grade level at which the median test score of all students in that grade is the same as that achieved by your child. (A median score is the score in a distribution which has one half of the remaining scores above it and the other half below it.)

Some test publishers are phasing out the grade equivalent score, and teachers are today not referring to it as often as in the past. People have a tendency to suggest that a high grade equivalent score indicates that a student should skip a grade or two and enter the grade identified by the grade equivalent score. While a high score indicates that the child who earned it performed above average among his grade level peers on his own grade level test content, it does not necessarily mean that he would do as well with content above his own grade level. A low grade equivalent score indicates that the child performed below average among his peers on his own grade level test content, but does not mandate that he should be put back a grade level or be retained, although it may be one consideration in making such a decision.

A relatively new score being currently used on achievement test score reports is this next one.

> Normal Curve Equivalent. The NCE scores range from 1 to 99 and coincide with percentile scores at 1, 50, and 99. NCE's have many of the characteristics of percentile ranks but have the additional advantage of being based on an equal-interval scale. This allows for mathematical manipulation of the scores, particularly desirable for supplementary programs such as "Chapter I." Like percentile scores, an NCE score that remains the same from one year to the next indicates one year's academic growth.

Two other achievement test scores, stanines and scaled scores, are seldom referred to by public educators in discussions with parents, and you are not likely to need knowledge of either of them during your annual evaluation process, but if you do, ask for a copy of the test publisher's written descriptions of these scores.

All standardized test scores leave room for a margin of error. Test publishers call this the "standard error of measurement." Thus all achievement test scores should be considered as estimates. We know that a true score exists for each child who takes a test, but the actual score he receives only falls within a band or range within which his true score would fall. We can't be sure what that true score is. In other words, a percentile rank of 70 is an estimated score which indicates that his true score may be 65 or 68 or 75 or some other score within a certain range.

It is important to remember, too, that the purpose of norm-referenced achievement test scores is primarily comparison. They are intended for comparisons among students as a measure of a common education. They further provide a basis for year-by-year tracking of an individual student's achievement. In some instances, test scores are used to evaluate particular instructional programs and may also be used to reflect upon the effectiveness of the teachers who teach the test-takers. The scores may in fact be used to reflect upon your teaching, and may be pointed to as cause to begin "remediation" measures or may jeopardize your right to home school. (Ironically, while public school educators have for years accepted normal curve results whereby one-fourth of the students may score in the lowest quartile, no one presumes these low scores, or their teachers, should be removed from their school setting.)

Standardized achievement tests are often also accorded much value in decision-making situations relative to individual students regardless of the tests' suspected flaws and of problems related to the testing situation. Among those flaws or problems may be those mentioned earlier, such as biases and a lack of correlation with a school's curriculum, an insensitivity to student reactions to the test-taking environment, inflexibility regarding student health on test day, and the possible ambiguity of test items. Further, we note the areas of learning that are missing from the tests that might speak well for home-schooled children — creative writing, art, music, health, values, character development, consumer education, entrepreneurship, and others. However, while home schoolers may want to participate in such watchdog organizations as The National Center for Fair and Open Testing, they may, in the meantime, need to continue meeting achievement test requirements.

What we're hoping for you and your children, at any rate, is at least a year's academic growth — reflected in achievement test scores. You now know how to determine if such growth has taken place. Also important to note is that achievement test results are (or should be) only one factor in determining growth. Your children's daily performance, routine quiz and test scores, portfolios, projects, social behavior and development, daily exhibition of a sense of well-being, attitudes toward learning, zest and zeal, and so on, are all indicators of growth. Unfortunately, arguing this point with school officials may not prove successful.

Local or State Competency Tests

A school district or state department of education may use standardized achievement test results in combination with local or state competency tests or may rely on competency tests alone. Competency tests typically cover writing as well as reading and mathematics, at a basic level, and they are not ordinarily given below junior high level. They are shorter and narrower in scope than standardized achievement tests, are typically not normed and usually provide what are called "criterion-referenced" scores identifying the number of items a student answered correctly. The writing subtest, however, is likely to be holistically scored (the *whole* composition as a single scoring unit is responded to by the scorer) often on a 1-5 or 1-10 point basis. Usually the formats are familiar to students and the content is based directly upon local or state curriculums. Some schools now use the competency test results as a means of screening students eligible for diplomas.

If you live in one of the states where local public schools use competency tests, you may be expected to arrange for your home-schooled children to take these tests. Scoring may vary among different tests, so ask for thorough explanations of the scoring procedures as well as for information related to the competency test content and formats. The results of such tests will probably become a part of your home-school annual evaluation.

Other Evaluative Documents

Also considered as part of an evaluation may be your children's portfolios for each subject area. In some states you may be asked to submit the portfolios to officials. (See p. 138 for details on portfolios.) Other items that may be a part of your ongoing record-keeping procedure and that may become important in your annual evaluation are your curriculum outlines, lesson plans, report cards, schedules and calendars. You may be asked to have these items reviewed by a consultant, to account for them yourself in an evaluative report, or to submit them to school officials at year's end. If lesson plans are required, you may be asked to account for them or to submit them routinely throughout your home-school year.

You may also be asked to arrange for the writing and submittal of a narrative report on student progress in each subject area and/or on student social progress. You can base your student progress narrative on student work, cumulative projects, tests, etc., and on your lesson plans for the year which show what has been taught to each child. You may need to show what is called "curriculum mastery" which involves concrete demonstration that your student has achieved the skills and knowledge that were designated as goals or objectives in the curriculum. In the narrative, then, you would need to discuss what your child's curriculum goals and objectives were at the year's beginning and which of the goals and objectives he had mastered by year's end. In a few states you may also be requested to describe your children's social, cultural, and/or character development. You may find helpful Annual Evaluation Sample One: Narrative on page 104.

You may not be expected to write the narrative yourself. Instead a consultant may be asked to investigate factors demonstrating your child's progress and to write the evaluation narrative. The consultant may, on the other hand, be asked to review and summarize evaluations that you and she had completed on a quarterly basis throughout your home-school year. She may further be asked to discuss with your child his year of home schooling.

Another possible inclusion in a yearly evaluation is a home teacher's daily diary, journal, or log which documents home-school attendance, lessons, and activities. Your personal observations of your child's academic and social progress and strengths and weaknesses may also be included. Your home teacher's log would be kept in a notebook of some sort, such as an inexpensive spiral notebook, and you would probably write in an entry each day or every other day or perhaps write a fairly detailed overview at the end of each home-school week. If turning in your log is a requirement, remember that the primary purpose of a log is to demonstrate your children's coverage of the required curriculum. So you'll want to make note of all curricular areas on an ongoing basis. A daily log might look like Annual Evaluation Sample Two: Home Teacher's Log on page 105.

Official Visits

Perhaps state statutes or procedures necessitate a visit by school officials. Such a visit may be part of an annual evaluation or separate from it. If a visit is imminent, try to identify ahead of time those elements of your home-school program about which school officials will be curious. Review the home-school requirements in your state to be sure you can demonstrate compliance with each of them. Also consider your physical setup, home library, the location and safe-keeping of your home-school records, and so on. You might create a small checklist for yourself as you prepare for the visit. Include items such as the following eight.

1. My curriculums for each child — Are they written, available, used? Do I have student work available that demonstrates that the curriculums are being taught? Am I familiar enough with the curriculums to discuss them? Do I have teaching materials on hand that I may want to show and discuss?

2. Progress assessment — Can I demonstrate how I will carry out or am carrying out ongoing assessments of each child's progress and achievement?

3. Required paper work and deadlines — Have I completed all required documents?

4. Attendance — Are my attendance records for each child available and up-to-date? Do they show that my children have been schooled the required numbers of hours and days? Are these records kept in a safe place?

5. Our home-school setup — What special aspects of our home-school arrangement will I want to point out to the visitors? Our home library? Our aquarium? What else?

6. Special services — Do I need for any reason to explain our use of special services by people such as a certified consultant, speech or hearing therapist, physical therapist, school psychologist? Or of facilities such as a library, gym, or science lab?

7. Socialization — Am I prepared to discuss the ways in which my children are involved in social activities that include other children, as well as adults?

8. Do I have any questions or issues I want to discuss with the visitors?

Add whatever items you wish to your checklist. Base the checklist upon those factors that involve requirements, expected procedures, exemplary teaching, and good or excellent student achievement. Then, using your checklist, prepare yourself for the official visit.

Finally, in some states you and your consultant can develop your own plan for an annual evaluation of your children's progress and of your home-school program. Whichever the case in your state, when you submit your statement of intent or a home-school proposal you may be expected to include your plans for either the required annual evaluation process or for an evaluation process planned by you. Once you have determined the choices regarding an annual evaluation that your state allows, do the needed planning for any required evaluation. At the end of your home-school year and/or at other appropriate times, you'll need to implement your evaluation plan.

An annual evaluation usually takes place when one's curriculum for the year has been completed or nearly completed. To truly reflect upon the effectiveness of your teaching and on your child's learning, the evaluation should logically correlate with goals and objectives outlined in your curriculum. If you are the designer of your evaluation, you could ensure such correlation. In most situations, however, correlation between evaluation and curriculum will be only partial. Standardized achievement tests, for instance, are based upon sets of goals and objectives unique to each test. Curriculums are established without regard for the specific content of standardized achievement tests, although curriculum framers often are generally aware of or informed of the content of the test which will be taken by the students who will use their curriculum. In your case, as a home-school teacher, you will probably have to draft your curriculum without benefit of such awareness or information. This fact does not, however, mean that your curriculum can not be at least partially correlated with standardized tests or other evaluation devices that are used. By following the curriculum design method delineated in the next portion of this section, you will be able to plan a curriculum that does include commonly evaluated content, as well as other content that you wish to include. Let's step next, then, onto the pages of your home-school curriculum.

Annual Evaluation Sample One: Narrative

Annual Evaluation Narrative

Home Student: Billy Miller   Grade: one

Please note: General curricular categories of Billy's studies appear in capital letters below. Specific learning objectives are underlined.

With respect to CHILDREN'S LITERATURE, Billy has logged a total of 144 children's books, including 19 Caldecott Award Books and other selections of children's literature, in his self-illustrated "Books I Have Listened To" scrapbook. He has spent no less than 30 minutes each home-school day listening to complete stories and to books of children's poetry.

Having enjoyed hundreds of poems by a wide variety of poets, including young poets featured in the children's magazine *Stone Soup*, Billy has developed a roster of his favorite poems and poets which he names and discusses with anyone interested and he can identify poetry by both its visual configuration in magazines and books and by its cadences when he hears it aloud.

He is also happy to pull out stories by his favorite authors and children's book illustrators whenever friends visit after school or on weekends. Prior to his "reading" of the book to a friend, he will identify the story characters and offer an overview of the events in the story. At times, he and a friend will abandon the books in our 60-volume library and simply tell stories of their own and now and then even create skits to depict their stories and present them to any available adults.

Billy has developed a great love of books during his first years of storybook experiences. Certain books have even become his "teddy bears" for bedtime sharing and cuddling. And his favorite building in Sky, Kansas, is the Sky Public Library. At the library he has also enjoyed the monthly Storybook Puppet Shows put on by the local arts association.

[Note: This narrative is based upon the Children's Literature Curriculum outlined in "Sample Seven: Curriculum and Materials" on page 82 at the end of Section Two. This portion would be only one segment of a larger evaluation narrative which would refer to all areas of the curriculum. Although actually writing the narrative will be time-consuming, if you rely on your curriculum outline and your records of daily lessons, you should quickly and easily come up with the information you need for your narrative.]

Annual Evaluation Sample Two: Home Teacher's Log

Home Teacher's Log

School Year: 1994-95
Home Student: Billy Miller   Grade: one
Home Teacher: Mazie Miller

Sept. 1: Morning, <u>phonics</u> — beginning consonant sounds; <u>reading</u> — oral paragraphs in the form of a simple recipe for no-bake cookies which Billy followed as I read; <u>literature</u> — an oral reading of *Frederick* by Leo Lionni followed by discussion of the central character, a mouse; <u>math</u> — counting and measurement — as we made the cookies; <u>social studies</u> — continued work on Billy's cardboard model of a metropolis he calls "Megalapatropolis. During lunch, <u>science</u> — watched a video documentary on African wildlife which Billy later discussed with his dad. Afternoon, <u>literature</u>, <u>science</u>, & <u>socialization</u> — we joined other home schoolers for a trip to the library for the monthly Storybook Puppet Show, followed by a walk through the park to find leaf samples and to play with the other kids. Later, <u>art</u>, <u>literature</u> — Billy did a painting of a giraffe on the African plains and the usual bedtime story — this time *The Grey Lady and the Strawberry Snatcher* by Molly Bang.

Sept. 2: Morning, <u>phonics</u> — review and on to new consonants; <u>reading</u> — a letter from Billy's Aunt Goldie after which Billy reiterated to me the main things about which Aunt Goldie had written; <u>writing</u> — Billy dictated a letter to Aunt Goldie which I typed and read back to him and then he attempted with some success his own reading of the letter; <u>art</u> & <u>science</u> — Billy made a crayon rubbing of three of the leaves he'd found in the park yesterday and then dictated to me brief paragraphs describing each leaf and the tree from which each came; <u>math</u> — counting the leaves he'd gathered and gluing them to a sheet of paper in order of size, smallest to largest, and discussing the comparative sizes of the trees from which the leaves had come. Afternoon, <u>literature</u> — *On Market Street* by Arnold Lobel, followed by Billy's oral story of what he'd do during a day on Market Street; <u>music</u> — piano lesson; <u>physical education</u> — fast-walking with his sister and the planning of what they called "A Super Health Nut Backyard Picnic Supper."

Sept. 3: Morning, <u>math</u> — counted people lining up for our home-schoolers' field trip bus ride and compared the number of children with the number of grown-ups, the number of boys with the number of girls, and the number of bus seats with the number of people; <u>social studies</u> — discussed with other home schooled children and their parents the many transportation systems available in the U.S. and their advantages and disadvantages; <u>science</u> — visit to the Kansas City Nature Museum. Evening, <u>literature</u> — read *Ferdinand*, Billy's current favorite children's book.

Curriculum and Materials

A written curriculum is one of the most frequently required components of a home-school program proposal. In public school terms, a curriculum is a set of goals and objectives or outcomes for student learning in each of the subject areas that will be taught. The goals and objectives usually relate to or stem from a personal (home-school) or institutional philosophy of education and life. Suggested textbooks, materials, and methods are also often listed as tools with which the curriculum may be taught. You may even see the term *curriculum* used to refer to the materials themselves. However, materials in themselves are *not* a curriculum and should not be used as such. When a school uses a set of materials as the curriculum, that school has turned over its educational philosophies, its courses and course structures, and often its teaching methods to the publisher of the materials! Educational materials should only be used as *aids* to teaching the goals, objectives, and outcomes or philosophies of a school's curriculum. You should establish your home-school curriculum before searching for and selecting materials. During the school year, lesson planning will allow for means by which you can carry out the curriculum, and materials will aid you.

Typically, the states delineate specifically which subject areas must be included in a home-school curriculum, and the regulations or procedures often require that the selection of subject areas must demonstrate that "the same," "comparable," or "equivalent" instruction to that given in public schools is being provided in home schools. To the required curricular areas you may add courses of your own choosing. You can check the "Basic Information Chart" and your state's summary in Section Four of this book, and other legal information you obtain to determine if your state has such requirements.

If your state makes no mention of curriculum requirements for home schoolers, it is still possible that *expected* procedures have been established either statewide or locally that include the selection or writing of a curriculum. You need to identify and study such procedures. Check with experienced local home educators. Your ability to show evidence that a suitable curriculum does exist for each of your home-schooled children may determine whether or not you'll be able to legally continue to home school should you be challenged at any time by school officials. In the minds of many public school officials, no written curriculum equals no schooling.

Regardless of the requirements, your children's interests and your own academic passions should play a role in designing your curriculum and lesson plans and also in designing methods and materials with which to teach and learn. Interests, passions, philosophies, beliefs, even going off on a tangent now and then, should play a role, a significant role. We should recognize, too, that the social, emotional, philosophical, and spiritual aspects of living that we wish to develop in our children can be and should be interwoven into the academic. The academic does not need to control a child's life. Instead, while academics are given full opportunity for development, values and philosophies can be integral to the academic content of a child's home-school curriculum to whatever extent you wish.

Realize first that having a written curriculum does not dictate invariability. You may exercise some variance from any curriculum as you implement it throughout the year. It isn't, after all, your daily implementation that will be approved (if approval is necessary in your state), it is your *written* curriculum. You see, even public school teachers do not strictly adhere to curriculums. Curriculums are guides. The listed materials and methods, likewise, can be altered, deleted, and added to throughout the teaching year. But the officials who may approve, evaluate or challenge your home-school program will look for solid written curriculum outlines as the foundation of your academic program. They may also look through your student portfolios, home teacher log, or other records to determine that the curriculum areas are being addressed in some manner.

To carry out the process of designing or outlining a curriculum for each of your home-schooled children; i.e., a curriculum for each grade level you will teach, you can follow these six steps:

1. State your educational philosophies and general learning goals for your children.

2. Decide the subject areas that will be included in each child's curriculum for one home-school year. Include those areas required and those of your own choosing.

3. Locate sample curriculums. Select items from them that are age and grade-level appropriate, and in more personal ways suitable for your children's curriculums.

4. Create rosters or charts of general subject categories.

5. Insert specific goals, objectives, or outcomes to complete the guide for each curricular area.

6. Engage in an initial search for materials and methods that you feel will be appropriate for teaching your curriculums. Add those materials and methods you select to your curriculum guide.

Don't be discouraged; writing a curriculum can take time, but the process outlined below will make the task less complicated than you might expect. Let's take each of the above steps one-by-one. Please keep in mind that what you will end up with here is a curriculum format the public schools and state departments of education typically use. My purpose here is to show you a process and curriculum format that comes as close as possible to guaranteeing its acceptability to public school officials. Let's give the process a try.

1. State your educational philosophies and general learning goals for your children.

Usually a curriculum is prefaced by a statement of the educator's basic philosophy and/or goals for the overall focus of the curriculum. This preface may include beliefs about how children best learn, the lifelong aims of education, the lifestyle and learning style emphasis that is integrated into the curriculum, basic values related to reasons for learning that are held by the framers of the curriculum, and so on. The basic, broad goals for the curriculum may be given in outline form. Educational goals reflect the quality of life and uses of knowledge and skills towards which the curriculum aims. There are as many possibilities for philosophies and goals as there are parent educators. You are as capable as any other parent or teacher to establish educational philosophies and goals. Curriculum Worksheet One on pages 117-118 will help you explore and express yours. As you explore them, think deeply. What are your true and sincere philosophies and goals for your children's education? Remember that these are continuously revisable; they can be altered and added to intermittently, especially at the beginning of your next home-school year.

2. Decide the subject areas that will be included in each child's curriculum for one home-school year. Include those areas required and those of your own choosing.

Look first at your legal information. Check for confirmation of any subject areas for your children's ages/grade levels that are noted in Section Four. Check with experienced local home educators for reconfirmation. Make a list of these required subjects. Let Curriculum Worksheet Two on page 119 help.

With the required subject areas listed, you'll have the beginnings of the legal skeleton of your curriculum. Now add subject areas that are not required, but that you wish to include. Some state's subject area requirements for home schools are very basic — math, English, reading, for example — allowing for much fleshing out. Also, of course, there may be subject areas never listed as requirements for home schoolers, but that are areas you feel important for inclusion. As long as you are careful to include the required subject areas, you can feel free to include others of your own choice. It is quite possible that you will design a curriculum that reaches far beyond the public school curriculum in offering a rich educational experience for your children.

You may, for example, be more in tune than public schools with what is being termed "the curriculum of the 21st century." In this curriculum you may wish to include critical thinking, computer literacy and practicum, entrepreneurship or home careers. Perhaps, instead, you feel environmental science is of greatest importance and will want to consider zoology, botany, ecology, conservation, earth science, ornithology, etc., for inclusion in your curriculum. Or perhaps you are a person for whom religious instruction is of vital significance and you want to integrate such instruction throughout your curriculum. You may, on the other hand, feel that physical education and wellness subject areas must be included. You may feel that the "core curriculum" should have an entirely different core. Public school academics may be of least importance; values, creativity, critical thinking, etc., may be of greatest or of core importance. Whichever, enrich your required curriculum list with subject areas of your choice.

3. Locate sample curriculums. Select items from them that are age- and grade-level-appropriate, and in more personal ways suitable for your children's curriculums.

Many curriculums can be purchased or borrowed. Some private and church satellite schools sell them. See "Home-School Curriculum Suppliers" in Section Six for a list of schools that offer curriculums. Also, state departments sometimes offer curriculums to home schoolers. If your state department has no curriculums available, you might try another state's department of education. Several have designed curriculums and made them available nationwide, and they are just as usable in one state as another, generally speaking. Curriculum guides may be available, too, for loan from local public schools. Fellow home schoolers may have curriculums you can borrow for reference as you write yours. Available, too, especially in college libraries, are books which outline recommended curriculums in certain subject areas. Moffett and Wagner's *Student-Centered Language Arts and Reading K-13: A Handbook for Teachers* is an example. Also, it's possible to develop your curriculum by selectively integrating items covered in a grade level textbook into your curriculum framework. The outcome of your curriculum search should be a sampling of several curriculums to which your can refer as you design you own.

Remember that if you wholly adopt a textbook publisher's "curriculum" or buy a set of curriculums from some other source, you may be locking yourself into prescribed courses, prescribed item-by-item coverage, sometimes prescribed materials and methods, and possibly prescribed philosophies. So select curriculum sources carefully. If you want to buy curriculums but maintain flexibility, look for those sources that allow for flexibility. If you want those that espouse philosophies and beliefs similar to your own, search for curriculums that satisfy such needs. In addition, look closely at teaching approaches integrated into any curriculums which you examine. Are the approaches compatible with what you believe will be your style as a teacher and with your children's learning styles? Read Appendix A for descriptions of common teaching approaches that may be built into curriculum programs. If you buy curriculums, remember that they must satisfy state requirements. If they don't, you can choose others or design and add on the missing subject areas yourself.

I recommend that you obtain two to four curriculum guides from such sources as those noted above in your listed subject areas, study them, and then create your own guides. In this way you can allow for the inclusion of your own and your children's interests and also for curricular areas that seem especially appropriate in your particular home-school environment. An estimated fifty to seventy-five percent of all home-schooling parents design their own curriculums. In other words, a solid majority have found the task not to be formidable. To make it easy, you may want to purchase a copy of *How to Write a Low Cost/No Cost Curriculum for Your Home-school Child.* (See Section Six) Keep in mind, too, that curriculum guides can be reused and revamped for younger children as they advance to the levels for which you have designed guides for an older child. Also, one year's guide can provide the basic outline, advanced skills inserted, for the next year's guide for one student. If your state department of education offers guides, you would be wise to include them among those you obtain. By following them to even a modest extent in the core subject areas, you will come closer to ensuring that your curriculum will be age appropriate, grade-level appropriate, and that you will be viewed as providing "equivalent instruction" at home. That means, of course, that your curriculums are more likely to be approved and/or to not be successfully challenged.

Curriculum Worksheet Two provides a column for listing any subject areas you may wish to adopt from your curriculum samples. When you've completed Worksheet Two, you'll have choices to make. Which of the possible subjects you've listed will become your final list of subjects? Do you need your children's input regarding these choices? Of course, required subjects should be included. Beyond that, think about the ages, abilities and interests of your children, the amount of time available to you each day and week for schooling, the availability of resources that you may need to teach each subject, and so on. Also, which subject areas will allow the best opportunity for your educational philosophies and your goals for your children's education to be put into action?

4. Create rosters or charts of *general* subject categories.

After rummaging through your sample curriculums, selecting, deleting, adding, and sorting items, and finalizing some selections, it's time to convert your rough list and notes into a more formal-looking curriculum. Begin with the general or broad subject areas you've selected. As you do this, remember that implicit within the phrase "equivalent instruction" is the concept of *complete* curriculums. Let your sample curriculums serve as models in your effort to create fairly comprehensive curriculums without overdoing. When you've finalized your subject area choices, create subject area rosters or charts, leaving room between each subject area heading for additional writing. Look back to Sample Seven in Section Two (p. 82) for an acceptable format and ahead to Curriculum Worksheet Three on pages 120-122 for guidance. Then go on to step 5 below:

5. Insert *specific* goals and objectives to complete the guide for each curricular area.

You may be one who is philosophically opposed to utilizing specific learning objectives. You may, in other words, oppose the step-by-step, task-by-task approach to learning and prefer more holistic learning. We need not debate the value of one versus the other approach to learning here, but only to note that public school people largely still use the specific learning objectives method of designing curriculum. If you want public school officials to approve your curriculum, you will probably be wise to frame it in writing as they would frame it, as they would expect any teacher to frame it. Again, it is worth repeating here that your actual daily methods of teaching what you have written down in the curriculum is not under scrutiny during the approval process, nor could it be easily observed during an inspection of or challenge to your home-school program. Only the *written* curriculum is up for approval or denial, and likewise, the *written* curriculum is what school officials would look at were they to inspect your records. Once approved, your curriculum goes home under your arm: yours. You may then teach in whatever fashion you wish, as long as the end result is student progress which is *related to* the approved curriculum.

In other words, step 5 suggests that you offer the officials a curriculum format they expect to see. Approval and continued acceptance of your curriculum are your aims. So let's look at step 5 in greater detail.

You'll need to think, one at a time, about each of the broad subject categories you have listed. Let your sample curriculums help you decide which specific tasks or skills a student at the designated grade level would need to learn and perform successfully in each subject category. A first grade reading curriculum, for example, might include the twenty-one consonant sounds and the five vowel sounds under the word attack subcategory. In math perhaps counting objects from 1 to 20 would be included. You can let your sample curriculums (and textbooks) *suggest* specific items that you might add. Add your own ideas, too, of course. Also, refer again to Sample Seven in Section Two for examples.

In your curriculum each of the tasks or skills is called a "specific learning objective." You should begin your statement of each learning objective with the words, "The student will be able to..." A verb follows, a verb which reflects an act on the student's part. In other words, the student must in some way demonstrate the task or skill in order for the teacher to see that the student has mastered the learning objective. For example, you might write for the first grade reading student, *"The student will be able to* <u>say</u> all the beginning consonant sounds when presented with each consonant letter visually." For the math student, you might write, *"The student will be able to* <u>count</u> from 1 to 20 objects."

You'll want to avoid repeatedly writing "The student will be able to...," so just write it once at the beginning of each list of learning objectives. It may appear as shown on pages 120-122 and in Sample Seven, Section Two.

The lists of objectives under each category should be relatively short, as should be evident in your sample curriculums. Don't be surprised, however, to discover that at home you and your children are able to cover a typical curriculum at a much faster pace than public school teachers and children. First, the amount of time per day most public school classes spend on actual learning activities is three to four hours. The remainder of the time is basically wasted on routines, transitions, etc. At home you won't be involved in such *etcetera*. Also, you'll be functioning in a one-on-one, or two, or three, situation which is much more conducive to faster learning than the full classroom situation. With respect to your curriculum then, you may wish to add an objective or two that branches out or up into more advanced skills, to embellish your curriculum with additional subject areas that interest your children, to take frequent academic field trips, or even to conduct a shorter school day than public schools.

One final but very important note regarding step 5 — learning objectives: A curriculum must be sequential. Sequential means that the specific tasks or skills the student will master are listed in order of increasing difficulty. Also, the sequential nature of any one grade level curriculum should suggest that the sequence is sustainable from grade level to grade level, K-12, at least in the core subjects. In other words, you would not list letter identification after letter-sound association in a kindergarten reading curriculum. You would not list subtraction before counting in a first grade math curriculum. You would not list polysyllabic (many-syllable) words before two-syllable words in a third grade spelling curriculum. Obvious degrees of difficulty make it logical to list the learning objectives sequentially. Again, the sample curriculums you obtain should serve as models of the sequential nature of curriculums.

Use Curriculum Worksheet Three to formalize your rough list and to add specific goals and objectives. Ignore the "Materials/methods" line until you have read through Step 6 below. I suggest that you not write directly on these worksheet pages but that you make copies since you will need several sheets to complete an entire curriculum.

Moving now to our last step in curriculum design, we should note that some, not all, curriculums include materials and methods lists. If your state requirements for approval indicate that you will need to provide an account of materials and methods, you should complete step 6 below. If your state does not request that you submit such an account, you may want to complete this step now anyway, but not necessarily as part of your curriculum plan.

6. Engage in an initial search for materials and methods that you feel will be appropriate for teaching your curriculums. Add those materials and methods you select to your curriculum guide.

To start with you will need to engage in an initial search for materials and methods. It can take a lengthy, exhaustive search to find every and all materials and methods you may use in a year's time. Initially, you just want to locate major texts that you think you'd like to use, at least for core subjects (reading, math, social studies, science) or plan for other key resources to use and key methods and approaches for teaching. Many curricular areas may be taught, perhaps even best taught, without textbooks. However, if you are able to list one major textbook for each core subject along with, if you wish, any correlated activity books, you should satisfy school officials for the sake of approval. For other subjects, list textbooks or any of a myriad of non-textbook resources or teaching methods. Again, please realize that the materials you list initially are part of the guide, and as a guide list, not binding. You may, for instance, elect to use portions of the textbooks you choose and to supplement with other materials or let the textbooks be springboards to *real* and lively activities. You may elect to use some of the student activities presented in the texts and to supplement with activities of your own design. You may supplement, too, with field trips, activity days, resource persons, educational props or equipment, and so on, to whatever extent you wish. You may simply decide to not use the textbooks you listed for any direct teaching. In this case, the listed textbooks can sit on your library shelf and serve as reference books in the way that atlases, encyclopedias and dictionaries do. You may want, too, to reread the answers to questions 7 and 9 in Section One of this book at this time. At any rate, as long as the end result is student achievement, you are free to use a wide variety of materials and methods.

You can begin your search for materials by browsing through the "Teaching Materials, Aids, and Information Suppliers" portion of Section Six in this book. Write for catalogs from which you can select. Visit bookstores. Speak with other home schoolers about useful materials they've located. Check to see if your state department of education and your local school district have lists of recommended texts — good places to begin if you need official approval of your list. Look through your sample curriculums for any included materials lists and through home-schooling magazines and books which include materials and resource lists. (See "Readings" and "Periodicals of Interest to Home Teachers" in Section Six.) As you search, begin deciding on materials and creating a simple list of basic texts. Then, to your basic list add any other materials and resources that come to your attention that you think you'd like to use and also any methods with which you are familiar and which you plan to use. Materials can be literally anything — your kitchen as a science lab, the local forest for botanical studies, purchasable educational equipment of various sorts, local tide pools for studies of sea life, etc. Other resources can include museums, libraries, experts, home-school group activities, etc. Methods, too, can be varied and innovative. Perhaps, for example, for primary math you will emphasize the use of manipulatives and practical application as methods. Perhaps for music instruction, you will use the Suzuki method. Perhaps for creative writing instruction your methods will involve what is known by educators (and explained in Appendix A of this book) as the full "writing process" rather than product oriented writing lessons and activities. Perhaps for science you will use exploration and experimentation as methods. At this point in your efforts, on the other hand, you may not be aware of these kinds of methods and will need to limit your list to materials. That's fine for now. The longer you work with your children at home the more aware you will become of teaching materials and methods.

For the time being, then, just list those materials and methods of which you are aware and that you think you would like to use. List them on the "Materials/methods" line on the curriculum worksheets you have copied for each subject area. You don't necessarily need to be specific, but you may be. For instance, you may not wish to list specific book titles for your children's literature subject area, but rather list "a variety of children's books" as your materials. However, if one of your objectives under children's literature is "The student will be able to cite aloud examples of goodness versus evil found in children's literature," then you may wish to list specific titles in which goodness versus evil is a factor. When listing actual textbooks and workbooks, you should give the specific titles. But when listing your local forest as an environment for botanical studies, you needn't list specific items in the forest.

After initial approval has been granted, if necessary, for your curriculum and materials list, both will become ongoing aids to your teaching. By ongoing I mean that you will add to them and alter them as the year progresses. Having created them yourself and then worked with them for a period of time, you will probably find them to be marvelously helpful guides for your teaching. They will function like cookbooks in your kitchen functioned when you first began cooking on your own or for your family. Although neither of them — curriculums nor materials lists — will dictate how you teach or what you teach, you *may choose* to follow their "recipes" exactly. You can refer to them frequently to determine your next step, next unit of study, next lesson, all throughout your home-school year.

Mention of lessons here brings us to our next topic. Once you have completed your curriculum and materials/methods list, you and your children are on the brink of beginning your home-schooling year. You'll need to gather your materials, settle on your schedules and calendars, gain any needed approval, and so on. Then you're ready to teach...almost. Actually, lesson planning comes first; then teaching. Although you won't be submitting a year's worth of lesson plans as part of your program proposal, we should take time to discuss them as they relate to curriculum, as part of your preparation to home teach, and because in some states lesson plan samples or lesson plan books are required.

Curriculum Worksheet One: Philosophies and Goals

<u>My Educational Philosophies</u>

1. I believe children learn best by: _____
_____
_____
_____

(State *how* they learn best.)

2. I believe teachers teach best by: _____
_____
_____
_____

(State *how* they teach best.)

3. I believe the lifelong aims of my children's educations are:
_____
_____
_____
_____

4. I believe my children's learning should lead towards this kind
of adult lifestyle:_____
_____
_____
_____
_____

5. I believe my children's lifelong learning attitude should be:
_____
_____
_____
_____
_____

6. I believe the following basic values should be integrated into
my children's curriculum: _____
_____
_____
_____

7. _____
_____
_____

Curriculum Worksheet One continued

<u>Basic Learning Goals for Your Children</u>

My children's curriculum should enable them to develop the ability to:

1. _____
2. _____
3. _____
4. _____
5. _____
6. _____
7. _____
8. _____
9. _____
10. _____
11. _____
12. _____
13. _____
14. _____
15. _____

Examples: access and use information
             acquire no less than survival literacy
             develop a sound sense of self-worth
             develop a sense of brotherhood with other people
             establish strong moral self-guides
             understand and respect cultural differences
             acquire a perception of *excellence*
             develop personal drive
             develop steadfast character traits
             function successfully in the free enterprise system
             understand the value of a healthy environment
             be curious and explorative

[Note: There are dozens of other possible long-term goals for a child's learning. The above are merely examples.]

Curriculum Worksheet Two: Subject Areas

Selecting Subject Areas to Include in Your Curriculum

Required Subjects for Home Schoolers	Subjects I Noted in Sample Curriculums	Other Subjects I Just Want to Teach

Now you have a rough list. Ponder your possible subject areas until you can settle on those you must teach and those you additionally want to teach. Circle them. Then go on to Step 4.

Curriculum Worksheet Three: Home-School Curriculum

<u>Home-School Curriculum</u>

Curriculum for _____ (student's name)
Academic Level/Grade _____

Broad Subject Area: _____(e.g.: SCIENCE)

Focus Area 1: _____(e.g.: zoology)

    The student will be able to:

      a. _____

      b. _____

      c. _____

      d. _____

      e. _____

      f. _____

      g. _____

      h. _____

      i. _____

    Materials/methods: _____

    _____

    _____

    _____

    _____

    _____

    _____

    _____

    _____

Curriculum Worksheet Three: continued

Focus Area 2: _____ (e.g.: botany)

    The student will be able to:

      a. _____

      b. _____

      c. _____

      d. _____

      e. _____

      f. _____

      g. _____

      h. _____

      i. _____

    Materials/methods

      _____

      _____

      _____

      _____

      _____

      _____

      _____

      _____

      _____

      _____

      _____

      _____

      _____

Curriculum Worksheet Three: continued

Broad Subject Area: _____ (e.g.: LANGUAGE ARTS)

Focus Area 1: _____ (e. g.: reading)

    The student will be able to:

    a. _____

    b. _____

    c. _____

    d. _____

    e. _____

    f. _____

    g. _____

    h. _____

    i. _____

    Materials/methods:

    _____

    _____

    _____

    _____

    _____

    _____

    _____

    _____

    _____

    _____

Lesson Planning

I'm sure some resistance will crop up here: "Must I write lesson plans?!" The answer? No, not always (unless required, of course). It is possible to teach effectively, at least at certain junctures within the progress of a unit of study, without lesson plans. Sometimes mid-lesson inspiration or intuition will steer you in the directions you and your children need or wish to go. In fact, unusually effective teaching and learning can result from taking spur-of-the-moment advantage of unplanned but excitingly teachable moments. On other occasions you may elect to let a text in some curricular area, such as intermediate math, lead the way, and student progress will probably occur just as well as with lesson plans. Many times, too, your children will lead the way. Should they become enamored, for example, with a week-long project, you may want to suspend regular lesson plans during certain hours each day. Some projects, such as a small business, will lend themselves to unstructured studies in several curricular areas at once. On a smaller scale, should your children become fascinated with watching a snail crawl up a tree, and snails aren't in your lesson plan, please do not stop this spontaneous, momentary, child-led lesson. In fact, take advantage of the opportunity to lend a bit of the academic to the situation: "How do you suppose he crawls? Does he have legs? How does he see? Where are his eyes? Why does he lug around that shell all the time? What does he eat? Why is he crawling up this tree? How long do you think it will take him to get wherever he's going?" Open ended questions are excellent mind-stretchers for such teachable moments even if never answered. Curiosities may lead your youngsters to animal books or encyclopedias in search of snail information once you are all back home. Then, too, you can look for lead-ins back to your lesson plans or study unit, so the snail becomes an integral part of what you had planned all along.

Back, then, to lesson plans. It is true, as we saw above, that in many situations you can teach effectively without lesson plans. Yet, especially if you are new to home teaching, you may very well benefit from sketching out some form of lesson plan weekly for each subject and grade level you teach, and in some states lesson plans may be inspected at your home or need to be submitted or maintained as records. In some school districts or states the format for lesson plans may be prescribed. In others, lesson planning is an option, or the form of the plans is an option.

Lesson planning can occur in various forms, but perhaps the most commonly referred to form in our nation's public schools is the written 5-step lesson plan. Its commonness in public school rhetoric does not, of course, necessarily indicate that it is the best form to use for a home school. However, we could conclude that the 5-step plan should be most acceptable to any school officials in a position to approve or review your home-school plans. Also, you may at some point find yourself in a discussion regarding the 5-step plan and, therefore, need to know its components.

The 5-step plan is based upon a research-supported lesson format. That is, a specific format for the progress of an effective lesson has been researched and defined for use by educators. That lesson format, *per se*, is not our direct concern here, but is presented for your information in Appendix C. We are concerned with the planning process that stems from that format. The plan is presented here to inform you, to enable you to prepare, if you must, lesson plan samples that will be acceptable to school officials, and to give you some examples to work with as you develop your own lesson plan design and procedure.

The 5-step lesson plan, then, is the design basis for the samples given on pages 126 and 127. As you can see in Samples A and B, for application of the 5-step lesson we would have to include learning activities for each of five steps. The terms for the five steps are numbered and appear in bold italics in Sample A. Note that one lesson may carry over for several days before it has been completed. Looking over the Formal 5-step Lesson Plan sample, you can see that not much is actually written down for each day. However, in this case, a science lesson noting activities for a period of five school days, writing the entire plan could take fifteen to thirty minutes.

It isn't likely that you will be expected to write out plans quite this complete, nor wish to, but by reading the sample you can begin to understand the concept of the 5-step lesson plan. After you've studied the formal plan a bit and understand its parts, you can use briefer statements to complete the plan in less time. Sometimes the briefer method omits the writing down of the objective — the objective will, after all, already appear in your curriculum for science. In fact, it is from your curriculum that you will get the objectives for your lessons. If you follow your curriculum, you may find it unnecessary to write objectives into your lesson plan, unless required. You can see how the same lesson plan would look if it were written in briefer form by reading through Lesson Plan Sample B: Brief Plan.

The brief lesson plan example would only take about five to ten minutes to complete. All the components of a 5-step lesson are present; they would relate directly to an objective in the science curriculum, and should anybody ask, you could explain all of this. Your lesson plans should then be acceptable. Not only acceptable, they'll probably be effective; that is, they'll help you do a good job of teaching.

If you feel working with the fuller plan at first would help you focus on each lesson's objective and do a better job of teaching, or if you think you may need expertly written plans in order to pass inspection, by all means use the fuller form. Perhaps later on you'll want to ease into the briefer form.

Typically, public school teachers use the briefer form but may have to account for how their lessons fit into the fuller form, and they almost universally write their plans in what is called a "lesson plan book." You may be able to secure one, if you wish, from your local school administrator, or order one from a school supply catalog, or make one designed like those public school teachers use or designed in a fashion that works better for you. The public school lesson plan book is about the size of a large looseleaf binder and is much like a combination schedule and calendar with pages full of large boxes, one for each subject area lesson included each day. It is a schedule in the sense that the time of day each period occurs is noted. It is a calendar in that each pair of opened pages makes up one school week, and there are enough pages for a full year's lessons. (See Lesson Plan Sample C on page 128.)

Lesson plans and lesson plan books of this type or of your own design may be useful to home teachers for the following reasons:

- They help the home teacher complete the year's curriculum in a year's time.

- The planning procedure helps assure that the objectives outlined in the curriculum of each subject area will be addressed.

- Reviewing her own plan book from time to time can help the home teacher retain focus on her stated educational philosophies and children's long-term learning goals.

- The plan book can serve as a lesson review guide.

- The plan book serves as an ongoing student assessment guide. The home teacher can review the information noted in the plan book in order to develop means for assessing what has been learned.

- The plan book can satisfy any official requirements that exist regarding lesson plans.

- The plan book can double as a log if necessary.

- This record of lessons can serve as the raw material from which the home teacher or a certified consultant can write an annual evaluation narrative, if one is required.

- If ever legally challenged, the home teacher may use the plan book as evidence of instruction.

Lesson Plan Sample A: Formal Plan

Formal 5-Step Lesson Plan

Subject Area: SCIENCE   Dates _____

Focus: turtles as representative of reptiles

Learning Objective: Students will be able to identify body parts of the turtle and their functions, explain the turtle life cycle, needs, food, dangers, reptilian characteristics, and habitat.

Monday *1. anticipatory set (or introduction):* Observe turtle. Elicit and offer open-ended questions. One child records observations on a large sheet of poster paper.

2. instruction: (a) Together set up a terrarium and include two turtles for further observation. Spend some time today and each day this week observing and recording our observations.

Tuesday (b) Biologist Kelly Green will demonstrate and discuss characteristics of turtles. We will review and summarize his presentation and add items to our chart, then look through the items on the chart and try to organize them by body parts and functions, life cycle stages, needs, etc. We will also determine what information we still need.

Wednesday (c) Using our list from yesterday of those items of information we still need to find, we'll conduct further observations and also do library research using our set of wildlife encyclopedias and our book on reptiles. Then we will add reptilian characteristics and additional other findings to the chart.

3. guided practice: Using a large drawing of a turtle on butcher paper and the items recorded on our chart, the children will work together to identify and label the body parts and also write down the functions of each body part. Then we'll begin painting a mural showing turtles' natural habitat, food, etc.

Thursday *4. closure:* One-by-one, the children and I will observe the turtles in the terrarium and I'll orally quiz each child about all aspects of turtles we've covered. Finish mural.

Friday *5. independent practice:* Each student will be given a worksheet on which will appear a drawing of a turtle. Each student will be asked to independently label the body parts of the turtle and to write down the functions of those body parts, identify the turtle's reptilian characteristics, and draw in an appropriate environment for the turtle.

Lesson Plan Sample B. Brief Plan

Brief 5-Step Lesson Plan

Subject Area: SCIENCE   Dates _____

Focus: turtles as representative of reptiles

Learning Objective: Students will be able to identify body parts of the turtle and their functions, explain the turtle life cycle, needs, food, dangers, reptilian characteristics, and habitat

Monday

Observe turtle.

Assess prior knowledge of turtles and establish directions for further study by asking open-ended questions.

Record observations and questions on chart.

Build terrarium, using library references as needed.

Tuesday

Biologist Kelly Green

Observe turtle.

Review, summarize, and add items to chart.

Assess gained knowledge and reorganize chart items.

Determine what information students still need.

Wednesday

Further observations and library research.

Students identify and label turtle body parts and functions on turtle drawing on butcher paper and begin a mural showing habitat, food, etc. While doing this, assess what students have learned, determine any final needs for observation or research, and do that observation and/or research.

Thursday

Orally quiz individual students.

Finish mural.

Friday

Individually complete turtle worksheets.

Give immediate feedback with butcher paper drawing.

[Note: In Appendix C explanation is give of each of the five lesson steps — anticipatory set, instruction, guided practice, closure, and independent practice.]

Lesson Plan Sample C: Plan Book

	subject: time:	subject: time:	subject: time:
Monday			
Tuesday			
Wednesday			
Thursday			
Friday			

Lesson Plans

School _____   Teacher _____
Grade Level(s) _____   Week _____ 19__ — 19__

As you complete your lesson plans, you'll want to be conscious of the time blocks needed for the planned activities of each subject area session and the schedule of your whole day. Try to balance substantial coverage of a day's learning objectives with your need to compress the lesson segments of your day into reasonable time periods. Also consider the ages of your children and their correlated attention spans and toleration for active versus quiet activity. Aim for a mixture of types and lengths of activities. If you have more than one child, you may need to plan for some separate lessons for your children to accommodate their academic levels. However, many lessons can be taught to students of varied levels simultaneously. Children's literature, science, and language usage, for example, could be taught to more than one level, as long as the levels are not too far apart. A subject like math, on the other hand, may require separate lessons for separate levels, although practical application situations could involve more than one level. In that case, the more advanced child would perform the more difficult applications and the less advanced child the less difficult. But they could, nevertheless, work together.

When your children must be taught separately, schedule independent work for one child while you teach the second child. Then switch. Also, education research has demonstrated that students teaching students is highly effective. Consider letting an older child help you teach a younger at times. Eventually the younger child may become skilled in areas which he can in turn teach the older.

When you teach your children together, you may want to provide instruction to them jointly, but vary the difficulty levels of their independent learning activities. Your plans can allow for this.

Obviously you will need to streamline your regular daily routine to accommodate home-school lessons. However, be flexible, look for options and alternative timing possibilities. You don't, for example, need a nonstop block of lessons. You could schedule two hours in the morning and one or two in the afternoon, or vary the hours from day to day. Evening schooling hours may enable you to share the teaching of your children with your spouse. You may even discover that your children function best as learners during certain hours of the day and you will want to adjust scheduling to capture those best times. At home, you control the time choices and can allow for much variety and flexibility in the activities that fill your children's time.

You may find yourself planning activities not as a part of a particular lesson or unit of study, but simply as good learning activities. This is fine. You may find a subject area category for the activities. For example, if you plan to attend a matinee play production, you can label that time block "language arts" or "literature," since a stage play is a live performance of a written play — a work of literature. If it's an historical play, you could call it a history lesson. After a few weeks of home schooling, your children may even begin to design their own lessons. Many home educators are successfully letting their youngsters lead the way with "lesson planning." You'll just need to record in lesson plan format, if necessary, those lessons your children design.

In closure here, I'd like to urge you to first consider your own educational philosophies and learning goals for your children and then use them as a foundation for designing your curriculum and further then to attempt, as needed, to write lesson plans in the manner described above. Doing so can provide you with useful guides and *evidence* that your home school program is and consistently has been in operation.

Next we'll consider the various kinds of other evidence that you may want or need to keep as you home school your children.

Keeping Records

While *Why?* may be one of the first questions you answer about home schooling, in many states or school districts it may be the last question school officials ask. They are likely to be more interested in *How? Where? When? Who?* and *What?* and in many states they will want to see the answers on paper, as evidence. They may want to see your records.

Their responsibility to both educate and protect all children within their boundaries is the primary reason many states and school districts expect home schoolers to keep, and often submit, records. While keeping home school records may not be enjoyable, a majority of home schoolers do so to avoid breaking the law. Most admit, too, that keeping several of the required types of records simply makes sense. Home schoolers themselves, for example, are likely to want some acceptable form of attendance, curriculum, and assessment records to demonstrate that their children have been schooled, have achieved certain academic levels, and are ready to go on to the next academic level, or to high school or college, or to a job. Home-school parents, like other parents, are preparing children to someday enter the adult world for which they need to be realistically equipped. Entrance to training programs, colleges, and/or jobs usually involves "admittance tickets" in the form of school records. Children don't necessarily need diplomas and degrees to enter that world, as discussed in question 11 in Section One, but usually do need evidence of having been schooled.

Also, if you think you may enroll your children in public school or in a private school at some future time, you are likely to need records to verify to those schools that your children have been attending home school, have studied certain subjects, have achieved certain levels, demonstrate special skill in certain areas, need particular assistance in other areas, and so on.

Another reason for keeping good records is as a contingency for potential home-school litigation. In 1984 John Holt estimated that well over ninety percent of this country's home schoolers function with no hassles from authorities, but that estimate left room for a hassled ten percent. While the latter percent has probably decreased since 1984, keeping careful records, and keeping them all the years you home teach and longer, may be the key to ensuring that you remain within the unhassled group. In one instance, for example, when one longtime home-school mother, upon request, emptied two boxfuls of well-prepared and well-kept home-school records on a local school superintendent's desk and proceeded to provide a two-hour description of her program, she was politely thanked and dismissed. No further questions were asked. *Evidence* easily won the debate. While what is outlined below is certainly not meant to be a legal brief, nor am I qualified to offer one, should you become one of the hassled at some point in time, the presentation of complete records as outlined here would surely be welcomed by a lawyer.

There are several kinds of records you either may be required to maintain and/or submit, or may simply want to maintain:

1. Home-school legal and procedural information
2. Statement of intent (potentially eleven segments)
3. Annual evaluation documents
4. Lesson plans, logs, and curriculum outlines
5. Ongoing progress assessment results and report card
6. Schedules and calendars
7. Communications with officials
8. Consultant's activities
9. Home-school attendance register
10. Portfolios of student work
11. Student socialization activities log
12. Special student services information
13. Year-by-year, cumulative, permanent records

Sounds like quite a drawerful? To some extent it is, especially if you elect to maintain all of these possible records. While all of them could be important in your case, you'll need to determine for yourself which you must keep or wish to keep. Realize too that to begin you may need to complete some records, such as schedules and a calendar, but for other records only set up a design or system for later maintenance. The greatest amount of work occurs in setting up your record-keeping system; later, routine should take over. Also, as your home-school year progresses, you'll find yourself fine tuning your record-keeping routines to save yourself time and trouble.

Several of the records you might keep have already been noted in Section Two and earlier in this section, Section Three, but we will touch upon these again here to clarify fully which initial and continuing records may be kept. Let's take a closer look now at the possible contents of your records drawer.

First, if you've been working on gathering legal information and on the segments of your statement of intent since your reading of Section Two, you have already begun two record files:

1. **Home-school legal and procedural information**. As you recall, in your legal file you'll include statutes, codes, regulations, requirements, guidelines, procedures, etc., related to home schoolers in your state.

2. **Statement of intent**. In your statement of intent file you'll insert those of the eleven segments of the statement that you've selected to complete, as outlined in Section Two.

Several of the items in your statement of intent file initiate the need for further record keeping, as you'll see below. Also, other records aside from those that stem from your statement may need to be kept.

3. **Annual evaluation documents.** As indicated in Sections Two and Three, at the end of each home-school year or intermittently during the year, you may need to conduct or arrange for some form of formal evaluation of your children's progress and of your overall program. If such an evaluation is a requirement, you will want to document the evaluation activities and results.

The evaluation records may take one of the many forms noted on page 91 in this section. Each item included should be dated to show that the elements of the evaluation were carried out when appropriate. You should complete the evaluation records and file them in your file drawer as soon as possible after each element of the evaluation is carried out, keep the records or copies of them in a permanent file at your home, and submit original copies, if required, to the local school district.

4. **Lesson plans, logs and curriculum outlines.** Keep your ongoing lesson plans and/or logs in a notebook, plan book, or logbook throughout each of your home-schooling years and at least until your youngsters finish school. Also, once you have created your curriculum outlines or charts, plan to keep them indefinitely.

As explained earlier, you may be asked to submit lesson plan samples as a portion of your initial home-school proposal, or to submit lesson plans throughout the year, or to maintain lesson plans in a lesson plan book open to inspection throughout the year. In some states a log or diary/journal may do. Likewise, you may be asked to submit or maintain your written curriculum. On the other hand, you may not be asked to write or keep any of the three. In any case, as noted, it is wise to keep at least sketchy lesson plans, even if completed in log or journal form after the lessons are taught, and to create some form of written curriculum that documents your effort to teach required subjects in your state. (Refer to Section Two and earlier portions of this section for detailed information about and samples of lesson plans, logs, and curriculums.)

5. **Ongoing progress assessment results and report cards** (if needed). As noted in Section Two, in most cases ongoing progress assessments must be periodically carried out and results recorded. Assessments may include quizzes, tests, observed progress, paperwork that demonstrates progress, oral responses to assessment situations, projects, and so on. See Section Two for other possibilities. Some form of recording the results of those assessments is often required, and in a few states, report cards must be completed and submitted.

The assessments themselves may be kept — most likely in a student portfolio for the appropriate subject area. Assessment papers would provide hard evidence that your children have progressed and that they are studying the approved curriculum.

If you are required to complete a traditional report card, you might choose to record assessment results in a grade book of some sort. You could secure one from the local school administrator, buy one from a school supplier, use a simple ledger book or sheets of graph paper, or make copies similar to Record-Keeping Sample One: Grade Book on page 144. Write your children's names in the farthest left column, write dates and identify the assignments or assessments atop the vertical columns whenever you are about to enter a grade, and consistently enter either percentage scores or letter grades. (If you have some flexibility in "grading," you may want to create an alternative, such as recording tiny arrows (→) to indicate *forward progress* and a pyramid (▲) to indicate *further work needed*. You may record significant daily assignments and assessment results, or just assessment results (with some of the assignments stored in portfolios). In a few states, progress reports or narratives are required in lieu of report cards. Such reports would likely include various areas of growth — academic, social, cultural — and be written in a fashion similar to Annual Evaluation Sample One: Narrative on page 104.

As explained in Section Two, even casual observations can be recorded as assessments. Your daily observations of student progress — academic, social, behavioral, emotional, etc. — are valid measures as long as they are recorded somewhat consistently, objectively and in sufficient detail. You could keep such observation records quite easily in a log or journal. Doing so could prove to be fun, and at year's end you and your children will have a wonderful account of their growth. If your children attend public school before home school, you may be able to use the observation journal to document affective as well as academic improvements that result from removing your children from the public school environment. In fact, such a journal may be your only means of verifying affective progress.

Sometimes you will find commercial progress charts that could be useful for recording assessments. They may be found in teacher's manuals that are companions to textbooks your children use. They may be separately published checklists, such as the "Barbe Reading Skills Check List" published by Prentice-Hall. They may accompany a mastery learning or diagnostic/prescriptive program if you are using one. You can create your own checklists or progress charts by using your curriculum objectives. Such charts or checklists are not mandatory, of course, but could provide an easy means for recording student progress.

You may have occasion to record the results of an oral assessment during which you informally quizzed your children. Then you could jot down the contents of your quiz and the degree of success your children demonstrated by their answers. A score or evaluative comment could sum up the results.

As you can see, a variety of assessment records are possible. Remember, it is imperative that such assessment records show that you have been assessing those curricular areas required by your state for home-school education programs. It will be obvious to school officials that if you have been assessing achievement in the required curricular areas, you have indeed been teaching the required subjects to your children.

6. **Schedules and calendars.** As indicated in Section Two, schedules of daily and weekly home-school hours and semester or yearlong calendars must be established by home schoolers in some states and maintained with other home-school records. Please see Section Two for a complete explanation of this form of record keeping.

Let's move on now to records not previously discussed in Section Two or earlier portions of this section, but which you would likely be wise to keep and some of which you may be required to keep.

7. **Communications with officials.** As a parent teacher you may engage in several sorts of interactive situations with school officials, particularly while you are setting up your program and trying to secure official approval for it, if needed, and/or while carrying out evaluations. You should record the focus and results of each of those situations in log or journal format and keep copies of all written communications, yours and theirs.

This could be one of the more important of your sets of records. As you progress through the home-school approval process, if approval is mandatory in your state, you will interact with school officials by phone, by letter, or face-to-face. It is important that you record each and every one of those communications so that you will not skip over something you have agreed to do, so that you can keep tabs on what the officials have agreed to do, so you can prevent deviations from or inconsistencies in the officials' dealings with you by reminding them of their communicated statements and yours. Using communication records to keep the process moving along according to agreed upon dates or dates acknowledged as required deadlines can also be important.

Many states, in fact, provide a chronology for the approval process whereby you must follow certain timelines, and likewise must the officials. Only if you have dated copies of communications exchanges can you justifiably prompt procrastinating officials. Remember, too, that should your own communications to the officials reveal laxness on your part, the officials may have reason to delay or deny approval. Furthermore, most states have well-defined appeal processes for parents whose home-school proposals are denied. But in order for an appeal to succeed, you very likely would need to demonstrate that you had followed carefully all timelines and met all deadlines. It could also obviously be beneficial to provide written evidence that the officials did not follow the timelines, if, of course, such is the case. Only by keeping regular, dated records of all communications with officials, beginning with your very first contact with them, would you be prepared to provide such evidence.

If program approval by school officials is not required of potential home schoolers in your state, you will probably be wise to keep communications records just in case questions or challenges arise weeks, months, or even years later.

> **8. Consultant's activities.** If you will use the help of a certificated consultant, create a file into which you can slip a calendar or simply a lined sheet of paper that can be dated and filled in periodically as your consultant completes the items of your mutual agreement. You can begin this calendar/log by listing and dating items the two of you established as to-be-completed by her. Then as she becomes a participant in your program, record all of her activities, with dates, on the calendar or log and continue to record them throughout your home-school year. Be especially sure to clearly show that the consultant has assisted you in any activities for which you are required to have assistance.

If your state is one that requires you to work with a consultant, this log will serve as proof of your consultant's active involvement in your home-school program. If your state doesn't require a consultant but you've independently secured one anyway, you still will want to keep track of your consultant's activities, your interactions with her, dates you need to remember with respect to her activities, and so on. Always remember, too, that if your right to home school is ever challenged or your program ever questioned, you can demonstrate with your consultant's activity file that in your attempt to be a legitimate and effective teacher to your children, you've gone so far as to secure the assistance of a certified teacher — someone whose legitimacy the state already recognizes. Then, too, with the specifics of her activities recorded and dated consistently by you, you will be able to demonstrate exactly how she has participated in your planning or teaching, in assessing your enrollees' ongoing progress, or in the overall evaluation of your program.

9. Home-school attendance register. The attendance register is typically a record booklet, somewhat like a ledger, with columns and squares and lines at the left for entry names. In it are kept students' names and a record of their days of absence and attendance in school.

You can design a register yourself by making or purchasing a few sheets of graph paper, by actually using a few ledger sheets, by securing a register booklet from you local school if possible, or by making a few copies of a page from a local school register booklet. If you use separate sheets, bind them together, write your children's names on lines in the column furthest to the left, and write in the dates that will be included in your home-school year (a week or month at a time will do) at the top of each vertical column of little squares. It would look like Record-Keeping Sample Two: Attendance Register on page 144.

Once you have the graph or register itself set up, you'll need to devise a marking system. For example, an "A" could be inserted in a square whenever one of your children is "absent" from home school. A "P" could represent "present." An "H" could represent "present half the day, absent the other half." Or you could use a system of plus and minus and zero symbols. You might even check with a local school teacher to find out how local teachers mark their registers and then use that system for your register. Write a note at the top of the first page or on a cover sheet explaining your marking system. You could later teach the system to your children and let them record the marks.

You will also need to reserve a section of your register for noting the reasons for absences when they occur. If you wish instead, you could attach an extra sheet of paper for this purpose, dating each entry as you record it.

A grade level line at the top of the register page would appear if the register were a published one. The teacher would write in the grade level of the students in the particular class listed on each page. If you are teaching more than one of your children at home, you probably are teaching more than one grade or academic level. In that case, you may wish to record grade levels.

Then all you need to do is regularly record your marks for each child's days of absence and attendance. Remember, *absence* means *no school* for that child on the date recorded. If you take your children on a science field trip or to an art workshop or a piano lesson, and those activities are a part of your day's lesson plan and reflect your curriculum, then your children are indeed in attendance.

At the end of each quarter, semester, and year, tally the total numbers of days of absence and attendance for each child. You will want to be sure that by year's end your attendance register shows that your children attended home school the number of required hours and/or days noted in the "Basic Information Chart" in Section Four of this book and in the material you've received from your state department of education and had confirmed by experienced local home educators. If you are expected to turn in your register, compliance with these time-in-school requirements will be what the officials will look for.

Another routine form of record keeping, but one frequently asked for by officials and oftentimes fun to keep, is the student portfolio. Let's look at what might constitute student portfolios for your home-schooled children.

> **10. Portfolios of student work.** Home-school student portfolios contain samples of work that a student has completed. Typically a portfolio would be kept for each subject of the student's curriculum, and the samples would include a wide array of student work — drawings, reports, worksheets, project reviews, creative writings, lists of books read, cassette tapes of musical performances, photographs depicting learning activities, pressed and identified plants — virtually any student work small enough to fit into the file.

In most portfolios you would not insert *every* item of student work that your children complete. Select such items as those that are exemplary, that demonstrate the central focus of a unit of study, or that culminate a unit of study. Yet in some portfolios you may wish to include every item completed in an area of study — an art portfolio, for example. Remember, you'll be maintaining portfolios in order to document that your children have been truly studying those curricular areas that are required and those that you indicated in your home-school proposal you would cover.

You and your children will probably discover that keeping portfolios is actually quite rewarding because you'll be able to concretely see an accumulation of work that represents learning. Also, if you date the items you include and keep them in chronological order in your children's portfolios, you and they can use them to measure progress. Your children may find themselves amazed at their own productivity as they return to their portfolios throughout the home-school year. In fact some portfolios, such as an art or creative writing portfolio, can become treasures, kept and enjoyed for years to come.

Looks like your record file drawer is going to fill up fast. The next category of home-school records, however, won't become quite so portly. Let's consider the records that we hope will show that you can answer with a confident smile one of the questions asked most frequently of home schoolers, "How will your children learn to socialize?" The answers can be found in this file:

11. **Student socialization activities.** These records can appear in the form of logs or journals, written by you or perhaps written at least in part by your children. In these logs or journals, one for each child, date and enter brief descriptions of any activities that involve persons in your children's learning community other than you, their teacher.

The socialization logs may become a fun writing activity for your children. As you or your children complete them, recognize that school officials, who often worry about the socialization of home-schooled children, will want particularly to know that your children have contacts with other children. So be sure to note even out-of-school-time interactions that your children have with their peers. Of course, also note interactions with children other than their peers and with other adults. You can include family activities, too, noting sibling and parent-child relationships in action. Write your descriptions with an emphasis on common socialization factors — teamwork, cooperation, self-confidence, adaptability, independence, conversational skills, friendliness, etc.

12. **Special student services information.** In this record file you would keep notations of any special needs of your children that led to the services of such people as a physical therapist, speech therapist, school psychologist, special education teacher, or a Chapter I remedial reading or math teacher. Then you would date and record those services that were delivered by such people. If one of your children meets on a regular basis with a special services person, you may want to slip a service calendar into this file.

As noted above, this set of records may be nonexistent in your case if none of your children have the special needs that would necessitate the services of the persons listed above. If, however, you are aware or become aware that one of your children has a physical or speech problem, emotional problem, or a reading problem, or is learning disabled or mentally retarded, check your state statutes and procedures regarding such home-schooled children, and seek help. Child neglect could become the charge against you if you are aware of such special needs and try to handle them entirely on your own. However, there are two potential exceptions.

First, it is possible that school officials won't have identified any of your children as learning handicapped, especially if your children are in the primary grades. If you have never been contacted by school officials to discuss a special need of one of your children, then probably the school has not officially identified such a need. (Federal law dictates that school personnel contact parents in cases of identified handicaps to discuss special services.) In this case, you would not need to seek special services yourself, unless you wanted to. I would suggest, in fact, as noted in answers to question 11 in Section One, that you may be able to do a better job of facilitating the learning of a learning handicapped child than can the public schools. However, you may want to explore, rather quietly, the available services.

Second, if your child is severely mentally retarded, school officials may be delighted to let you school your child without interference from them. It may be necessary to go through legal channels to home school a retarded child, but you may be able to function quite independently after that.

One final note about special services. You may at some time be offered an opportunity for your child to participate in a special instruction program, such as Chapter 1 remedial reading or math. Be skeptical, however, of remedial programs, especially if the services will be carried out by an aide. Aides are indispensable persons on public school staffs, but they are not typically trained in methods of teaching reading or other subjects, remedial or otherwise. Usually they simply follow a teacher's instructions and present brief skills lessons. Perhaps you would want to schedule an observation session before deciding to utilize the services of a remedial program.

At any rate, if you do perceive a need for special services for any of your children, investigate the possibility of securing those services. Record your observations, those that led you to realize your child's special need, the steps you take to secure appropriate services, the responses you get, and the services that actually are delivered. You want to be able to demonstrate that you did not neglect any of what school officials would consider your children's special needs.

13. **Year-by-year, cumulative, permanent records.** At the completion of each year's schooling a simple record is prepared of the student's courses for the year with grades or pass/fail status or other symbol of achievement for each course. The student's total days present and absent are also recorded. These are written in a file or on a sheet of paper which has room for twelve, or with kindergarten, thirteen such yearly records. Typically achievement test results are also recorded or glued onto these records.

When a public school student finishes his schooling, he would have a cumulative, permanent record that included courses and grades from which a *transcript* can be prepared and sent to college admissions departments and potential employers. The permanent record is photocopied and sent as well from one school to another whenever a student transfers between schools. It serves as a record of all the courses he has completed thus far and his achievement levels in those courses, as well as a year-by-year attendance record. Having such a cumulative record for your home-schooled children could prove useful, particularly if you give your home school a schoolish sounding name and create a "perm record" that looks somewhat professional. The permanent record or transcript should be mailed from the old school (yours in this case) to the new, or to the employer, or to the college, rather than delivered by hand by you or your child.

Legally you have a right to see and copy any public school permanent record that might already exist for your child if she has previously been a public school student — if you can do so without removing the record from the school. If the school has a copying machine, just ask to use it to copy your child's permanent record. Then you will have not only a sample of a legitimate perm file, but a record you can continue for your child. If you can't copy your child's school file, perhaps a friendly school secretary, teacher or administrator would let you have one blank permanent file folder in which the cumulative record format is printed. (Public schools buy them already printed.) Also, some of the home-school support organizations or a satellite school might supply you with a cumulative record folder.

If your child has not previously been a public school student, or if you are unable to secure a permanent file folder, you can create your own. Type it out or print it on a computer printer. It should include segments that look like those in Record-Keeping Sample Three: Cumulative Permanent Record on page 145.

We've come to the end of our roster of records to keep. You can refer to the Record-Keeping Checklist on page 143 for a quick review. Then select those records you want to maintain, and finally plan for and set up your record-keeping system.

I'd like to conclude this segment with a final acknowledgment. I know there are many potential home schoolers and practicing home schoolers who immediately cringe at restrictions placed upon any aspect of their lives, including home schooling, by *the authorities*. It follows, too, that these home schoolers will not take lightly the states' claim to a right to require that certain records be kept. I understand and concur in many instances, but can only advise you here to try to determine the most efficient route to gaining the right to educate your children at home, and to follow that route. Doing so will no doubt mean that you will select from above the types of records you feel you should and must keep in the interest of establishing for your children schooling at home. My purpose in presenting the full range of records that can be kept is to show you how to set up a reliable body of documents that you may need in order to demonstrate that you have planned your program well, that your plan correlates closely *on paper* with public school expectations, and eventually that you teach your children successfully. Then if you did choose the route your state has laid for home schools, chances are you'll make it, legally and efficiently, all the way *home.*

❇❇❇

With this we close the home-school planning process — in this book, but not in your life. Still in the offing are working through each of the components you elect to complete, preparing those you must for presentation to school officials, and using the completed components to seek approval and/or to begin your home-school year. Thus you will have taken that first major step towards your home-school door. When you arrive, you will discover an extraordinary world of educational possibilities for you and your children. And the steps continue — pathways to choose, trees to climb, rivers to swim — educational byways winding into and around and over and through your home and your family. A wonderful journey — enjoy.

❇❇❇

Record-Keeping Checklist

Required	Desired	Type of Record	Record Ready and Active
		Home-school legal and procedural information	
		Statement of intent. (See checklist at end of Section Two for those segments you elected to include)	
		Annual evaluation documents	
		Lesson plans	
		Log — Purpose: _____	
		Curriculum outline	
		Ongoing progress assessment results and/or report card	
		Schedules and year's calendar	
		Records of communications with school officials	
		Consultant's activities record.	
		Home-school attendance register	
		Portfolios of student work Subject areas: _____ _____ _____	
		Record of student socialization activities	
		Special student services information	
		Year-by-year, cumulative permanent records	

Record-Keeping Sample One: Grade Book

School _____   Teacher _____
School year _____   Semester ____   Quarter ____
Course/Subject _____

	M	T	W	T	F	M	T	W	T	F	M	T	
students													
1. Mary Miller													
2. Susie Miller													
3. Tom Miller													

dates

Record-Keeping Sample Two: Attendance Register

School term _____   School _____
Teacher _____   Academic Level(s) _____
                             Month _____

dates   (A=absent, P=present, H=present half-time)

students	M	T	W	T	F	M	T	W	T	F	M	T	
Mary Miller													
Susie Miller													
Tom Miller													

Record-Keeping Sample Three: Cumulative Permanent Record

<u>Cumulative Record</u>

School _____

Student's full name _____ Birthdate _____

Father's name _____

Mother's name _____

Parents' address_____

_____

Elementary

s p e l l i n g	r e a d i n g	m a t h	s c i e n c e	s o c s t	m u s i c	a r t	h e a l t h				a b s e n t	p r e s e n t	g r l e v e l	teacher

[Subjects may vary; use blank columns to add others.
Final grades for each subject area are recorded on the grid.]

**Junior High
High School**

[Grids similar to the one on the right are used to record each year's academic work for grades 7-12]

	Grade ____				
	course	sem 1	sem II	final grade	teacher
1.					
2.					
3.					
4.					
5.					
6.					
7.					

State
Regulations
and
Procedures

From the States

The regulatory details in the "Basic Information Chart" below have been gleaned from state laws, regulations, and other documents and commentaries provided by staff of the fifty state departments of education and the District of Columbia's Public Schools Office. The chart provides quick reference to four home-school regulatory items: 1) compulsory school ages, 2) home teacher certification requirements, 3) whether or not certain courses are required and 4) homeschooling time requirements. The "Summary of State Regulations and Procedures," following the chart, provides further information and explains established procedures for home schoolers in each state.

As you use both chart and summary, confirm all procedural and legal information with currently active and experienced home schoolers in your state. Keep in mind, for instance, that home-school regulations change from time to time in individual states, and you are responsible for securing updates. Thus, you would be wise to confer with established home schoolers in your state regarding any procedural changes and adaptations and their current application in your own school district. Practicing home schoolers may be aware not only of changes in statutes and procedures, but of legitimate loopholes and alleyways through which you can most easily take your first step to home schooling.

While Idaho law, for example, not long ago indicated that a home school teacher must be certified unless the certification requirement was waived by the local school board, in parts of Idaho, the issue was often not addressed. Many home schoolers in those areas did not approach their local school boards regarding certification or any other matter, and were not sought out by school officials. Only by contacting an experienced home schooler in those locales would a newcomer have found out about this mutual silence. However, while rare, prosecutions were not unheard of. In one town, for example, a home educator was taken to court because she had no written curriculum to present. On the other hand, the educator mentioned on page 132 in Section Three overcame a superintendent's challenge (out of court) when she presented complete home-school records. More important than all of this now, however, is the fact that this Idaho requirement has since been eliminated. Further, the elimination of the requirement is currently an issue of debate in parts of the state, a sign that at some future date, it is possible that the requirement will be reinstated or that some alternative requirement will be instituted. The point made by this Idaho example is that the states' home-school laws and regulations often aren't uniformly applied locally and do indeed change from time to time, so regardless of what you find in the following chart and summary, you should **proceed only after confirming the procedural information with practicing home schoolers**.

One further reason to do so is that beginning home schoolers may not be aware of other categories of laws and regulations that have bearing upon home schooling practices and possible litigation. There are some laws headed by the category "Home Schooling," but in most cases the "Compulsory Education" or "School Attendance" laws lay the rules for home schooling. However, other legal categories may apply to home schooling. State driver's licensing laws, for example, may mandate that an approved driver's education course precede anyone becoming licensed, and a high school level home schooler would need such a course. Laws related to child health may require that immunization records be kept at a home school. "Conscientious religious objection" laws may apply to schooling. Laws related to handicapped students may apply to one or more of your children. Also, some laws pertain to procedures for the development of state department of education regulations, which are binding once put in place. In the early 1990s, for example, several states began considering regulations that mandate or encourage school district's to allow home school students' participation in public school classes and activities on a part-time basis. Practicing home schoolers or home-school organizations that monitor the creation of new laws and regulations can apprise you of legalities such as these, of how they relate to your situation, and of how well followed they are by school district personnel in your locality.

The most commonly found requirement is that the home-school curriculum "equally well serve," be "the same as," or be "equivalent to" that of the public schools. In the Summary below, the specified course requirements for "equivalency" are given for most states. Be aware, however, that *equivalency* is a vague term in some of the education laws; in other words, it is a term still open to interpretation in some states. Recognize, too, that the equivalent curriculum requirement represents minimums, not maximums. You may freely add other courses as you wish. Also, as noted in Section Three, to remain able to demonstrate equivalency you should keep your curriculum in written form and store it in a file at home as well as submit it if required.

Usually, scheduling requirements also allow some freedom. The mandated number of home-school days is most often stated; the number of hours, less often. But seldom are how-to-use recommendations given for scheduling those hours and days. In other words, having to home school four or five hours daily does not mean you must spend those hours at desks as if you and your children were literally in school. Many possible uses of those hours can be justified as home-school learning time. Sometimes the hours requirement will be stated as *contact time.* This means that you must be present with your children in educational pursuits during the specified number of hours. *Contact time* does not mean contact with a desk and chair!

Another frequent requirement is standardized achievement testing. As you study your state's summary, be sure you understand if achievement testing is legally required, and if so, which test must be administered, when and where the test is to be given, and by whom. This understanding will aid you in deterring any public school attempts to test your children beyond the degree required. Psychological, IQ, readiness, textbook, and interest tests, for example, are not commonly the kinds of tests to which your children must submit. Standardized achievement tests are common. You may be opposed to all testing, but if ignoring a testing requirement will result in the closure of your home school or lure school officials into the courtroom in a case against you, think carefully about your decision to test or not. As you consider this issue, you may wish to return to Section One's question *2, e,* regarding home-school test results and to the discussions of annual evaluations in Sections Two and Three.

If you walk through the planning procedure and compose as complete a plan as you deem advisable and yet find your proposal denied by school officials, ask them to tell you exactly how it is deficient. What must you add or alter for your plan to become acceptable? Then revise as you see fit, relative to your rights and theirs.

Recognize, too, that some local school officials may take the law into their own hands in zealous attempts to live up to their self-perceived responsibilities by molding home-school regulations to their own perspectives. To prevent yourself from being taken in by such overstepping of school officials' rights and responsibilities, you need to be well-informed of the extent and the limits of your state's home-school laws. Then, should inquiries be made by school officials, you can review the limits of their authority as defined by the laws in your state and confidently respond to the officials with written assurances that you are meeting the specific legal requirements of your state, notations of those requirements, and explanations and/or documentation of your means of meeting those requirements.

Let's set out then to informally map the legal footpath to your home school, to draw in the route that will take you and your children home. Note that wording in the "Basic Information Chart" is as found in the actual state statutes. Thus, for example, "between 7 and 16" and "7 through 15" both appear in the chart in order for the wording to remain consistent with each state's laws. However, please remember that **what follows here is a layperson's summary and does not constitute legal consultation**. Once again, remember, **ALWAYS ask practicing home schoolers —perhaps a local and a state support group— for their experience-based interpretations of the laws and local and statewide application of the laws.**

Basic Information Chart

state	compulsory attendance	certification required	state-required subjects/courses	hours per day days per year
AL	between 7 and 16	yes, as 'private tutor'	yes, same branches of study as in the state's public schools	3 hours daily between 8 a.m. and 4 p.m.; 140 days
AK	between 7 and 16	no	no	180 days
AZ	between 8 and 16	no	yes	175 days or equivalent
AR	5 through 17	no	no	
CA	between 6 and 18	yes, if 'private tutor;' no if in independent study with local school, or established as a private school or as a satellite of one, or doing correspondence study	yes, same branches of study required by the public schools	3 hours daily; 175 days
CO	7 and under 16	no	yes	average 4 hours daily; 172 days
CT	between 7 and 16	no	instruction equivalent to public schools	equivalent to public schools
DE	between 5 and 16	no	same as public schools	180 days
DC	between 5 and 18	no	equivalent to public schools	substantially equivalent to public schools; 3 hours daily; 5 days weekly
FL	6 and under 16	no	sequentially progressive instruction	same as public schools

state	compulsory attendance	certification required	state-required subjects/courses	hours per day days per year
GA	between 7 and 16	no	yes	4.5 hrs daily; 180 days
HI	6 through 17	no	basically yes	3 hrs daily average
ID	7 up to 16	no	subjects usually taught in the public schools	equal to that of the public schools
IL	7 up to 16	no	no	176 days
IN	7 up to 17; or with parental consent: 16	no	equivalent to public schools	same number of days as public schools where you reside
IA	6 to 16	no	no	at least 148 days
KS	7 and under 16	no	yes	substantially equivalent hours; 186 days
KY	between 6 and 16	no	yes	185 days
LA	7 through 17	no	a sustained curriculum at least equal to that of public schools	180 days
ME	7 to 17	no (See Summary for conditions.)	yes	adequate hours to accomplish proposed education plan; 175 days
MD	5 and under 16	no	studies as usually taught in the public schools	regular instruction of sufficient duration to implement year's instructional plan
MA	between 6 and 16	no	yes	180 days

state	compulsory attendance	certification required	state-required subjects/courses	hours per day days per year
MI	between 6 and 16	yes, unless the home school is "based upon a sincerely held religious belief"	yes	comparable to the local public schools
MN	between 7 and 16	no	yes	170 days
MS	6 and under 14	no	no	5-8 hrs daily; 155 days or a term sufficient for promotion from grade to grade
MO	between 7 and 16	no	yes	1000 hours yearly (See further note in Summary.)
MT	7 through 15	no	yes, comparable to public schools	180 days or equivalent
NE	between 7 and 16	no	yes	elementary:1,032 hours yearly; secondary: 1,080 hours yearly; 175 days
NV	between 7 and 17	yes, with exceptions (See Summary.)	equivalent instruction	days of appropriate length; 180 days
NH	between 6 and 16	no	yes	
NJ	between 6 and 16	no	academically equivalent to public schools	equivalent to public schools
NM	5 to 18, or high school completion	no, but must have a high school or GED diploma	a basic academic educational program	daily hours: 2.5, grade K; 5.5, grades 1-6; 6.0, grades 7-12; 180 days

state	compulsory attendance	certification required	state-required subjects/courses	hours per day days per year
NY	6 to 17 in NYC; 6 to 16 elsewhere	no	substantially equivalent	hours comparable to that of the public schools; equivalent of 180 days
NC	from 7 until 16	no, but must have at least a high school diploma or equivalent	no	9 calendar months, on a regular schedule
ND	7 to 16	no, with certain provisions (See Summary.)	same as local schools	at least 4 hours daily; 175 days
OH	between 6 and 18	no	yes	900 hours yearly
OK	5 and under 18	no	equivalent to public schools	180 days
OR	between 7 and 18	no	courses usually taught in public schools	equivalent to that required by public schools
PA	8 to 17	no, but must have at least a high school diploma or the equivalent	yes	daily hours: 2.5-grade K 5.0-grades 1-6 5.5-grades 7-12; annual hours: 450-grade K 900-elementary 990-secondary; 180 days
RI	between 6 and 16	no	yes	4 1/2 hours daily; 180 days
SC	5 to 17	no, but must have at least a high school diploma or the equivalent	yes	4.5 hours daily; 180 days

state	compulsory attendance	certification required	state-required subjects/courses	hours per day days per year
SD	6 and under 16	no	competent alternative instruction in basic skills	equivalent to public schools
TN	7 through 17	no, but for K-8 a high school diploma; for 9-12 a baccalaureate degree, unless waived	K-8 no; 9-12 yes	4 hours daily; 180 days
TX	6 through school year including child's 17th birthday	no	yes	180 days
UT	between 6 and 18	no	yes	daily hours 2.5 - grade K 4.5 - grade 1 5.5 - grades 2-12; 180 days
VT	between 7 and 16	no	yes	175 days
VA	5 through 18	no	yes	same as the public schools
WA	8 and under 18	no	yes	(For hours see Summary below.)
WV	6 to 16	no	yes	equal to local county schools
WI	between 6 and 18	no	yes	875 hours yearly
WY	7 and under 16	no	must provide a sequentially progressive curriculum of instruction	175 days

Summary of State Regulations and Procedures

In all states you *may choose* to follow the procedures outlined in Sections Two and Three of this book. The home-school regulations and procedures of your state, summarized below, are in most instances already incorporated into the contents of those sections, although you may need to *adapt the form* of required documents as indicated by your state's procedures.

You'll discover below that many states require fewer, some far fewer, than all of the procedures shown in Sections Two and Three, yet still maintain that you must be ready and able to *prove* that your children are being satisfactorily educated. Completing all or several of the procedures outlined in Sections Two and Three, regardless of the requirements noted below, will enhance if not ensure that you will be able to provide such proof. However, after reading the requirements below and considering how you can best maintain "proof," consult with other homeschoolers in your locality and your state to find out which procedures they feel confident with following.

The term **core curriculum** is used below to refer to the typical, basic five courses of reading, language arts, math, science and social studies. Language arts typically includes spelling, grammar, creative writing, and related areas. Although reading is often listed as a separate subject area, it is actually one of the language arts subcategories and, when understood as such, is not listed separately. Math courses are sequential, progressing in plateaus of prerequisite skills and include the usual roster of math skill areas — number recognition, counting, measurement, basic geometry, problem solving, fractions and so on up to the higher math skill areas and courses. Computer education may be included in the math sequence. Science and social studies may include any or all of the commonly taught, age-appropriate knowledge and skill areas. For typical course lists, check state or local curriculum guides, private or satellite school curriculums, or commercial home-school curriculums as recommended in the curriculum portion of Section Three, or look to the lists in my book *How to Write a Low Cost/No Cost Curriculum for Your Home-School Child*. Also, take advantage of your at-home freedom to embellish any required basic curriculum. You may need a written account of your curriculum that reflects compliance with regulations, but in everyday practice, remember this most important home-school word: *flexibility*.

The summary provided below for your state is meant to be read in combination with the above chart on pp. 152-156. Both, of course, are to be considered along with any information you obtain from your state's department of education and from experienced home schoolers in your state. Again, **remember that all home schoolers should remain alert to any changes in laws affecting them. One of the best and most important ways to do this and to gather information about the legal applications and atmospheres in your local area and in your state is to communicate with active home-school organizations**, many of which continually monitor state legislative activity and local legal actions. In addition, current state statutes are available in many libraries, particularly regional libraries or libraries in the largest cities within a state and in law libraries.

Understand that the following are a lay person's summaries, aided by direct communication from state education department personnel in each state and copies of the laws. Nevertheless, what follows here does not constitute legal consultation.

Note that the word *form* appears in italics below if a prepared form is provided for your use by your state or local school officials. This is to signal you that you will need to secure the designated form.

ALABAMA: In Alabama "private tutor" laws apply to home schooling. To establish yourself as a home schooler, you must be certified, and, prior to beginning instruction, file with the county or city superintendent a statement naming your students, the subjects to be taught, and the period of time instruction will be given, and thereafter file the required report *form*. Instruction must be in English and be offered in the branches of study required in the public schools. Courses of study are available from your state department, but at the outset plan for no less than a core curriculum. During the instructional year, you will need to keep a register of course work completed, hours and attendance (See Section Three), and submit any reports that the state board, state superintendent, county superintendent, or local board may require. If a certified teacher is not available, nonpublic school options include enrolling your children in a nonprofit church school, which operates as a "ministry" of a local church, group of churches, denomination, and/or association of churches. Enrollment and attendance of church school students must be filed with the local superintendent on a *form* provided by his office. A second non-public option is private schooling. If this option interests you, write to your state department of education for "Certain Laws that Pertain to Private Schools in Alabama" and for the private school registration procedure and report forms. You may also wish to review question 3 in Section One. If your have a physically or mentally limited child or live at a remote location distant from public transportation, write to your state department of education to request information regarding "Children exempt from attending public school."

ALASKA: Obtain the packet for establishing a religious or home school from the department of education. You will need to name your "private school," designate a "Chief Administrative Officer," complete required *forms* and submit them to the state department of education. These forms include: an Affidavit of Compliance (optional), a School Calendar, and an Annual Enrollment Report, which must also be submitted to your local school district. Immunization reports are to be sent to the state department of health and social services. If your own children are the only students taught at your school, you are not required to have fire, safety, or asbestos inspections and do not need a corporal punishment policy. The state also offers Centralized Correspondence Study as another nonpublic schooling option. (See *Alyeska*...under "Home-School Curriculum Suppliers" in Section Six.)

ARIZONA: You will need to file with the county school superintendent in the county of your residence an affidavit stating that your children are being taught at home. Each child must take a nationally standardized norm-referenced achievement test during the first year of her home school program after she reaches eight years of age.

AR-CO

Each is then required to take the test, at a minimum, every third year thereafter. The test is administered between March 15 and May 15 of each year under the auspices of, and at a site designated by, the county school superintendent in the county of residence. You may elect to follow the procedures outlined in Section Two and Section Three, particularly the curriculum and record-keeping segments.

ARKANSAS: A completed state department of education Notice of Intent *form* and Notice of Achievement Test Selection *form* must be delivered to your public school superintendent by August 15th of each year (or December 15th for second semester). (See "Statement of Intent" and "Annual Evaluation," in Sections Two and Three.) If new to the state, you have twenty school days to file these documents. Request "Regulations and Procedures for Home-schools" from your state department for yearly standardized test requirements, approved test list, test administration process, and satisfactory test results information. You may wish to include no less than a core curriculum.

CALIFORNIA: You have five options: private tutoring with a certified teacher, independent home study through your public school under the supervision of a certified person, independent study as a satellite student of a private school, independent study through a correspondence school, or filing between October 1st and 15th each year an affidavit (obtained from your local county office of education) establishing your home as a private school. Whichever option you select, you'll be expected to provide your child instruction in the areas required for public education (English & all language arts, math, social sciences, fine arts, health, science, physical education), to keep necessary records (See "Keeping Records" in Section Three.), and to demonstrate your competency; but each of the options comes with its own set of requirements. Write to your state department of education or contact a state home-schoolers' organization (See Section Five) to obtain specifications of each of these options and for all available information regarding the procedures for each option.

COLORADO: Fourteen days prior to the beginning of your home-school program each year you must provide written notification to the local school district of the establishment of your home school, including basic personal information; i.e., names, ages, address, and attendance hours, for each child. You should plan for a record-keeping system including attendance data, test and evaluation results, and immunization records. (See "Keeping Records" in Section Three.) If the superintendent of your local school district has probable cause to believe that your home-school program is in noncompliance with your state's home-school guidelines, he may request that you submit your records to the district within fourteen days of his written notice.

CT-DC

Plan for a sequential program of instruction including communication skills (reading, writing, speaking), math, history, civics, literature, science, and the U.S. Constitution. (See "Curriculum and Materials" and "Schedules and Calendars" in Sections Two and Three.) Arrange for achievement tests at grade levels 3, 5, 7, 9, 11, using the same standardized test as used by the local public schools. Results must be submitted to your local district or an independent or parochial school in Colorado whose name is then submitted to your local district. If composite test results for your home-schooled children are not above the 13th percentile, you will need to select another educational alternative for your children — although you may retest with another approved test first. Ask your state department for a current copy of "Rules for the Administration of an Established System of Home Study" and a copy of Senate Bill 56 passed in 1988.

CONNECTICUT: Annually, within ten days of the start of your home instruction program, you must file with your local school district superintendent a Notice of Intent *form* for each home-school student. The form asks for basic information demonstrating compliance with school attendance laws: name, address, birthdate, and phone number of the student; home teacher's name, address, and phone number; a list of subjects to be taught; total number of days scheduled for instruction; methods of assessment of student progress that will be used; and the date an annual portfolio review will be held with local school officials. Plan to include reading, writing, spelling, grammar, geography, arithmetic, U. S. history, citizenship, and local/state/U.S. governments. Science is also "recommended." Upon receiving your Notice, the local school district will check it for completeness and file it as a permanent record, and will, near the school year's end, determine compliance with course requirements through the annual portfolio review process. (See Section Three regarding portfolios.)

DELAWARE: Delaware rules and regulations do not speak directly to home schooling, but rather to school attendance. However, proceed as you deem advisable with Sections Two and Three for your own benefit. The state asks that you submit an enrollment statement to your local superintendent both before July 31st and by the last school day in September. Include a statement and evidence to the effect that your child is receiving a regular and thorough education at home. Some means of measuring progress should be shown. By selecting and privately following procedures found in Section Two and Three, you are likely to be equipped to respond to any challenges.

DISTRICT OF COLUMBIA: Your home school must be registered by presenting for D.C. school board approval a completed "Notice of Intent to Provide Home Instruction" *form*. Information required

FL-GA

includes your home-schooled children's names, ages, and grade levels; the qualifications of the home teacher; your curriculum (See Section Three); the place, amount, and character of instruction; and an annual summary report of student progress for each home-school student. Plan to maintain attendance records, available for inspection by authorized school board personnel.

FLORIDA: You must *either* hold a Florida teaching certificate for the grade levels you intend to home teach *or* comply with the following requirements: 1) File with your local superintendent a notice of intent to home teach. Include names, addresses, and birthdates of all children you will home teach. 2) Maintain a portfolio, including a daily teacher's log which shows titles of textbooks used, sample writings and other work, worksheets, workbooks, creative materials used or developed by the student. The portfolio is to be kept for two years and be available for inspection. Better yet, keep the portfolio at least as long as your children are home schooled. Upon any future discontinuation of your home school, you will be expected to submit requested records to your local district. 3) Arrange for annual student evaluation by one of the following methods: a) review of portfolio and discussion with student by a certified teacher; b) standardized achievement test administered by a certified teacher; c) state student assessment test; d) "any other valid measurement tool" agreed upon by you and your district superintendent. (See Section Three.) The results of the evaluation will be reviewed by your superintendent, and if he determines that student progress has been unsatisfactory, you will be placed on one-year probationary status. This allows you one more year of home teaching to help your student improve his progress. Plan to include no less than a core curriculum. Finally, your state maintains a data base of educational institutions for which you are required to file a data base survey *form.*

GEORGIA: You must submit a declaration of intent to your local school superintendent on a *provided form* by September 1st or within thirty days after you have begun home-schooling. Names/ages of your enrollees, address of your home school, and your school year calendar should be included. If you parent teach, you must have a high school or GED diploma. If a tutor teaches, the tutor must hold a baccalaureate degree. Plan to include no less than a core curriculum. You will need to submit monthly attendance reports — *forms available* from your local superintendent. Arrange to administer standardized achievement tests in consultation with a person trained in test administration and interpretation, every third year beginning at the end of third grade. You will be expected to write annual progress assessment reports in each subject area for each of your home-schooled children. (See "Annual Evaluation" in Section Three.)

HAWAII: You will need to submit either an "Exceptions to Compulsory Education" *form* or a self-written notice of intent letter to the local school principal prior to your home-school year. Include your child's name, address, phone number, birthdate, grade level, and your signature. Maintain a written, "structured," cumulative and sequential curriculum that is based upon educational objectives and provides "a range of up-to-date knowledge and needed skills, and takes into account the interests, needs and abilities of the child." (See Section Three.) Your records should include the beginning and ending dates of your home-school year, the number of instructional hours per week, subject areas you will cover, methods you will use to determine mastery (assessments and evaluations), a list of texts and other materials (in bibliographical format). Plan to include in your elementary curriculum: language arts, math, social studies, science, art, music, health, and physical education. For a secondary curriculum: social studies, English, math, science, health, physical education, and guidance. Arrange for standardized achievement tests for grades 3, 6, 8, and 10, either administered privately or at the local public school. At each year's end, you must submit an annual report of your child's progress to the local school principal. The report should consist of one of the following: a) a nationally-normed standardized achievement test score showing grade level achievement, b) standardized test scores demonstrating at least one year's academic growth, c) an evaluative report prepared by a certified instructor who indicates your student has demonstrated appropriate grade level achievement, or d) a narrative assessment prepared by you, including descriptions of progress in each subject area covered in your child's curriculum, samples of your child's work, representative tests and assignments, and course grades if you give them. If progress is deemed unsatisfactory, the local principal "shall meet with" you to establish a plan for improvement.

IDAHO: Idaho law indicates that parents alone are responsible for their child's home-school attendance and for the quality of their child's home education, and that public school trustees have no legal authority to require proof. However, the potential for litigation does exist. You may want to maintain a curriculum outline showing that your children are receiving an education comparable to that offered in public schools. Include a core curriculum plus health, physical education, art, and music. Also, keep any records that demonstrate that you are meeting any special physical or psychological needs of your children and attempting to ensure their social development. Some local districts are becoming more cooperative in offering curricular aid and part-time public school class and activities participation to home schoolers; however, check with active home schoolers in your area about the local atmosphere before asking about assistance and participation opportunities.

IL-IA

ILLINOIS: In your state a home school is for the most part unregulated. Truancy laws alone apply and will be brought into action if someone reports to a county's regional superintendent that certain children are actually not being home schooled. In this instance, the regional superintendent investigates and consults with the home-school parents in an attempt to resolve the matter. If not resolvable, charges may be brought and the parent will have to "prove attendance." The best proof may be the kinds of records found in Section Three of this book, including a written curriculum that includes no less than a core curriculum. If your child is home schooled through eighth grade and then wants to enter ninth in a public school, she will have to take a placement test. All county superintendents have copies of the "nonpublic school enrollment and staff *form*" for use by private schools and home-school parents who opt to complete it and turn it in. It asks basic information and is "used primarily to gather statistical information" for the state, which in 1993-'94 included eight hundred home school students in its statistical records.

INDIANA: Home schools in Indiana are treated as private schools, subject only to requirements including a core curriculum and the same number of days as public schools. Contact other home schoolers in your area or a state home-school organization to determine your school district's expectations regarding the submission of any information. Plan to keep attendance records, which may be reviewed by the state or local school superintendent. The language of instruction must be English.

IOWA: In your state the person who instructs a home-school student must be either the student's parent, guardian, or legal custodian or a person who possesses a valid Iowa teaching certificate or practitioner license appropriate for the age/grade of the student. By the first day of school in your school district, you must file with the local school board secretary a completed report *form* (available from your local school district), which includes your name and address, names and birthdates of your children, a planned minimum of 148 days of instruction, the name and address of the home-school teacher providing "competent" instruction and an indication of whether that person holds a teacher certificate or practitioner license, an outline of courses of study (including subjects covered, lesson plans, and time spent on the areas of study), titles and authors or publishers of your textbooks, and evidence of immunizations. The report also asks whether and to what extent dual enrollment of the student in the public school is desired (academic or activities participation), whether the child has been identified as one requiring special education, and which form of annual assessment is to be administered (test or portfolio). If you withdraw your child from a public school mid-year in order to home school, you have fourteen calendar days to file the report. If a certified or licensed person other than yourself will instruct your child, refer to "Title V, Chapter 31: Competent Private Instruction and Dual Enrollment" (available from your state department) for guidelines. Annual evaluation, either through testing (several options available, see document noted above) or portfolio, must be completed by May 1. Portfolios must be evaluated by a parent-designated practitioner licensed for the appropriate age/grade level and trained in portfolio assessment. (For details of portfolio contents, see document noted above.) The portfolio evaluator must submit an assessment narrative documenting the child's achievement and progress in reading, language arts, and mathematics for students of grade five and below, and those subjects plus science and social studies for students of grade six and above.

KANSAS: To establish your home school you must register it with your state board of education as a private school. Although you may not be challenged, do be prepared to show evidence that you are "competent" as an instructor. See "Evidence of Home-Teacher Qualifications" in Section Two and follow as you feel advisable the other procedures outlined in Sections Two and Three, particularly with respect to curriculum and record keeping. Maintain copies of your curriculum design, records, daily plans, etc. Plan to include no less than a core curriculum, plus health.

KENTUCKY: Within the first two weeks of the local school district's school year, you must submit by letter to the local school district the names, ages, and address of your home-schooled children. The superintendent of schools may request further information necessary to carrying out state laws regarding compulsory attendance and employment of children. Keep an attendance register, which should remain available for intermittent inspection. (See "Keeping Records" in Section Three.) It is also recommended by your state department that you keep portfolios of each student's work in the several areas of study and an ongoing transcript of work completed. (See "Cumulative Permanent Record" in Section Three.) Plan to include no less than reading, writing, spelling, grammar, history, mathematics, and civics in your curriculum. The language of instruction must be English.

LOUISIANA: Within fifteen days after you begin home schooling, submit an application to the state department of education for review and recommendation to the state board of education. The initial application should include attached copies of your home-schooled children's birth certificates. (Yearly renewals are due Oct. 1 or within twelve months of initial approval, whichever is later.) You will need to demonstrate that you are providing a "sustained curriculum;" i.e., a

ME

curriculum that is sequential — provides for learning by steps or degrees of difficulty in a consistent fashion. You can offer evidence of a sustained curriculum in one of four ways: 1) documentation — complete outlines of each subject taught, a list of books and materials used, a portfolio of students' work and assessments, statements by third party observers of your children's progress, or other evidence; or 2) verification of your children's performances on the State Basic Skills Test — at or above the state performance standard established for their grade levels; or 3) verification of your children's performances on the state board-approved standardized achievement test — at or above their grade levels or progress at a rate equal to one grade level per year; or 4) a statement from a certified teacher indicating that his or her examination of your program reveals that your children are being taught a "sustained curriculum" of *at least equal* quality to that of the public schools. If you follow the procedures outlined in Section Two and Section Three, you should be able to accomplish *1* herein as evidence — if you wish to proceed according to *1*.

MAINE: At least sixty days prior to beginning home instruction, you must complete and submit for approval to the state commissioner of education (and a copy to the local public school superintendent) your state's "Application for Equivalent Instruction Through Home Instruction" *form*. The form asks for basic information — child's name, grade, age, birthdate; local school unit; parent's name, phone, address, legal residence; and includes a "proposal" or statement of compliance. You must be certified unless you are "assisted by a satisfactory support system" which may include one of the following: 1) a certified teacher consultant regularly involved a minimum of four times yearly; 2) a minimum of four times yearly assistance from a public or approved private school; 3) a minimum of four times per year assistance from another approved home instruction program which has been in operation for at least one school year; or 4) other support approved by the commissioner of education, such as, local home-school support groups. Prepare a sample of your typical weekly instructional "scheme" describing the subject areas to be taught; a syllabus (curriculum outline—See Section Three); a list of instructional materials; your plan for assessment of student progress at least quarterly; a plan for record-keeping (See Section Three); and an annual assessment plan including one of the following: 1) standardized achievement test, 2) test developed by the local school unit, 3) review of student's progress records by a certified teacher, 4) review of student's educational portfolio by a local home-school support group with a certified teacher member, or 5) review of student's progress record by a local advisory board selected by the local school superintendent. Plan to provide instruction appropriate to each child's grade level in English/language arts, math, science, social studies, physical education, health education, library skills, fine arts, and, in at least one grade between grades six and twelve, Maine studies. Also, at one grade level between grades seven and twelve, your student must demonstrate proficiency in the use of computers.

MARYLAND: You will be asked to complete and sign an "Assurance of Consent *Form*," regarding your compliance with Maryland education laws at least fifteen days before you begin home teaching. Plan to include no less than a core curriculum plus art, music, health, and physical education and to maintain thorough home-school records, particularly a portfolio of your initial and ongoing plans, materials, samples of your child's work, and assessments. (See Sections Two and Three.) Your portfolio will be reviewed by a local school official at the end of each semester to verify that you are providing "regular and thorough instruction." However, you may opt instead to step under the supervisory umbrella of a state-approved nonpublic school. You may volunteer to participate in the yearly standardized test administration carried out by the local public school. Secure and read your state's home-education bylaw, which delineates the procedure for setting up a home school and which sets limits on public school officials' involvement in your program.

MASSACHUSETTS: Prior to withdrawing your children from public school, you will need to gain approval to home school from your local school superintendent or school committee. You must demonstrate that you are complying with schooling requirements in the state by submitting curriculums to be taught, a list of materials and aids to be used, lesson plans, schedule and calendar, your qualifications as a home teacher, plans for ongoing student progress assessment, and plans for annual evaluation. (See Sections Two and Three.) You have the right to present your proposal and witnesses on your behalf, if necessary, during a school committee meeting. Should approval of your proposal be denied, its inadequacies should be delineated for you so that you may revise your proposal. The school committee *may* require standardized achievement testing and *may* arrange for visits to or observations of your home-school environment by school officials. Plan to include no less than a core curriculum plus art, music, physical education, and principles of "good behavior."

MICHIGAN: You must report your intent to home school to your state department of education annually by October 1 on a *provided form*. which asks whether you are certified or "claim an objection to teacher certification based upon a sincerely held religious belief" and will thereby function as a noncertified home-school teacher. The form also asks for your student count at each grade level, courses of instruction, hours and days of instruction, your own education level,

MN

number of low-income-family students, and whether or not you have established academic and/or attendance eligibility requirements for students studying driver education. Courses of study should include mathematics, reading, English, science, and social studies in all grades; and the United States and Michigan constitutions, and the history and present form of civil government of the United States, Michigan, and municipalities in high school. You may wish to secure a copy of your state board's "Model Core Curriculum Outcomes." (See "Support Services" in Section Five of this book.) Home school students may enroll in non-core courses at local public schools. You may ask your intermediate school district to maintain (store) your student records where they can remain available to college admissions officers and any prospective employers of your students. While you are not required to do so, you may choose to administer a standardized test and/or to utilize the Michigan Educational Assessment Program test, the latter of which may qualify your "graduating" students for a state endorsement on their high school transcripts and diplomas. Write to the Michigan Department of Education for the nonpublic school report *form* and for "Some Questions and Answers Regarding the State Regulation of Nonpublic Schools."

MINNESOTA: By October 1st of each year, you must note intent to home school to your local school superintendent by submitting the names, ages, and addresses of your enrollees and immunization statements for each; a 170-day instructional calendar, the name of each home-school teacher along with evidence that each is in compliance with one of the following six options: 1) holds an appropriate teaching certificate, 2) will be supervised by a certified person, 3) has completed a teacher competency exam, 4) will provide instruction in a school that is accredited by a state recognized accrediting agency, 5) holds a baccalaureate degree, or 6) is the parent of a child who is assessed yearly using a nationally norm-referenced standardized achievement test, arranged in cooperation with the local school superintendent. If you, as home-school teacher, only qualify under the sixth option above ("the parent of..."), then you will need to complete a quarterly report card which indicates your child's progress in each required subject. All nonpublic students must be assessed using a standardized achievement test, and if a child's total battery score is at or below the 30th percentile or one grade level below the performance level for children of the same age, the parent must obtain additional evaluation of the child's abilities and performance to identify any learning problems. Plan to include in your curriculum reading, writing, literature, fine arts, mathematics, science, history, geography, government, health, and physical education. You should keep and make available an annual instructional calendar and documentation, such as class schedules, materials used, and testing or other assessment methods, that reflects your compliance with subject area requirements. (See Section Two and Section Three.)

MISSISSIPPI: By September 15th each school year, you must complete a certificate of enrollment *form* which includes names, addresses, ages of your home-schooled children and a description of your educational plan and scope. (See "Curriculum" in Section Three.) Plan to keep an attendance register along with a log of valid reasons for your child's absence from any home-school lessons. (See "Keeping Records" in Section Three.)

MISSOURI: The state of Missouri places few regulations or restrictions upon home schoolers. Registration, for instance, is not mandatory. However, if you wish, you may file a declaration of enrollment and notice of intent to home school with your county recorder or local superintendent. While you need to provide at least 1000 hours of home instruction appropriate for your students' ages and abilities, at least 600 of those hours should be in the core curriculum areas, and at least 400 of the 600 should occur at home. Maintain a plan book or other written record of subjects taught and activities carried out, a portfolio of your child's academic work, and a record of tests and other measures of your child's academic progress which show evidence of ongoing instruction. (See Sections Two and Three.)

MONTANA: Notification of intent to home school must be submitted to the county superintendent of schools at the beginning of each school year. Plan to maintain attendance and immunization records, which are to be made available to the county superintendent upon request, and to provide "an organized course of study," including those subjects required of public schools as a core instructional program. (See Section Three.) Your home-school building must comply with applicable local health and safety regulations.

NEBRASKA: To obtain exemption from compulsory attendance requirements for your children, you will need to sign and have notarized a "Statement of Objection and Assurances" *form* indicating that the legal requirements for school approval and accreditation and the rules and regulations of your state board of education violate your "sincerely held religious beliefs." Then, thirty days prior to the beginning of your home-school session, you must file an "Affirmation of Appointment as Authorized Parent Representative" *form,* indicating your understanding of your duties as a "parent representative" of the parents of the children who attend your home school. Also, prior to your school session, you must submit to the commissioner of education an information summary, including a 175-day calendar; a list of names, addresses, ages, educational levels, and experience of any

NV-NH

instructional monitors who will work in your home school; a scope and sequence instructional chart or summary including no less than a core curriculum plus health; a list of all classes or courses and grade levels and the names of the monitors responsible for those classes or courses. You must show evidence of your basic literacy (your qualifications to teach) or take a minimum competency test. (See Section Two regarding home-teacher qualifications.) Your state or local superintendent may elect to visit your home school at mutually agreed upon times.

NEVADA: You will need to annually provide to your county school district's board of trustees "evidence" that your child will receive "equivalent instruction" and be instructed by any one of the following: 1) a teacher, other than the parent, who possesses a Nevada teaching license; 2) the parent, when the parent qualifies for a teaching license for the grade level to be taught; 3) the parent, in consultation with a person who possesses a teaching license or who has provided instruction in the home at the age level to be taught for at least three years; or 4) the parent, when the child is enrolled in an approved (licensed by the state board) correspondence program. If option 3 above is used, the county board of trustees must waive the consultant requirement if after one year it has been demonstrated that your child has "made reasonable educational progress in his educational plan." To provide the above-noted "evidence," you must submit a request that your child be excused from compulsory attendance on the ground that the child will be given equivalent instruction, including: 1) the home teacher and her qualifications as per 1-4 above; 2) an education plan, including learning goals, teaching methods, instructional materials; 3) a calendar including at least 180 days of instruction "of appropriate length;" 4) a weekly instructional schedule; and 5) your child's birth certificate or other documentation of his identity. Your child must be tested by the local school district or its designee when she is in grades 2, 4, 5, 7, and 8, unless enrolled in an approved correspondence program. Non-correspondence students in grades 10 and 12 may opt for testing, other measures agreed to by the parent and county trustees, or portfolio assessment. If your child attains a composite score at or below the third stanine on the test, you will need to provide to the local school board information describing the remedial measures you will pursue. Plan for no less than a core curriculum and check with school officials or experienced home schoolers regarding prescribed courses.

NEW HAMPSHIRE: By August 1st of each year, you must provide a "Letter of Notification of Intention to Provide Home Education" to the resident school district superintendent, the commissioner of education, or a nonpublic school principal, each of whom must assist you, upon your request and as needed, in making such notification. The "Letter" should include a list of names, addresses, and birthdates of your students; your name, address, and phone number; a list of the subjects you'll teach; and a description of those subjects which includes 1) the name of an established correspondence school used, if any; 2) the name of an established commercial curriculum provider used, if any; 3) a table of contents or other material which outlines the scope and instructional sequence for each subject, or both; and 4) a list of textbooks or other instructional materials to be used. Within twenty-one days of receipt of an acceptable notification, the official to whom you submitted it will reply by letter, acknowledging the establishment of your home education program. If not acceptable, procedures outlined in the booklet "Home Education Administrative Rules" will follow. (Secure a copy.) You will need to keep a portfolio each year consisting of a log which designates by title the reading materials used and also samples of writings, worksheets, workbooks, or creative materials used or developed by your child. You will also need to provide for an annual evaluation (results to be submitted annually on or before July 1st) including one of these options: 1) a written evaluation by a certified teacher (including name/address of teacher, evaluation date(s), description of the reviewed student work, summary of the child's progress, signatures of evaluator and parent); 2) the child taking either a nationally recognized standardized test or a state assessment instrument or test used in your local school district (composite results at the 40th percentile or above demonstrates progress); 3) an alternative method mutually agreed upon by you and the official to whom you submitted your notification. (See booklet for possible methods.) If "progress" is not made, you may be placed on probation for one year and notified of reasons and of conditions, if any, that you must meet to be released from probation in less than one year. The above booklet also outlines grievance/due process procedures for parent educators. As you develop your curriculum, include science, mathematics, language, government, history, health, reading, writing, spelling, the history of the constitutions of New Hampshire and the United States, and exposure to and appreciation of art and music. If you stop home schooling, you must give notice to school officials within fifteen days.

NEW JERSEY: One of your tasks in setting up and carrying out a home school is to maintain continuous records/documentation that show that you are providing your home-schooled children with "instruction academically equivalent to that provided in the public schools for children of similar grades and attainments;" that is, equivalent instruction in English, math, science, social studies, and other required academic courses. You are expected to annually submit a written curriculum as evidence to the local board of education,

NM-NY

which will either "accept" the curriculum or "show" that "the curriculum is not academically equivalent to that provided in the local public school." You may wish to complete other major components of the statement of intent outlined in Section Two as preparation for providing further evidence if challenged.

NEW MEXICO: You must hold a high school diploma or its equivalent and complete a "Notification of Establishment of a Home-school" *form* issued by your local school district. Attach immunization records for your home-schooled children, and submit the documents to your local district within thirty days prior to the beginning of your home-school year (and by April 1st for each subsequent year). Plan to include no less than a core curriculum. Plan to continue maintaining immunization records and to maintain attendance records. (See Section Three.) Between November 1st and 6th, you should complete a "Home-school Enrollment Report," a *form* issued by and returned to the local school district. Arrange with the local district for yearly standardized achievement testing. Ask your state department for a copy of "Procedures for Home-schooling in New Mexico."

NEW YORK: Although there is no statutory requirement in New York that a parent must obtain school district approval to remove a child from public school, you are *expected* to file a notice of intent by July 1st, or within fourteen days of moving into a school district or deciding to pursue home instruction. District officials will then send you a copy of the regulations on home instruction and an Individualized Home Instruction Plan *form* on which you must submit your curriculum and/or educational plan showing equivalent instruction to that of the public schools, including a full core curriculum and physical education and health (including drug abuse and AIDS prevention education). During the school year, you must submit quarterly progress reports and documentation of hours of instruction to the district. The annual evaluation of each child must include either results of a standardized test or, at certain grade levels, a narrative report on the child's progress. Standardized achievement tests are required alternate years in grades 4 through 8 and every year in grades 9 through 12. A composite score below the 33rd percentile or that fails to reflect one academic year's growth may cause your home-school program to be placed on probation, during which time school officials may visit your program. Plan to keep attendance records and maintain other evidence of your students' ongoing educational program and achievement. (See Section Three) The total amount of your instructional time per week should be generally comparable to that of the local public school. With mutual agreement between you and school officials, your home-school students may have access to public school facilities, such as the library, career information center, and gymnasium; may participate in intramural school-sponsored clubs and extracurricular activities, such as band and music; may borrow instructional items, such as library books, microscopes, and movie projectors; and may participate in occupational education programs and programs for the gifted or for special needs students. Also, school district summer school programs are open to home-school students.

NORTH CAROLINA: Prior to your initial home-school year you must notify the North Carolina Division of Non-Public Education of your intent to home school. To do so, secure from this office and complete a copy of the *form* "Notice of Intent to Operate a School in North Carolina." Attach to the completed form photocopies of documentation which verifies that you (as home teacher) hold at least a high school diploma or its equivalent. (Keep originals of documentation on file at home.) Keep accurate home-student attendance and immunization records for each child. Arrange for the purchase, administration and scoring of a nationally standardized achievement test covering English grammar, reading, spelling, and math annually for each of your children. Keep results on file, available for an annual review by a Division of Non-Public Education representative. While not mandated, you are advised by division officials to maintain a daily log or lesson plan book throughout your home-school year. Include a daily time log for each course of study and a chapter/units-covered daily log. These should be available for annual review by a Non-Public Education representative. If in the estimation of officials your home school meets legal requirements, it will be considered a private school.

NORTH DAKOTA: At least thirty days prior to the start of the public school year, you must request an exemption for your children from compulsory attendance at public school. To do so file a Statement of Intent *form* with the local school superintendent. The statement includes your home-school parents' and children's names and address, each child's birthdate and grade level, proof of identity and immunizations, a list of any public school courses or extracurricular activities in which your children plan to participate, and an oath or affirmation that you will comply with all provisions of the North Dakota law regulating home-based instruction. The statement should further indicate your qualifications to supervise home-based instruction. You are qualified if: 1) you are certified to teach in North Dakota; 2) you have a high school education or GED certificate and will be monitored by a certificated teacher; or 3) you meet or exceed the cut-off scores of the National Teacher Exam (NTE). Under option #2, the certificated teacher must spend one hour per week monitoring the program involving one student. If more than one student is involved, an additional one-half hour per month per student is

OH

required. The monitor must evaluate, on an ongoing basis, the progress that is being made by the student(s) and report such twice annually to the local school superintendent. You will need to maintain an annual record of courses taken by each student including copies of academic progress assessments and results of nationally standardized achievement tests administered annually beginning with grade three. The achievement tests must be given "in the child's learning environment" by a certified teacher and copies of the results submitted to the local school superintendent. All subjects required in statute must be included in your curriculum. Copies of the statutes addressing required subjects and graduation requirements can be obtained from the local school superintendent. The state Department of Public Instruction, Division of Independent Study, in Fargo, has correspondence studies available for a grades 9-12 curriculum. (Address in Section Five.) You may wish to write to the state department for its "Revised Administrative Rules for Quality Assurance."

OHIO: You must submit a notice of intent to home educate to the local school superintendent. The notice should include the school year for which notification is made, your name, address and those of any other adults who will teach your children, the full name and birthdates of the children being home educated, assurance that the home education program will include the required subjects and provide 900 hours of instruction annually, a curriculum outline, a list of textbooks and other materials, and assurance that the person providing instruction has one of the following: 1) a high school diploma, 2) a certificate of high school equivalence, 3) standardized test scores that demonstrate high school equivalence, or 4) other credentials found appropriate by the superintendent. Lacking one of the above, you must provide assurance that you will work under the direction of a person holding a baccalaureate degree until your children's test scores show "reasonable proficiency" or until you obtain a high school diploma or the equivalent. Plan to include reading and all other language arts, geography, United States and Ohio government, local government, mathematics, science, health, physical education, fine arts including music, first aid, safety, and fire prevention. The local superintendent may require additional information or revisions and request a conference. Approval for subsequent years will be based upon the academic assessment report that must be submitted with the request. The report may be based upon results of an approved nationally normed standardized achievement test administered by an approved person, a narrative of each child's program and progress written by an approved person, or an approved alternative form of assessment. If progress is unsatisfactory, remediation procedures must be undertaken until progress reaches a satisfactory level.

OKLAHOMA: To date, the state of Oklahoma recognizes your right to "in good faith" home educate your children and asks only that you provide 180 days of instruction and include the array of subjects typically taught in Oklahoma's public schools, including reading and writing, mathematics, science, United States constitution and citizenship, health and safety, physical education, and conservation. Plan for good record-keeping. (See Section Three.)

OREGON: At least ten days prior to home schooling, you should notify your education service district superintendent or county school district superintendent, who according to legal procedure should then notify your local district superintendent. When writing your state department for the Oregon laws, ask for the state board's approved comprehensive examination list (with publishers and addresses) from which you may select the test you wish to have administered to your child (yearly) by a qualified neutral person.

PENNSYLVANIA: The local school district superintendent's approval of your home school is not required. However, prior to your school year (and annually thereafter by August 1st), your home-school "supervisor" should file an affidavit with the superintendent verifying that you are teaching the required subjects for the required number of hours. The affidavit should also state the name of the home-school "supervisor" (must be a parent or legal guardian), names and ages of your children, address and phone number, and that instruction will be given in English. Attach a complete curriculum outline (See Section Three), immunization records, and a "certificate" verifying that the "supervisor" has had no criminal record for the past five years. You must maintain a student portfolio, including a daily learning activities and materials log and samples of student work (See Section Three). At year's end have the portfolio reviewed by a certified teacher, a non-public school teacher, or a licensed psychologist, who will also interview each home-schooled child. The evaluator must submit a written report demonstrating that the home-school student is making "sustained progress in the overall program" and that "appropriate education" is taking place. Arrange for standardized achievement tests at least in reading, language arts and math for students in grades 3, 5, and 8. (A list of approved tests is available from the state department of education. Also see Sections Two and Three herein.) For an elementary instruction plan, include English, spelling, reading, writing, arithmetic, science, geography, United States and Pennsylvania history, civics, safety education including regular and continuous instruction in fire danger and prevention, health and physiology, physical education, music, and art. For secondary instruction, English: language, literature, speech, composition (four years); science (three years); geography; social

RI-SC

studies: civics, world history, United states and Pennsylvania history (three years); math: general mathematics, algebra, geometry (three years), art and music (two years), physical education, health, safety education including regular and continuous instruction in fire danger and prevention. At the secondary level, feel free to also include economics, biology, chemistry, foreign languages, trigonometry, or other age-appropriate courses. Upon your request, the local school district must provide copies of planned courses, textbooks, and curriculum materials.

RHODE ISLAND: You will need to contact the local school committee for approval of your home school. However, before you contact local school officials, you may want to consult with practicing home schoolers to determine the home-schooling climate in your county. When you do proceed, follow carefully the procedures outlined in Sections Two and Three of this book so that you will have a sound home-school proposal to present for approval and well-kept evidence of the quality of your children's home schooling. In your curriculum, plan to include reading, writing, geography, arithmetic, United States history and government, English, health, physical education, and beginning at fourth grade include history and government of Rhode Island, and beginning at ninth grade include the United States and Rhode Island constitutions. The language of instruction must be English. You must keep an attendance register and may be wise to maintain evidence that your teaching of the above required subjects is "thorough and efficient" (See Section Three.) In some school districts, parents may present a certificate that their child attends a local private school's satellite program. Although standardized testing is not required, you may opt to test and your local school district officials do have the authority to require some type of evaluation as long as they consider your preferences regarding means of evaluation.

SOUTH CAROLINA: Each school district in South Carolina should have available an application process by which you provide: a description of your home-school education program, textbooks and materials to be used, methods of program evaluation, and the place of instruction. Your application will be taken up at a local board of trustees meeting, which you may attend. You, as home teacher, must hold a high school diploma or the equivalent. Plan for instructional days of at least 4 1/2 hours excluding lunch and recesses, access to a library for your children, and for a curriculum that includes no less than reading, writing, mathematics, science, and social studies, and in grades seven through twelve, also composition and literature. Maintain and keep available for inspection: a plan book, diary or other written record indicating subjects taught and learning activities, a portfolio of student work, and a record of academic progress assessments. A semiannual progress report including attendance records and individualized student progress assessments in each of the above instructional areas must be submitted to the local school district. Home students must participate in the annual statewide testing program and the Basic Skills Assessment Program approved by the state board of education and administered by a certified school district employee, either with public school students or at the student's place of instruction. If you have a home-school child who is eligible for enrollment in the public school's first grade, he must be administered the state board approved readiness assessment, after which you will be advised as to whether that child should be taught using a kindergarten or first grade curriculum. Home-school parents must agree in writing to hold school board members and school district staff "harmless for any educational deficiencies" a student may sustain as a result of home instruction. If local school officials determine that your home-school program is deficient and notify you of such determination, you will have thirty days to correct the deficiencies. Also, should a home student score below the test requirement of the promotion standard prescribed by the state board for one year, the local district board may decide whether or not that student must be placed in a public school, receive special services as a handicapped student, or continue home schooling with an instructional support system at the parent's expense. In lieu of the above requirements, if parents are *bona fide* members of and in continuing compliance with the academic standards of the South Carolina Association of Independent Home Schools, parents may home teach their children under the auspices of that organization, which is annually reviewed for compliance with the parent qualifications, instructional year, and curriculum requirements noted above.

SOUTH DAKOTA: You must file an "Application for Excuse from Attendance," a standard *form provided* by your state superintendent, which includes the location of the home school and the names of the home teachers. If approved, your local school board president will issue you a certificate of excuse — a right to home school. A teaching certificate isn't required, but your state superintendent may determine your "competency" for home teaching. English language mastery must be one of your child's goals, and your curriculum should include no less than a core curriculum plus free enterprise, United States and South Dakota constitutions, patriotism, and moral instruction. Your child must take the same achievement test as is administered at your local school (which will be provided by your local school) and test administration may be monitored by a school district designee. Plan to keep records of attendance and reasons for absences for your child. (See Section Three.)

TN-UT

TENNESSEE: By August 1st you must submit a notice of intent to your local superintendent, including basic enrollee information, home-school location, curriculums, instructional hours, your qualifications. Plan to include no less than a core curriculum. Grades 9-12 curriculums must include courses required by the state board of education for high school graduation. Immunization records must also be submitted. Standardized achievement testing is required at grade levels 2, 5, 7, and 9 (same test as approved by state board for public schools) to be administered by the state commissioner of education or a designee on public school premises or by a professional testing service (if you wish to hire one) which is approved by your local school district. Public school facilities may be used by home schoolers upon the approval of the local superintendent, particularly for special needs courses (lab sciences, special education, etc.). Maintain attendance records, which are subject to periodic inspection and must be turned over to your local superintendent at year's end. (See Section Three.) If you do not have a baccalaureate degree but wish to home teach secondary students, you may apply to the state commissioner of education for an exemption to the degree requirement.

TEXAS: Your children are legally exempt from compulsory attendance in the public schools if they are attending a private or parochial school that teaches no less than reading, spelling, math, grammar, and good citizenship. A home school is considered a private school. However, selectively plan well, as outlined in Section Two and Section Three, so you can build a valid record of your child's achievement and demonstrate that you are using books, workbooks, and other written materials. In particular, you must write out or purchase and maintain a well-planned curriculum including reading, spelling, grammar, citizenship, and math. (See "Curriculum and Materials" in Section Three.) School officials may verify your education program and the attendance of your school-age children in home school and request assurances from you that you are complying with the law.

UTAH: You are *expected* annually to seek a public school attendance "release" for your children from the local school district by completing an annual application *form* available in the district office. On the application you will list courses you'll teach and a schedule/calendar showing the required courses and number of hours/days. For grades K-6 include language arts, math, science, social studies, arts, healthy lifestyles, and information technologies. For grades 7-8, add pre-vocational education and electives of your choice. For grades 9-12, include English, language arts, math, science, vocational education, special studies, arts, healthy lifestyles, and electives of your choice. Request information from your local school district about the number of "units" (credits) you need to provide of each subject for grades 7-12. You should maintain evidence sufficient to satisfy the local school board that your curriculum and days/year-length meet requirements, that your home-school materials are adequate, and that academic progress occurs. Also keep attendance records.

VERMONT: Any time after March 1st of the year prior to the beginning of your home-school year, you must complete and send to your state's commissioner of education an "Enrollment Notice for Home Study Program" *form provided* by the state department. The form asks for the names and ages of the home-school children; names, addresses, phone numbers, and signatures of the parents and of persons providing instruction; an assessment of progress for each child enrolled the previous year; "independent professional evidence on whether [a] child is handicapped" for each child not previously enrolled in school; an outline of each course of study; and identification of your school district. Plan to include reading/English, science, mathematics, and social studies including citizenship, history, United States and Vermont government; plus physical education, health, and fine arts. You may home teach children residing in your home and no more than two other children of one other family. Within fourteen days of receipt of your Enrollment Notice, the commissioner will reply with an "acknowledgement of compliance," or ask for missing information, due in fourteen days, or order a hearing. Arrange for yearly assessment of your child's progress in each subject area by one or more of the following: 1) a certified teacher, 2) a teacher from an approved Vermont school, 3) a commercial curriculum publisher's teacher advisory service report along with a portfolio of your child's work, 4) a report prepared by you along with a portfolio, or 5) standardized achievement test results (administered by a qualified person or by an approved Vermont school).

VIRGINIA: In August each year you must notify your local superintendent of your intent to home school by letter or other form of written notice, including your children's names, a description of your planned curriculum, and verification that *one* of the following four conditions exists: 1) you hold a baccalaureate degree; 2) you meet the qualifications for a teacher prescribed by your state board of education; 3) you enroll your children in an approved correspondence course; 4) you provide in writing a program of study (curriculum) which, in your local superintendent's judgment, includes your state's "Standards of Learning Objectives" for language arts and math and provides evidence that you are able to provide an adequate education for your children (demonstrated by how well you write the document and thereby show your own literacy, your plans for instructional activities, and whether your curriculum presents a

WA

reasonable scope and sequence of content). Plan to include no less than a core curriculum. Ask the state department of education for a copy of its "Standards of Learning Objectives" and see "Curriculum and Materials" in Section Three. If you decide to enroll your children in a correspondence school, ask your state department for a copy of its approved "Correspondence Courses for Home Instruction." Plan to arrange for achievement testing (ITBS or TAP test supplied) with your local superintendent or to provide for an alternative evaluation or assessment to be approved by your superintendent. (See "Annual Evaluation" in Section Three.) If one of your children scores below the 23rd percentile on an achievement test, further assessment may be conducted by the local superintendent to determine if a probationary year of remediation is needed. Keep immunization records for your children, as these records may be requested by the local school superintendent. If you have a student with a disability, you are entitled to seek special services for him through the local public school.

WASHINGTON: By September 15th of each school year or within two weeks of the beginning of any public school quarter, trimester, or semester, you must file with the local public school district superintendent a signed declaration of intent *form* indicating that you will home teach your children. The statement must include the names and ages of your home-schooled children and specify whether a certificated person will be supervising the instruction. You will need a certificated supervisor unless you have 1) earned forty-five college quarter credits, or 2) completed a course in home-based instruction, or 3) have been deemed qualified by your local superintendent. (Contact the Washington Homeschool Association or the Family Learning Organization for information about home-based instruction courses. Addresses in Section Five.) In your curriculum include "the basic skills of" occupational education, science, mathematics, language, social studies, history, health, reading, writing, spelling, and art and music appreciation. Hours of instruction should include 2700 over a 3-year period for grades 1-3, 2970 over a 3-year period for grades 4-6, 1980 over a 2-year period for grades 7-8, and 4320 over a 4-year period for grades 9-12 "in sufficient units for meeting the State Board of Education graduation requirements." Your home-schooled children must either annually take a standardized achievement test approved by the state board of education and administered by a qualified person or an annual assessment narrative of your students' progress must be written by a certificated person currently working in the field of education. If it is determined that any home-school child is not progressing at a reasonable level for his age or stage of development, you must make a good faith effort to remediate any deficiency. Maintain immunization records, instructional and learning activities records, and progress assessment records.

WEST VIRGINIA: Two weeks prior to withdrawing your child from public school or prior to the beginning of the local school year, you must submit a notice of intent and a plan of instruction for the upcoming year to your county superintendent or school board. (See Sections Two and Three.) Your curriculum should cover "the basics," including language, reading, math, social studies, and science. You must also include evidence that you hold a high school diploma or equivalent *and* that your formal education extends four years beyond the most academically advanced of your home-schooled children. You need to arrange for the administration of a standardized achievement test by a certified educator at your local public school, or by a licensed psychologist, or by a person authorized by the test publisher, or by a person authorized by your county superintendent or board. If composite scores fall below the 40th percentile, a remedial program must be initiated. If such score occurs a second year, home schooling will no longer satisfy the compulsory school attendance requirement. Your county superintendent or a designee "shall offer" textbooks, other teacher materials and resources, subject to their availability, that may help you home teach, and your child may, as deemed appropriate by the home instructor, enroll in any class offered by the county board, subject to approval of the board and subject to normal registration and attendance requirements. Plan to maintain attendance, instruction, and progress records, which the local superintendent or board may request. (See Section Three.)

WISCONSIN: On or before each October 15th, each "administrator" of a home-based private education program must submit, on *forms* provided by the department of public instruction, a statement of the home-school's enrollment on the third Friday of September. On the form you must state that the program of instruction is provided by the child's parent or guardian or by a person designated by the parent or guardian; that the primary purpose of the program is to provide private or religious-based education; that the program is privately controlled, provides a minimum of 875 hours of instruction each year, provides a sequentially progressive curriculum of fundamental instruction in six mandated subject areas; and that the program is not operated or instituted for the purpose of avoiding or circumventing the compulsory school attendance requirement. It is recommended by the department that you maintain at home a copy of your home-school calendar verifying hours of instruction and a course outline verifying a sequential curriculum of fundamental instruction.

WYOMING: Each home-school year you must submit a curriculum to your local school board showing that your home-education program provides a "basic academic educational program;" i.e., a sequential curriculum including fundamental instruction in reading, writing, math, civics, history, literature and science. (See Section Three.) Maintain records which demonstrate that your teaching is based upon that curriculum and that your children are home schooled the required number of days.

State Departments of Education

Use the following addresses to request further information—education statutes, home-school procedural information, required forms, etc. Each entry below gives you the address of the state department of education division that deals with home schooling. Most of the entries also include phone numbers for both the department (or state board, or commissioner, or state superintendent's office) and for the office or division specifically responsible for addressing home-schooling matters. These addresses and phone numbers, as well as the divisions assigned responsibility for home schooling, sometimes change.

Alabama Department of Education, Office of General Counsel, P.O. Box 302101, 50 North Ripley Street, Montgomery AL 36130-2101. State superintendent at (205) 242-9700, or general counsel office at 242-1899.

Alaska Department of Education, Home Study, 801 Tenth, Suite 200, Juneau AK 99801. Commissioner at (907) 465-2800, or home study with state curriculum at (907) 465-2835, or home study with your own curriculum at 465-2026.

Arizona Department of Education, Director of Home Schooling, 1535 West Jefferson, Phoenix AZ 85007. Department of Education at (602) 542-5393, or divisional director at 542-5387.

Arkansas Department of Education, Home School Division, Education Building, 4 State Capitol Mall, Little Rock AR 72201-1021. Department of Education at (501) 682-4475, or division at 682-4233.

California Department of Education, Legal Office, 721 Capitol Mall, Room 524, Sacramento CA 95814. Department of Education at (916) 657-2451, or divisional office at 657-2453.

Colorado Department of Education, Home Schooling, 201 East Colfax Avenue, Denver CO 80203. Department of Education at (303) 866-6806, or home schooling at 866-6854.

Connecticut Department of Education, Division of Teaching and Learning, 165 Capitol Avenue, Hartford CT 06106. Commissioner at (203) 566-5061, or division at 566-3593.

Delaware Department of Public Instruction, Assessment and Accountability Branch, Townsend Building, Dover DE 19903-1402. State superintendent at (302) 736-4602, or branch at 739-4583.

District of Columbia, D.C. Public Schools, Educational Programs and Operations Division, 415 Twelfth Street Northwest, Washington DC 20004. Superintendent at (202) 724-4222, or division at 724-4310 or 724-2406.

Florida Department of Education, Student Services, 325 West Gaine Street, Tallahassee FL 32399. Department of Education at (904) 487-1785, or divisional services at (904) 487-3510 or 488- 8974.

Georgia Department of Education, 205 Butler Street Southeast, Local Support Unit, Room 1666, Atlanta GA 30334. Department of Education at (404) 656-2800, or divisional unit at 656-2446.

Hawaii Department of Education, Student Personnel Services Section, 2530 Tenth Avenue, Building A, Honolulu HI 96816. Department of Education at (808) 586-3230, or divisional section at 733-9109.

Idaho Department of Education, Division of Instruction, Len B. Jordan Building, 650 West State Street, Boise ID 83720. Department of Education at (208) 334-3300, or division at 334-2165.

Illinois State Board of Education; Planning, Research, and Evaluation Division; 100 North First Street; Springfield IL 62777. State Board at (217) 782-2221, or division at 782-3950.

Indiana Department of Education, Center for Community Relations and Special Populations, Room 229 State House, Indianapolis IN 46204-2798. Department of Education at (317) 232-6667, or divisional center at 232-9100 or 232-9111.

Iowa Department of Public Instruction, Grimes State Office Building, Des Moines IA 50319. Department of Public Instruction at (515) 281-5294, or home schooling at (515) 281-3198.

Kansas Department of Education, Accreditation Department, 120 Southeast Tenth Street, Topeka KS 66612. (913) 296-3201.

Kentucky Department of Education, External Liaison Services, 19th Floor Capital Plaza Tower, 500 Mero Street, Frankfort KY 40601. Department of Education at (502) 564-4770, or commissioner of education at 564-3141, or liaison services at 564-3421.

Louisiana Department of Education, P.O. Box 94064, Baton Rouge LA 70804-9064. State superintendent at (504) 342-3602, or home schooling at 342-3463.

Maine Department of Education, Division of Instruction, State House Station #23, Augusta ME 04333. Department of Education at (207) 287-5800, or division at 287-5922.

Maryland Department of Education, Home Schooling Division, 200 West Baltimore Street, Baltimore MD 21201. Department of Education at (410) 333-2000, or division at 333-2433.

Massachusetts Department of Education, Legal Department, 350 Main Street, Malden MA 02148. Department of Education at (617) 388-3300; or legal division at 388-3300, extension 109.

Michigan Department of Education, Home School Consultant, 608 West Allegan Street, Hannah Building 4th Floor, Lansing MI 48933. State superintendent at (517) 373-3354, or consultant at 373-0796.

Minnesota Department of Education, Government Relations Division, Room 710-Capitol Square Building, 550 Cedar Street, St. Paul MN 55101. Commissioner at (612) 296-2358, or division at (612) 296-6595.

Mississippi Department of Education, Community and Outreach Services, 501 Sillers Building, Jackson MS 39201. State superintendent at (601) 359-3513, or outreach services at 359-3598.

Missouri Department of Elementary and Secondary Education, School Laws Division, Box 480, Jefferson City MO 65102. Commissioner at (314) 751-4446, or division at 751-3527.

Montana Office of Public Instruction, Attn: Home Schooling, P.O. Box 202501, Helena MT 59620-2501. Office of Instruction at (406) 444-3095, or home schooling at 444-2509.

Nebraska Department of Education, Home Schooling Division, 301 Centennial Mall South, P.O. Box 94987, Lincoln NE 68509-4987. Department of Education at (402) 471-2465, or division at 471-2784.

Nevada Department of Education, Elementary and Secondary Education, Home School Consultant, 400 West King Street-Capitol Complex, Carson City NV 89710. State superintendent at (702) 687-3100, or consultant at 687-3136.

New Hampshire Department of Education, Attn: Home Schooling, State Office Park South, 101 Pleasant Street, Concord NH 03301. Commissioner at (603) 271-3144, or home schooling at 271-3741, or home-schooling legal information at 271-3453.

New Jersey Department of Education, Attn: Home Schooling, 225 East State Street, Trenton NJ 08625-0500. Commissioner at (609) 292-4450, or home schooling at 984-7814.

New Mexico Department of Education, Attn: Home Schooling, Education Bldg., Santa Fe NM 87501-2786. (505) 827-6635.

New York Department of Education, Deputy Commissioner, Room 875 Education Building Annex, University of the State of New York, Albany NY 12234. Commissioner at (518) 474-5844, or home-schooling program manager at (518) 474-3879.

North Carolina Division of Non-Public Education, 530 North Wilmington Street, Raleigh NC 27604-1198. (919) 733-4276.

North Dakota Department of Public Instruction, Elementary Education Division (or Secondary Education Division), 600 East Boulevard, Bismarck ND 58505-0440. Department of Public Instruction at (701) 224-2261, or elementary division at 224-4647, or secondary division at 224-2266.

Ohio Department of Education, Standards and Evaluation Division, 65 South Front Street, Columbus OH 43266-0308. State superintendent at (614) 466-3304, or division at (614) 466-2937.

Oklahoma Department of Education, Accreditation Division, 2500 North Lincoln Boulevard, Oklahoma City OK 73105-4599. Department of Education at (405) 521-3301, or division at 521-3333.

Oregon Department of Education, Office of Student Services, 700 Pringle Parkway Southeast, Salem OR 97310-0290. (503) 378-5585.

Pennsylvania Department of Education, Office of School Services, 333 Market Street, Harrisburg, PA 17126-0333. Department of Education at (717) 787-5820, or divisional office at (717) 787-4860.

Rhode Island Department of Education, Teacher Certification Division, 22 Hayes Street, Providence RI 02908. Commissioner at (401) 277-2031, or division at 277-6887.

South Carolina Department of Education, General Counsel Office, Rutledge Building, 1429 Senate Street, Columbia SC 29201. Department of Education at (803) 734-8458, or divisional office at (803) 734-8783.

South Dakota Department of Education, Office of Educational Accountability, R. F. Kneip Building, 700 Governors Drive, Pierre SD 57501-2291. Department of Education at (605) 773-3243, or divisional office at 773-4770.

Tennessee Department of Education, 100 Cordell Hull Building, Nashville TN 37243-0375. (615) 741-2731 or (615) 741-2963.

Texas Education Agency, Field Services Division, 201 East Eleventh Street, Austin TX 78701. Agency at (512) 463-9734, or division at (512) 463-9354.

Utah Office of Education, Instructional Services, 250 East Fifth Street South, Salt Lake City UT 84111. Office of Education at (801) 538-7514, or divisional services at 538-7743.

Vermont Department of Education, 120 State Street, Montpelier VT 05620-2501. (802) 828-3135.

Virginia Department of Education, P.O. Box 6-Q, Richmond VA 23216. (804) 225-2023 or (804) 225-2747

Washington Public Instruction, Attn: Home Schooling, Old Capitol Building, P.O. Box 47200, Olympia WA 98504-7200. Office of Public Instruction at (206) 753-6717, or home schooling at 664-3574.

West Virginia Department of Education; Division of Research, Technology, and Professional Services; 1900 Kanawha Boulevard East, Building 6 Room 330, Charleston WV 25305. State superintendent at (304) 558-2681, or division at 558-3788.

Wisconsin Department of Public Instruction, Financial Aids Management Services, 125 South Webster Street, P.O. Box 7841, Madison WI 53707. Department of Instruction at (608) 266-1771, or divisional services at 266-5761.

Wyoming Department of Education, School Improvement Unit, Hathaway Building 2nd Floor, Cheyenne WY 82002. Department of Education at (307) 777-7675, or divisional unit at 777-6268.

❋❋

Support for
Home Schoolers

Mutual-Support Groups

Wisely, most home schoolers communicate with other home schoolers. As pointed out at the beginning of Section Four, legal information and atmospheres can be clarified for you by practicing home schoolers in your area. Also, as noted in the introduction, when your faith in yourself lags or you begin to experience burnout, support from home-schooling friends may rejuvenate you. Important, too, are the idea exchanges, newsletters, issue updates, shared learning and social activities, joint field trips, resource libraries, meetings, workshops, conferences, and so on, that can be brought to you through interaction with other home schoolers. One way to reach other home schoolers is through involvement in a home-school support group. Hundreds of such groups exist throughout the United States.

Within the list below, you will find informal local support groups, larger regional or state networks, and national organizations. Those listed were respondents to my nationwide survey of hundreds of such organizations, but no doubt there are many others whose addresses were unavailable to me, but which you may locate as you begin making contacts with the home-schooling community. Remember, too, that most organizations listed here are primarily *mutual-support* organizations, although many offer services and resources well beyond "support." At the end of this section you'll find a list of organizations or institutions more formal in nature which offer services to home schoolers and, in Section Six, educational resource suppliers.

As you begin to contact support groups, you will learn that many have evolved around the shared philosophies of the members. Some groups, for example, may include mostly members who feel the Bible should underlie all curriculums, or who share a maverick attitude towards governmental controls, or who believe in integrating life with learning, or who espouse "unstructured" methods, or who focus on environmental, ethical, or multicultural education. Some simply feel they are the best teachers for their children. A few are composed of parents dealing with special educational situations, such as teaching a handicapped child. A growing number of groups are all inclusive, embracing varied educational philosophies and approaches, family lifestyles and belief systems, cultural backgrounds, and needs for support. You may want to shop for a group whose philosophies and purposes are most compatible with or most receptive of your own.

Useful to note, too, is that although you will want to contact support organizations within your state, you may also benefit by looking beyond your state to those organizations in other states whose offerings appeal to you and whose scope ranges across state boundaries. At the same time, don't avoid organizations that appear to be small, for even they are likely able to help you consider options, understand the laws, locate information, explore resources, and make needed connections. You will discover, in fact, that many of the larger organizations listed here will connect you with one of the yet hundreds of local groups not listed here.

Please note that support group contact persons, addresses, and phone numbers change from time to time, but frequently if a phone call or letter to a support group draws no response, it doesn't mean the group no longer exists. Usually, it just means the contact person has changed and you may have to do some tracking to locate him or her. Sometimes when one group actually does disband, another takes its place near the same locality or members join a regional or statewide group.

Since the organizations listed below are nonprofit, you are more likely to get a response if you enclose a stamped, self-addressed envelope with any mailed request for information. Also, be aware that phone numbers are sometimes voice mail numbers; that is, you'll need to leave your name and phone number or address with an answering machine.

Alabama

Homeschool Advocates (5962 Chalet Drive North, Mobile AL 36608): Offers support/encouragement, legal information, meetings and idea exchanges, newsletter, resource library, materials exchanges, consultations with certified teachers, activity days, field trips. (205) 344-3239

Alaska

Alaska Private and Home Educators Association (P.O. Box 141764, Anchorage AK 99514): Offers statewide group networking, legislative monitoring, annual convention, children's essay contest, newsletter. (907) 753-3018

Arizona

Phoenix Learning Alternatives Network (8835 North 47th Place, Phoenix AZ 85028): Offers support/encouragement through group meetings, idea exchanges, and "coffee talks;" in-state networking, newsletter, textbook and materials exchanges/fairs, annual conference, resource library, informal home-teacher training, parent educator workshops and courses, field trips, shared longterm study programs, shared learning and activity days. (602) 483-3381

SPICE (10414 West Mulberry Drive, Avondale AZ 85323): An all inclusive group offering mutual support, legal information, meetings, idea exchanges, newsletter. (602) 877-3642

TELAO Homeschooling Association (4700 North Tonalea Trail, Tucson AZ 85749): An all-inclusive organization offering support/encouragement, legal information, local and regional meetings and idea exchanges, in-state networking, newsletter, textbook and materials exchanges/fairs and workshops, consultations with home teachers, legislative monitoring, resource library for browsing before buying, newcomer's handbook, activity days and field trips, informal home-teacher training, parent educator workshops and courses, testing service, catalog of materials. (602) 749-4757

Arkansas

Arkansas Christian Home Education Association (P.O. Box 4410, North Little Rock AR 72116): Provides help and information to homeschoolers, organizes efforts to obtain and keep favorable homeschooling laws, helps organize local support groups. Offers monthly newsletter, information packet, newcomer consultations, activity days and field trips, seminars, conferences and materials fairs, legislative monitoring and lobbying. (501) 758-9099

CA

California

California Coalition of People for Alternative Learning Situations (P.O. Box 92, Escondido CA 92025): Supports learning situations that are alternative in intention, form, and content. Offers support and encouragement, sharing, information dissemination, newsletter, meetings, statewide communications network, field trips and activity days, publications of interest to home teachers, legislative monitoring and lobbying efforts, public awareness activities, statewide conference, consultation services. (619) 749-1522

Christian Home Education Association (P.O. Box 2009, Norwalk CA 90651-2009): Offers legal information, in-state networking, newsletter, legislative monitoring, annual conferences, newcomer's handbook. (800) 564-CHEA

Homeschool Association of California (P.O. Box 231236, Sacramento CA 95823-0403): An all-inclusive organization that supports and promotes home schooling by providing information, monitoring legislation, and cultivating connections among home schoolers and the society at large. Bi-monthly newsletter; annual conference; boutique of publications, conference tapes, and other items; statewide and in-county networking; social events; home school-to-school district liaison; meetings and idea exchanges. (707) 765-5375

Home Education League of Parents (Suite 131, 3208 Cahuenga Boulevard West, Los Angeles CA 90068): Offers support/encouragement, legal information, meetings and idea exchanges, in-state networking, newsletter, consultations with home teachers and informal home-teacher training, legislative monitoring, a newcomer's handbook, activity days and field trips, workshops, seminars, home school-to-school district liaison, small catalog of resources. (213) 874-9518

Humboldt Homeschoolers (688 South Westhaven Drive, Trinidad CA 95570): Offers support/encouragement, legal information, meetings and idea exchanges, in-state networking, newsletter, textbook and materials exchanges, legislative monitoring, resource library, newcomer's handbook, activity days and field trips, a support group bookstore. (707) 677-3290

Santa Clara Valley Homeschoolers (795 Sheraton Drive, Sunnyvale CA 94087): Offers support, field trips, academic classes, informal meetings. (408) 735-7525

SPICE (of Sacramento Valley) (P.O. Box 282, Wilton CA 95693): Offers support/encouragement, legal information, local/regional meetings and idea exchanges, in-state networking, newsletter, legislative monitoring, newcomer's handbook, activity days and field trips, home school-to-school district liaison. (408) 687-7053 or 362-1813

Colorado

Christian Home Educators of Colorado (1015 South Gaylord Street, #226, Denver CO 80209): Offers support/encouragement, statewide networking, annual conferences and resource fairs, legal information, newsletter, legislative monitoring, regional meetings, parent educator workshops and seminars, a catalog of materials. (303) 777-1022

Colorado Home Educators Association (200 Union Boulevard, Suite 430, Box 0358, Denver CO 80228): Provides a statewide voice for Colorado home educators without partiality to any one perspective or approach; statewide networking, newsletter, promotion and encouragement of local support groups, a home-school state fair, public awareness and education programs, promotion of favorable legislation and legal action, promotion of sound home-education programs, bibliography of home-school research studies. (303) 441-9938

Colorado Home Schooling Network (7490 West Apache, Sedalia CO 80135): Offers support/encouragement for unstructured home schoolers, meetings and idea exchanges, bimonthly newsletter, 30-page legal packet. (303) 789-4309 or 688-4136

Colorado Homeschooling Network (31 Pin Oak Drive, Littleton CO 80127): An all-inclusive group offering support/encouragement for unstructured home schoolers, legal information, meetings and idea exchanges, in-state networking, newsletter, legislative monitoring, activity days and field trips. (303) 972-0811

Colorado Springs Homeschool Support Group (P.O. Box 26117, Colorado Springs CO 80936): Offers encouragement, networking, meetings and idea exchanges, activity days and field trips, legislative monitoring and lobbying, seminars, conferences and materials fairs, teen group, testing service, newsletter, directory of members and their curricula and interests. (719) 598-2636

Front Range Eclectic Educators (%Mason, 5732 Stetson Court, Parker CO 80134): Offers Christian-oriented support/encouragement, in-state networking, activity days and field trips, consultations, newsletter. (303) 841-9494

Home Education League of Parents (P.O. Box 2865, Grand Junction CO 81502): Offers support/encouragement, legal information, meetings and idea exchanges, in-state networking, newsletter, materials exchanges/fairs, resource library.

Home Educators' Fellowship (138 45th Avenue, Greeley CO 80634): Offers support/encouragement, networking, meetings and idea exchanges, activity days and field trips, consultations, seminars, conferences, home-school materials, monthly newsletter. (303) 356-5243

CT — FL

INCH/Home Education League of Parents (1622 Monroe Street, Denver CO 80206): Offers support/encouragement, legal information, local/regional meetings and idea exchanges, in-state networking, newsletter, materials exchanges/fairs, consultation referrals, activity days, field trips, workshops/seminars, testing service. (303) 388-8292

Connecticut

Connecticut Home Educators' Association (P.O. Box 250, Cobalt CT 06414): Offers support/encouragement, information, networking, bimonthly newsletter, idea exchanges, meetings, field trips and activity days, legislative monitoring and action, conferences. (203) 267-4240

Delaware

Tri-State Home School Network (P.O. Box 7193, Newark DE 19714): Offers support/encouragement, networking, moms' meetings, idea exchanges, activity days/field trips, newsletter, mentor program.

District of Columbia

Community of Independent Learners (P.O. Box 16029, Alexandria VA 22302): An all-inclusive group for northern Virginia and the District of Columbia that offers mutual support, meetings and idea exchanges, in-state networking, activity days, field trips; and explores flexible alternative strategies that recognize children's uniquenesses. (703) 998-9626

Florida

Family Learning Exchange (2020 Turpentine Road, Mims FL 32754): Offers support/encouragement, legal information, meetings and idea exchanges, legislative monitoring, occasional activity days and field trips. (407) 268-8833

Florida Parent Educators Association (P.O. Box 1193, Venice FL 34284-1193): A statewide organization offering support/encouragement, in-state networking, newsletter, resource information, annual convention and curriculum fair, legal information, legislative monitoring and lobbying, public awareness activities, a home school-to-school district liaison service. (813) 497-2270

Parkland Home Educators (2111 Oakhurst Avenue, Winter Park FL 32792): Offers support/encouragement, legal information, local and regional meetings and idea exchanges, in-state networking, newsletter, materials exchanges/fairs, consultations by noncertified home teachers, legislative monitoring, annual conference, newcomer's handbook, activity days and field trips, informal home-teacher training, workshops and seminars, testing service, student assessment/ evaluation packages, materials catalog, home school-to-school district liaison.

West Florida Home Education Support League (711 Beauvais Road, Pensacola FL 32524): Offers support/encouragement, information hotline, newsletter, in-state networking, meetings and idea exchanges. (904) 478-8026

Georgia

Christians Concerned for Education (330 Concord Lane, LaFayette GA 30728): Offers support/encouragement, information, newsletter, legislative monitoring and action, curriculum assistance and consultations. (404) 397-2941

Free to Learn at Home (4439 Lake Forest Drive, Oakwood GA 30566-2414): An all-inclusive group that offers support/encouragement, legal information, meetings, in-state networking, newsletter, consultations with home teachers, legislative monitoring, newcomer's information packet, activity days and field trips, monthly teen nights, testing service. (404) 536-8077

Georgians for Freedom in Education (209 Cobb Street, Palmetto GA 30268): Offers support/encouragement, information, legislative input and monitoring, promotion of public awareness, meetings, newsletter, field trip planning assistance, seminars, workshops, consultation service. (404) 923-9932

Gwinnett Christian Home Educators (1981 Clinton Place, Lawrenceville GA 30243): Offers support/encouragement, legal information, newsletter, idea exchanges and meetings, resource library, informal consultations, curriculum assistance, materials fairs, in-state networking, public awareness activities, field trips and activity events, special classes, parent workshops. (404) 963-0713

Hawaii

Christian Home Schoolers (91-824 Oama Street, Ewa Beach HI 96706): Offers support/encouragement, legal information, meetings and idea exchanges, in-state networking, newsletter, materials exchanges/fairs, annual conferences, activity days and field trips, parent educator workshops and seminars. (808) 689-6398

Hawaii Island Christian Home Educators (P.O. Box 782, Keaau HI 96749): Offers support/encouragement, legal information, meetings and idea exchanges, in-state networking, newsletter, materials exchanges/fairs, legislative monitoring, members' resource library, newcomer's handbook, activity days and field trips, informal training and parent educator workshops and seminars, home school-to-school district liaison. (808) 965-9002

ID — IL

Homeschool Adventures (777 Kolani Street, Wailuku HI 96793): Offers support/encouragement, legal information, meetings and idea exchanges, in-state networking, legislative monitoring, newcomer's handbook, activity days and field trips, catalog of materials and a bookstore. (808) 242-8225 or 572-9289

Idaho

Idaho Home Educators (P.O. Box 4022, Boise ID 83711-4022): A Christian-oriented organization that offers support, information, idea exchange, resource/reading lists, testing/evaluation by fee, monthly skating parties, monthly mom's breakfasts, meetings, buddy system, home-teacher inservice training, school board liaison. (208) 345-1343

North Idaho Home Education Association (P.O. Box 1133, Post Falls ID 83854-1133): Offers support/encouragement, first-timer's assistance, information dissemination, newsletter, teen program, field trips, activity days (such as art fairs, field days and picnics, skiing), testing service, lending library, and periodically offers curriculum exchanges, workshops, and various cooperative educational or sports programs for home schoolers. (208) 769-6295

Port Cities Home Educators (1880 Old Spiral Highway, Lewiston ID 83501): Offers mutual support, meetings, field trips, special classes.

Illinois

Evanston Home Educators (%Berggren, 9214 Harding Avenue, Evanston IL 60203): Offers support/encouragement, legal information, meetings and idea exchanges, in-state networking, legislative monitoring, activity days and field trips. (708) 676-3855

Home Oriented Unique Schooling Experience (3934 North Kimball, Chicago IL 60618): Offers support/encouragement, legal information, local/regional meetings and idea exchanges, in-state networking, newsletter, materials exchanges/fairs, legislative monitoring, activity days and field trips. (312) 463-4304

Home Oriented Unique Schooling Experience (806 Oakton, Evanston IL 60202): Offers mutual support, legal information, local/regional meetings, in-state networking, newsletter, legislative monitoring, newcomer's handbook, activity days, field trips. (708) 328-6323

Illinois Christian Home Educators (P.O. Box 261, Zion IL 60099): A ministry to home educators in Illinois. A statewide organization that facilitates the formation of local support groups and statewide networking. Offers publications of interest to home educators, seminars, newsletter, encouragement.

Indiana

Fort Wayne Area Home Schoolers (P.O. Box 12954, Fort Wayne IN 46866-2954): Encourages home-schooling excellence. Offers a quarterly newsletter, book fair, orientation meetings, get-togethers and field trips, some materials, moms' meetings, achievement testing.

Indiana Association of Home Educators (1000 North Madison S-2, Greenwood IN 46142)): A statewide, Christian-oriented organization that offers support/encouragement, legal information, in-state networking, workshops and courses, public awareness activities, legislative monitoring and lobbying. (317) 885-3013

Wabash Valley Homeschoolers Association (2515 East Quinn Avenue, Terre Haute IN 47805): Offers mutual support, field trips and other group activities, meetings, information exchange. (812) 466-9467

Iowa

Network of Iowa Christian Home Educators (P.O. Box 158, Dexter IA 50070): A statewide organization that offers legal information, in-state networking, newsletter, materials exchanges/fairs, legislative monitoring, regional meetings, annual conference, parent educator workshops and seminars. (800) 723-0438

Southwest Iowa Home-Education (RR 3 Box 143, Missouri Valley IA 51555): Offers mutual support, information dissemination, public awareness activities, idea exchanges, meetings, field trips, activity days, legislative monitoring and action, consultations, curriculum assistance, publications, workshops, curriculum and materials fairs. (712) 644-2322 or 566-2802. Alternate address: Southwest Iowa Home-Education, Rural Route, Underwood IA 51576

Kansas

Christian Home Educators Confederation of Kansas (P.O. Box 3564, Shawnee Mission KS 66203): Statewide organization that offers support/encouragement, in-state networking, legal information, newsletter, legislative monitoring, lending library. (913) 651-4773

Lawrence Area Unaffiliated Group Homeschoolers (LAUGH) (RR 1 Box 496, Perry KS 66073): Offers support/encouragement, legal information, meetings and idea exchanges, in-state networking, newsletter, legislative monitoring, activity days and field trips. (913) 597- 5579

Teaching Parents Association (P.O. Box 3968, Wichita KS 67201): Offers support/encouragement, meetings and idea exchanges, legislative monitoring, consultations, conferences and seminars, monthly newsletter, field trips, testing service, networking. (316) 755-2159

KY-ME

Kentucky

Kentucky Christian Home School Association (1301 Bridget Drive, Fairdale KY 40118): A Christian-oriented group that offers support/encouragement, information dissemination, networking, bimonthly newsletter, public awareness activities, idea exchanges, meetings, field trips and activity days, legislative monitoring and action, curriculum packages, consultants/consultations, materials and aids, publications of interest to parent teachers, workshops, curriculum and materials fairs, science and craft fair. (502) 363-3104

Kentucky Home Education Association (P.O. Box 81, Winchester KY 40392-0081): Offers support/encouragement, networking, meetings, legislative monitoring and lobbying.

Lexington Homeschoolers (c/o Mandel, 615 Headley, Lexington KY 40508): Offers support/encouragement, information dissemination, networking, monthly newsletter, idea exchanges, field trips and activity days, informal consultations, assistance with materials and publications of interest to parent teachers, and an annual fair for the display of student projects. (606) 254-1799

Louisiana

Christian Home Education Fellowship of Louisiana (P.O. Box 74292, Baton Rouge LA 70874-4292): A statewide organization that offers support/encouragement, in-state networking, legal information, and more. (504) 642-2059

Southwest Acadiana Homeschoolers (507 South Arenas, Rayne LA 70578): Offers mutual support, legal information, local/regional meetings and idea exchanges, in-state networking, newsletter, legislative monitoring, annual conference, parent educator workshops. (318) 334-2812

Maine

Maine Homeschool Association (P.O. Box 9715-199, Portland ME 04104): A statewide nonsectarian association that offers legal information, in-state networking, newcomer's booklet, newsletter, legislative monitoring, list of certified teachers willing to help with annual assessment and meeting other requirements, public awareness activities. (207)353-5388

Southern Maine Home Education Support Network (76 Beech Ridge Road, Scarborough ME 04074): Diverse group that focuses on family empowerment and offers support/encouragement, legal information, newsletter, resource library, a variety of activity days and field trips and other events, sports programs, annual crafts fair. (207) 883-9621

Maryland

Maryland Home Education Association (9085 Flamepool Way, Columbia MD 21045): Provides longterm service and support for home educators regardless of political or religious orientation and functions as a legislative watchdog and initiates action in favor of home schooling. Offers legal information, statewide networking, statewide conferences and other similar functions, books at discount, research information, and a starter kit. (410) 730-0073

Massachusetts

Jewish Home Education Network (2 Webb Road, Sharon MA 02067): An international organization that offers support/encouragement, meetings and idea exchanges, newsletter, legislative monitoring, worldwide networking. (617) 784-9091

Massachusetts Home Learning Association (P.O. Box 1976, Lenox MA 01240): Offers support/encouragement, information dissemination, networking, newsletter, idea exchanges, quarterly activity days, legislative monitoring, informal consultations, information booklet. (413) 637-2169

Worcester Area Homeschooling Organization (246 May Street, Apt. #2, Worcester MA 01602): Offers mutual support. (508) 755-9553

Michigan

Heritage Home Educators (2122 Houser, Holly MI 48442): Offers support/encouragement, legal information, meetings and idea exchanges, in-state networking, newsletter, materials exchanges and fairs, resource library, activity days and field trips. (313) 634-4337

Information Network for Christian Homes (4150 Ambrose Northeast, Grand Rapids MI 49505): Offers networking, meetings, legislative monitoring, consultations, seminars, conferences, newsletter. (616) 364-4438

Older Homeschoolers' Group (9120 Dwight Drive, Detroit MI 48214): An all-inclusive group for home schoolers ages 12-18 in southeast Michigan, northern Ohio, and the Windsor, Ontario, Canada area. Offers mutual support, local/regional meetings, in-state networking, newsletter, educational programs (without tests or grades; with reliance on individual motivation and responsibility) in the arts, history, science, and other areas. Provides regular joint activities, and Girl Scouts, Boy Scouts, and Cub Scouts. (313) 331-8406

MN — MT

Minnesota

Families for Home Education (17020 Hamilton Drive, Lakeville MN 55044): Offers support/encouragement, legal information, meetings and idea exchanges, in-state networking, newsletter, resource library, newcomer's handbook, activity days and field trips. (612) 432-4657

Minnesota Association of Christian Home Educators (P.O. Box 188, Anoka MN 55303): Offers curriculum fairs, quarterly newsletter, seminars, picnics and other activities, support group networking, "out-state" meetings. (612) 753-2370

Minnesota Homeschoolers Alliance (P.O. Box 23072, Richfield MN 55423): A statewide organization that offers support/encouragement, in-state networking, newsletter, legislative monitoring, annual conference, workshops and other special events, phone line, support group listing, legal information, meetings and idea exchanges, materials exchanges/fairs, newcomer's packet. (612) 491-2828

Mississippi

Home Educators of Central Mississippi (% Bynum, 535 Luling Street, Pearl MS 39208): Offers support/encouragement, legal information, local/regional meetings and idea exchanges, in-state networking, newsletter, materials exchanges/fairs, consultations by noncertified home teachers, legislative monitoring, annual conference, resource library, activity days and field trips, parent educator workshops and courses, a bookstore. (601) 939-5927

Missouri

Christian Home Educators Fellowship (601 Madison Drive, Arnold MO 63010): Supports and trains Christian home educators, educates the Christian community about home education, works to protect parents' rights. (314) 296-1020

Homeschooling Network (47 Clermont Lane, St. Louis MO 63124): Offers mutual support, legal information, local/regional meetings, newsletter, materials exchanges/fairs, legislative monitoring, resource library, newcomer's handbook, activity days and field trips.

Ozark Lore Society (%Ozarks Resource Center, Brixey MO 65618): Offers support/encouragement, legal information, meetings and idea exchanges, in-state networking, monthly newsletter, resource library, newcomer's handbook, activity days and field trips. (417) 679-4773

Montana

Flathead Valley Homeschoolers (681 Shadow Lane, Kalispell MT 59901): Offers encouragement, networking, meetings and idea exchanges, activity days and field trips, consultations, curriculum packages, seminars and materials fairs. (406) 892-4052

Gardiner's Homeschoolers (P.O. Box 201, Gardiner MT 59030): Offers encouragement, networking, meetings and idea exchanges, legislative monitoring and lobbying, home-school materials. (406) 848-7226

Glendive Area Home Educators (44 FAS 254, Glendive MT 59330): Offers encouragement, meetings and idea exchanges, activity days and field trips. (406) 687-3890

Montana Coalition of Home Educators (Box 654, Helena MT 59624): Statewide organization offering support/encouragement, statewide networking, regional meetings, newsletter, biannual conferences, testing service, home educator workshops and seminars, legislative monitoring. (407) 443-5826

Nebraska

Lincoln Educated at Residence Network (7741 East Avon Lane, Lincoln NE 68505): Offers informal support and discussion of home-school issues, field trips, meetings as needed. (402) 488-7741

Nevada

Christian Home Educators of Nevada (1001 Sage Rock Way, Las Vegas NV 89031): A statewide organization that offers support and encouragement, legal information, in-state networking.

New Hampshire

Catholics United for Home Education (13 1/2 Parker Avenue, Manchester NH 03102): Offers support/encouragement, legal information, meetings and idea exchanges, in-state networking, legislative monitoring. (603) 623-3377

New Hampshire Alliance for Home Education (16 Winter Circle, RFD 3, Manchester NH 03103): Offers mutual support, legal information, local/regional meetings and idea exchanges, in-state networking, newsletter, materials exchanges, consultations with home teachers and certified teachers, legislative monitoring, newcomer's handbook, activity days, field trips, informal training, testing service, catalog of materials, home school-to-school district liaison. (603) 424-4060

New Hampshire Home Schooling Coalition (P.O. Box 2224, Concord NH 03301): Offers support/encouragement, legal information, meetings, in-state networking, newsletter, newcomer's handbook.

New Jersey

North Jersey Home Schoolers Association (P.O. Box 34, Hillsdale NJ 07642): Offers mutual support, legal information, local/regional meetings and idea exchanges, in-state networking, newsletter, materials exchanges/fairs, consultations with noncertified home teachers, legislative monitoring, a newcomer's handbook, activity days and field trips, parent educator workshops and courses. (201) 666-6025

Unschoolers Network (2 Smith Street, Farmingdale NJ 07727): Offers information dissemination, phone consultations, telephone question-answer service, support group networking, monthly bulletin, newsletter, workshops and seminars for parent educators, public awareness workshops. (201) 938-2473

Unschooling Families Support Group of Central New Jersey (150 Folwell Station Road, Jobstown NJ 08041): Offers mutual support, meetings and idea exchanges, activity days, field trips. (609) 723-1524

New Mexico

Family Educators (1766 Royal, Las Cruces NM 88011): Offers support/encouragement, meetings and idea exchanges, newsletter, legislative monitoring, resource library, activity days and field trips. (505) 522-1499

New Mexico Christian Home Educators (5749 Paradise Boulevard Northwest, Albuquerque NM 87114): Offers support/encouragement, annual convention/curriculum fair, how-to-start seminars statewide, resource referrals, legal information and seminars, support group networking, full-time information hotline, state newsletter, liaison with NM Dept. of Education and local districts. (505) 897-1772

New Mexico Family Educators (P.O. Box 92276, Albuquerque, NM 87199-2276): Offers support and encouragement, information dissemination, newsletter, idea exchanges, meetings, field trips and activity days, testing service, curriculum assistance, materials and aids of interest to home schoolers, parent workshops, curriculum and materials fairs, legislative monitoring. (505) 889-9775

New York

Albany Area Homeschoolers (46 Pershing Drive, Scotia NY 12302): Offers support/encouragement, legal information, local/regional meetings and idea exchanges, in-state networking, newsletter, materials exchanges/fairs, consultations with home teachers, legislative monitoring. (518) 346-3413

Families for Home Education (5458 Oxbow Road, Cazenovia NY 13035): Offers support/encouragement, legal information, local/regional meetings and idea exchanges, in-state networking, newsletter, legislative monitoring, activity days and field trips, informal home-teacher training. (315) 655-3238

Finglerlakes Unschoolers Network (249 Coddington Road, Ithaca NY 14850): Offers support/encouragement, legal information, local and regional meetings and idea exchanges, in-state networking, newsletter, materials exchanges/fairs, legislative monitoring, resource library, newcomer's handbook, activity days and field trips, parent educator workshops/seminars. (607) 277-6300

Home Educators' Alliance (341 East Fifth Street, New York NY 10003): Offers mutual support, legal information, meetings and idea exchanges, newsletter, legislative monitoring, resource library, activity days and field trips. (212) 505-9884

Loving Education at Home (P.O. Box 332, Syracuse NY 13205): A Christian-oriented statewide network that offers support, statewide networking, meetings, student activities, curriculum information, resource assistance, regulatory information manual, newsletter, annual convention, inservice programs. LEAH groups exist throughout state.

NYC Home Educators (341 East Fifth Street #1R, New York NY 10003): Offers legal information, meetings and idea exchanges, newsletter, resource library, a newcomer's flyer, a home school-to-school district volunteer liaison. (212) 505-9884

TLC Home Educators (P.O. Box 270, Ray Brook NY 12977): Offers support/encouragement, legal information, meetings and idea exchanges, consultations by noncertified home teachers, annual conference, resource library, newcomer's handbook, activity days and field trips, catalog of materials. (518) 891-5657

Tri-County Homeschoolers (%Lewis, 130 Blanchard Road, Stoney Point NY 10980): Offers mutual support, legal information, in-state networking, regional meetings, activity days, field trips. (914) 429-5156

North Carolina

Ed Venturous Learning Families (412 Thunder Creek, Franklin NC 28734): Offers support/encouragement, planning meetings, activity days and field trips, resource shelf at the county library, mentorship arrangements, newsletter. (704) 369-6491

Families Learning Together (412 Thunder Creek, Franklin NC 28734): An all-inclusive statewide network which offers family gatherings, quarterly newsletter, family directory, media resource file of articles about home schooling, home-schooling information. (704) 369-6491.

ND - OH

Islamic Homeschool Association (1312 Plymouth Court, Raleigh NC 27610): Offers phone/mail, networking, newsletter, newcomer's handbook. (919) 832-1960

North Carolinians for Home Education (419 North Boylan Avenue, Raleigh, NC 27603): Offers mutual support, home-schooling information, networking, newsletter, annual conferences. (919) 834-6243

North Dakota

North Dakota Home School Association (P.O. Box 486, Mandan ND 58554): A statewide organization that offers legal information and referrals, in-state networking, newsletter, materials exchanges/fairs, legislative monitoring, annual conferences, newcomer's handbook, home school-to-school district liaison.

Ohio

Christian Home Educators of Ohio (P.O. Box 262, Columbus OH 43216): Offers support and encouragement, information dissemination, phone consultations, conventions, educational materials, information phone tree, newsletter, speakers bureau, legislative and state board liaison and monitoring. 1-800-274-CHEO

HELP-Columbus (P.O. Box 14296, Columbus OH 43214): Offers mutual support, legal information, local/regional meetings and idea exchanges, in-state networking, materials exchanges/fairs, consultations with home teachers, legislative monitoring, resource library, newcomer's handbook, activity days, field trips, informal home-teacher training, bookstore, home school-to-school district liaison. (614) 268-5363

HELP-Oberlin (10915 Pyle - South Amherst Road, Oberlin OH 44074): Offers mutual support, legal information, meetings and idea exchanges, in-state networking, newsletter, consultations with certified and noncertified teachers, resource library, activity days and field trips, informal home-teacher training, parent educator workshops/seminars, student assessment/evaluation packages, catalog of materials, home school-to-school district liaison. (614) 774-2720

HELP-Toledo (%Jablonski, P.O. Box 98, Perrysburg OH 43552-0098): Offers support/encouragement, legal information, meetings and idea exchanges, in-state networking, newsletter, consultations with certified teachers and with noncertified home teachers, legislative monitoring, resource library, newcomer's handbook, student assessment/evaluation packages. (419) 478-9729

HELP-Tri County (P.O. Box 93, Pitsburg OH 45358): Offers mutual support, legal information, meetings and idea exchanges, in-state networking, newsletter, materials exchanges and fairs, legislative monitoring, resource library, newcomer's handbook, activity days and field trips, catalog of materials. (513) 692-5680 or (513) 968-4942

HELP-Unlimited (P.O. Box 93, Ashland OH 44805): Offers mutual support, legal information, meetings and idea exchanges, in-state networking, newsletter, legislative monitoring, activity days and field trips, informal home teacher training, parent educator workshops and seminars, materials catalog. (419) 281-0546 or 868-7916

HELP-Yellow Springs (P.O. Box 63, Yellow Springs OH 45387): Offers mutual support, legal information, meetings and idea exchanges, in-state networking, newsletter, materials exchanges/fairs, legislative monitoring, activity days and field trips, catalog of materials, home school-to-school district liaison, legal assistance. (513) 767-2346

Home Education Resource Organization (%Janovyak, 4 Erie Street, Norwalk OH 44857): Offers support/encouragement, legal information, meetings and idea exchanges, in-state networking, consultations with home teachers, activity days and field trips, parent educator workshops and seminars, assessment/evaluation packages, a home school-to-school district liaison.

Homeschool Network of Greater Cincinnati (5166 Romohr Road, Cincinnati OH 45244): Offers mutual support, legal information, meetings and idea exchanges, in-state networking, newsletter, materials exchanges, legislative monitoring, participation in National Homeschool Association meetings, annual conferences, resource library, newcomer's "Welcome Packet," activity days, field trips, student assessment/evaluation. (513) 772-9579 or 732-6455

National Homeschool Association (P.O. Box 157290, Cincinnati OH 45215-7290): An all-inclusive national organization which offers nationwide networking, quarterly newsletter, resource referral service, annual family campout/conference and regional conferences, legislative monitoring. (513) 772-9580

Ohio-Home Educators Network (P.O. Box 23054, Chagrin Falls OH 44023-0054): Offers mutual support, legal information, local/regional meetings and idea exchanges, in-state networking, newsletter, consultations with certified teachers and with noncertified home teachers, legislative monitoring, annual picnic, reading list, activity days and field trips, informal home-teacher training, parent educator workshops and seminars, assistance compiling student assessment/evaluation portfolios, home school-to-school district liaison.

Older Homeschoolers' Group (9120 Dwight Drive, Detroit MI 48214): An all-inclusive group for home schoolers ages 12-18 in southeast

OK — OR

Michigan, northern Ohio, and the Windsor, Ontario, Canada area. Offers mutual support, local/regional meetings, in-state networking, newsletter, educational programs (without tests or grades; with reliance on individual motivation and responsibility) in the arts, history, science, and other areas. Provides regular joint activities, and Girl Scouts, Boy Scouts, and Cub Scouts. (313) 331-8406

Oklahoma

Christian Home Education Fellowship (P.O. Box 471363, Tulsa OK 74147-1363): A statewide organization that offers mutual support, in-state networking, legal information, newcomer's information packet, orientation classes, annual curriculum fair, newsletter, members' library and resource center. (918) 583-7323

Home Educators Resource Organization (475 College, Norman OK 73069): Offers mutual support, legal information, meetings and idea exchanges, in-state networking, newsletter, materials exchanges and fairs, consultations with certified teachers and with home teachers, resource library, newcomer's handbook, activity days and field trips, informal home-teacher training, materials catalog. (405) 321-6423

Oklahoma Central Home Educators (P.O. Box 270601, Oklahoma City OK 73137): Offers support, legal information, local/regional meetings, in-state networking, newsletter, materials exchanges/fairs, legislative monitoring, annual conference, newcomer's handbook, testing service, record keeping service, resource catalog. (405) 521-8439

Oregon

Douglas County Home Schoolers' Connection (1350 Elgarose Road, Roseburg OR 97470): Offers assistance and connections for new home schoolers. (503) 673-7594

Oregon Christian Home Education Association Network (2515 Northeast 37th Avenue, Portland OR 97212): Offers encouragement, networking, legislative monitoring and lobbying, consultations, seminars, conferences and materials fairs, newsletter, idea exchanges.

Oregon Home Education Network (4470 Southwest Hall Boulevard #286, Beaverton OR 97005): Offers support/encouragement, legal information, in-state networking, newsletter, legislative monitoring, annual conference, newcomer's handbook, testing service, legal assistance, moms' weekends, family retreats. (503) 321-5166

Parents Education Association (P.O. Box 1482, Beaverton OR 97075): A political action group that promotes quality Godly education outside the state school system and ensures like-minded supporters a voice in the political arena. Offers legislative monitoring and lobbying, seminars, information exchanges. (503) 693-0724

Pennsylvania

Center City Homeschoolers (2203 Spruce Street, Philadelphia PA 19103): Offers support/encouragement, legal information, meetings and idea exchanges, in-state networking. (215) 732-7723

Creative Education Network (%Lounsbury, Star Route, Mechanicsville Road, Carversville PA 18913): Offers mutual support, legal information, group meetings and idea exchanges, in-state networking, activity days and field trips. (215) 297-0642

Pennsylvania Home Education Network (285 Allegheny Street, Meadville PA 16335): Offers mutual support, legal information, local/regional meetings and idea exchanges, in-state networking, newsletter (including membership directory, group listings, and standardized tests source lists) materials exchanges/fairs, legislative monitoring, annual conference, newcomer's handbook, informal home-teacher training, parent educator workshops/seminars, statewide phone tree, catalog of materials and bookstore. (215) 265-2734

Pennsylvania Homeschoolers (RD 2 Box 117, Kittanning PA 16201) Offers support and encouragement, networking, statewide newsletter, public awareness activities, idea exchanges, legislative monitoring, certificated consultants, conferences, announcements of field trips, statewide events, activity days, high school diploma program. (412) 783-6512

South Hills of Pittsburgh Support Group (3485 South Park Road, Bethel Park PA 15102): Offers support and encouragement, information, annual seminars, monthly field trips, reading club, 4-H club. (412) 854-4188

Rhode Island

Rhode Island Guild of Home Teachers (P.O. Box 11, Hope RI 02831): A statewide organization that offers networking, an annual curriculum fair, newsletter, special academic events. (401) 821-1546

South Carolina

Piedmont Home Educators' Association (P.O. Box 2681, Greenville SC 29616): Offers support and encouragement, information dissemination, networking, newsletter, idea exchanges, meetings, field trips and activity days, legislative monitoring and political action, consultations, workshops, curriculum and materials fairs, annual spelling bee, science fair, art show and field day. (803) 834-0241

SD — TX

South Carolina Association of Independent Home Schools (P.O. Box 2104, Irmo SC 29063-2104): An accrediting and policing organization for home-school families who choose not to home school through their local school district. (803) 551-1003

South Carolina Home Educators Association (P.O. Box 612, Lexington SC 29071-0612): A statewide organization that offers support/encouragement, legal information, statewide networking, newsletter, legislative monitoring, annual conference, newcomer's handbook. (803) 951-8960

South Dakota

South Dakota Home School Association (P.O. Box 882, Sioux Falls SC 57101): Offers support/encouragement, in-state networking, quarterly meetings, activity days and field trips, newsletter, legislative monitoring. (605) 334-2213

Tennessee

Tennessee Home Education Association (3677 Richbriar Court, Nashville TN 37211): A statewide organization with 175 to 200 or more support group affiliates. Offers support/encouragement, information dissemination, networking, bimonthly newsletter and monthly chapter newsletters, public awareness activities, legislative monitoring and lobbying, meetings and idea exchanges, consultations, publications of interest to home educators, conferences, workshops/seminars, curriculum and materials fairs, field trips. (615) 834-3529

Texas

Alternative Education Alliance (11702-B Grant Road, Suite 112, Cypress TX 77429): Offers mutual support, legal information, meetings and idea exchanges, in-state networking, newsletter, newcomer's handbook, materials catalog. (713) 480-6856 or (713) 370-3756

HAEA/HELP (14222 Ridgewood Lake Court, Houston TX 77062): Offers mutual support, legal information, local/regional meetings and idea exchanges, newsletter, activity days, field trips. (713) 480-6856

Home-Oriented Private Education for Texas (P.O. Box 17755, Austin TX 78760-7755): Offers Christian-oriented mutual support, legal information, in-state networking, newsletter, newcomer's handbook, materials catalog. (512) 280-4673

North Texas Self-Educators (150 Forest Lane, Double Oak/Lewisville TX 75067): An all-inclusive group that offers mutual support, legal information, beginner's information packet and 4-hour workshop, local/regional meetings and idea exchanges, in-state networking, newsletter, legislative monitoring, activity days, field trips. (817) 430-4835

Texas Advocates for Freedom in Education (%Jackson, 13635 Greenridge Street, Sugar Land TX 77478): Offers mutual support, legal information, in-state networking, newsletter, materials exchanges and fairs, legislative monitoring, regional meetings, annual conference, parent educator workshops and seminars.

Utah

HELP-Four Corners (Castle Valley Star Route, Box 1901, Moab UT 84532): Offers mutual support, meetings, consultations with home teachers, activity days, field trips, parent educator workshops/seminars, home school-to-school district liaison. (801) 259-6968

Latter-Day Saint Home Educators' Association (2770 South 1000 West, Perry UT 84302): Offers a newsletter, consultations with home teachers, annual conference, newcomer's handbook, parent educator workshops/seminars, catalog of materials. (801) 723-5355

Utah Home Education Association (P.O. Box 50565, Provo UT 84605-0565): A statewide organization that offers mutual support, legal information and assistance, local/regional meetings and idea exchanges, in-state networking, newsletter, materials exchanges and fairs, consultations with home teachers, legislative monitoring, annual conferences, resource library, newcomer's handbook, activity days, field trips, informal home-teacher training, parent educator workshops/seminars, testing service, catalog of materials, bookstore, a home school-to-school district liaison. (801) 535-1533 or 342-4027

Vermont

Addison County Homeschoolers (RD 2 Box 2850, Vergennes VT 05491): Offers mutual support, legal information, local/regional meetings and idea exchanges, newsletter, materials exchanges and fairs, consultations with home teachers, resource library, activity days and field trips, informal home-teacher training. (802) 877-3959

Christian Home Educators of Vermont (2 Webster Avenue, Barre VT 05641-4818): Offers mutual support, legal information, in-state networking, local/regional meetings and idea exchanges, newsletter, materials exchanges/fairs, annual conferences, newcomer's handbook, activity days, field trips, bookstore, legislative monitoring. (802) 476-8821

Covenant Christian Home Schoolers (47 North Main Street, Windsor VT 05089): Offers support/encouragement, networking, meetings, activity days, workshops, newsletter.

Northeast Kingdom Christian Homeschool Support Group (P.O. Box 55, Lyndon Center VT 05850): Offers support/encouragement, legal information, meetings and idea exchanges, resource library, activity days and field trips, annual talent show. (802) 626-4264

VA

Vermont Home Schoolers' Association (RD 2 Box 4440, Bristol VT 05443): Offers mutual support, home-schooling information, networking, meetings, newsletter, legislative monitoring, informal consultations. (802) 235-2457

Virginia

Blue Ridge Area Network for Congenial Homeschoolers (Route 3 Box 602, Afton VA 22920): Offers support, legal information, local/regional meetings and idea exchanges, in-state networking, newsletter, consultations with home teachers, legislative monitoring, resource library, activity days, field trips, catalog of materials. (703) 456-9822

Children's Circle (Route 1 Box 132A, Mouth of Wilson, VA 24363): Offers mutual support, legal information, meetings and idea exchanges, activity days, field trips. (703) 579-4252 or (919) 982-9072

Community of Independent Learners (P.O. Box 16029, Alexandria VA 22302): An all-inclusive group for northern Virginia and the District of Columbia that offers mutual support, meetings and idea exchanges, in-state networking, activity days, field trips; and explores flexible alternative strategies that recognize children's uniquenesses. (703) 998-9626

Home Educators Association (P.O. Box 1810, Front Royal VA 22630-1810): Offers support/encouragement, legal information, in-state networking, newsletter, materials exchanges/fairs, legislative monitoring, annual conference, newcomer's handbook. (703) 635-9322

LEARN/Northern VA Homeschoolers (2520 Rocky Branch Road, Vienna VA 22181) A network of home-schooling families in Northern Virginia which publishes a newsletter and whose members offer legal information, local/regional meetings and idea exchanges, regional networking, materials exchanges/fairs, legislative monitoring, newcomer's handbook/information packet, activity days, field trips. (703) 281-9049

Richmond Educational Alternatives for Children at Home (%Pleasant, 1805 North Junaluska Drive, Richmond VA 23225): Offers mutual support, legal information, local/regional meetings, in-state networking, newsletter, materials exchanges/fairs, legislative monitoring, annual conferences, resource library, activity days, field trips, parent educator workshops/seminars, assessment/evaluation packages. (804) 233-2831

Virginia Home Education Association (Route 1 Box 370, Gordonsville VA 22942) A statewide organization which monitors legislative and regulatory activity and helps local home-school groups interact effectively with local school districts. (703) 832-3578

Washington

Family Learning Organization of Washington State (P.O. Box 7256, Spokane WA 99207-0256): A statewide organization that offers family learning advocacy, legislative representation, school district liaison, networking, information, testing and evaluation, courses and workshops for home schoolers. Also sponsors the Family Learning Fair, a curriculum fair which attracts hundreds of home schoolers and would-be home schoolers from throughout the Pacific Northwest and southwest Canada. (509) 467-2552

Homeschoolers' Support Association (P.O. Box 413, Maple Valley WA 98038): Assists potential and novice home schoolers, fosters community awareness of home schooling, supports and informs home schools of all philosophical persuasions. Offers support meetings, information, monthly newsletter, home-school family activities and school membership with the Pacific Science Center. (206) 432-9805 or 537-7192

Kittitas Valley Homeschool Association (P.O. Box 1492, Ellensburg WA 98926): Offers support/encouragement, legal information, meetings and idea exchanges, newsletter, materials exchanges/fairs, activity days and field trips, materials catalog. (509) 925-4033

Washington Homeschool Organization (18130 Midvale Avenue North, Suite C, Seattle WA 98133): A statewide organization that offers networking, annual convention, information dissemination, newsletter, public awareness activities, idea exchanges, meetings, testing and record keeping services, legislative monitoring and action, consultations, curriculum assistance, certificated consultants, publications of interest to home educators, curriculum and materials fairs, and workshops, seminars, and courses. (206) 546-9483

West Virginia

Christian Home Educators (P.O. Box 8770, South Charleston WV 25303-0770): A statewide organization that offers support and encouragement, in-state networking, legislative monitoring, annual conference, annual research project fair competition, high school graduation ceremony, testing service, annual fine arts festival, newsletter.

West Virginia Home Educators Association (P.O. Box 3707, Charleston WV 25337-3707): Offers support/encouragement, legal information, meetings and idea exchanges, in-state networking, newsletter, materials exchanges/fairs, legislative monitoring, annual conference, newcomer's handbook, activity days and field trips, testing service, catalog of materials and a bookstore, a home school-to-school district liaison. (800) 736-8943

WI-WY

Wisconsin

Families in Schools at Home (5009 Holiday Drive, Madison WI 53711): Offers support/encouragement, legal information, local asnd regional meetings and idea exchanges, newsletter, materials exchanges/fairs, consultations with noncertified home teachers, legislative monitoring, annual conference, activity days and field trips, parent educator workshops and seminars and informal training, home school-to-school district liaison. (608) 271-4075

H.O.M.E. (5745 Bittersweet Place, Madison WI 53705): Offers support/encouragement, legal information, meetings and idea exchanges, in-state networking, newsletter, resource library, activity days and field trips. (608) 238-3302

Unschooling Families (1908 North Clark Street, Appleton WI 54911): Offers support, legal information, meetings and idea exchanges, newsletter, resource library, activity days, field trips. (414) 735-9832

Wisconsin Parents Association (P.O. Box 2502, Madison WI 53701-2502): A statewide organization that offers support/encouragement, in-state networking, legal information, newsletter, materials exchanges/fairs, legislative monitoring, support for regional meetings, annual conferences, home-schooling handbook, information regarding interactions with local school districts and court proceedings.

Wyoming

Homeschoolers of Wyoming (P.O. Box 926, Evansville WY 82633-0926): Offers networking, legislative updates, state annual convention and curriculum fair, state home-school fine arts day and science fair, and support/encouragement. (307) 237-4383

Unschoolers of Wyoming (23 Dance Hall Road, Lander WY 82520): Offers support/encouragement, legal information, in-state networking, newsletter, regional meetings, annual conference.

Support Services

Many of the following organizations and institutions are non-profit, but be aware that some are commercial enterprises. Also, some function from single-purpose philosophical foundations while others are all-inclusive. Further, like the support group list, this list is incomplete. There are many other services available in each state to home schoolers, including some of those offered by such obvious public institutions as libraries, museums, environmental organizations, art galleries and arts/crafts workshop centers, mentorship and apprenticeship situations, community schools programs, and college courses and special activities.

Alaska

Alyeska Central School, *"Alaska's Centralized Correspondence School"* (3141 Channel Drive #100, Juneau AK 99801-7897): A fully accredited public correspondence school that offers a complete K-12 curriculum in all subject areas, issues a high school diploma, provides free enrollment with materials-return (for Alaskans), and certified teacher assistance. (907) 465-2835

California

"The Adventist Home Educator" (P.O. Box 836, Camino CA 95709-0836): A newsletter linking Seventh-day Adventist home educators together with mutual encouragement, idea exchanges, legislative monitoring, legal information, an AHE handbook, and a subscriber directory. (916) 647-2110

Baldwin Park Christian School (13940 East Merced, Baldwin Park CA 91706): Assistance with materials choices, curriculum planning and quarterly evaluations, teaching advice, start-up counseling. (818) 337-8828

Cascade Canyon School (P.O. Box 879, Fairfax CA 94930): Offers home schoolers enrollment in sign language, arts, physical education and foreign language classes (Spanish, French, Russian); field trips and overnight programs. (415) 459-3464 or 488-4502

Center for Educational Guidance (P.O. Box 445, North San Juan CA 95960): Aims to empower family, child and community as an interrelated whole and to serve as a model for Integrated Holistic Education. Offers programs designed to allow family and community to reclaim responsibility for the education of the young, community courses for

CO

home-school children and parents in academics, the trades, crafts, art, movement, computer literacy, etc.; an apprentice program; a learning tools library; assistance to support groups; family counseling and conflict resolution; cooperative game days for kids, families, and others; workshops in California and Oregon about such topics as how children learn, communicating with children, conflict resolution, holistic curriculums, evaluating educational options; a Special Events Program through which professionals are brought to the community to share their expertise; an outdoor education Ropes Course program geared to the whole family; family retreats. (916) 292-3623

HCL (P.O. Box 4643, Whittier CA 90607): An accredited private school which encourages and supports "invited teaching" in the home and community. Offers group networking, individual consultations, skills exchange service, materials catalogs, special events and field trips, joint educational projects. (310) 696-4696

"Home Educator's Almanac" (18515 Murphy Springs Court, Morgan Hill CA 95037): A newsletter serving over four hundred families in the northern California/Silicon Valley area. Offers support/encouragement, legal information, networking, local and regional meetings, idea exchanges among members of various support groups, newcomers' consultations by certified and noncertified teachers, legislative monitoring, newcomer's handbook, activity days and field trips, testing service, materials catalog/bookstore.

Montessori World Education Institute (P.O. Box 3808, San Luis Obispo CA 93403): Offers training in Montessori teaching methods for use in home schools.

Pilgrim School (P.O. Box 820, Springville CA 93265): Aims to provide legal cover and accountability and to challenge families to live Godly lifestyles. Offers local support group, seminars, records, newsletter, tapes, and an Independent Study Program based on individually prescribed and negotiated learning plans. (209) 539-0500

Colorado

Grace Academy (6060 Hollowtree Court, Colorado Springs CO 80918): Offers supplemental classes to home-schooling families in such subjects as speech, drama, art, choir, drafting. (719) 593-8396

Pinewood School (112 Road D, Pine CO 80470): Aims to individualize the learning process to meet the interests and needs of the students and parents involved. Provides a full and a basic home-based education program, an educational resource center, test filing service, on-line computer services, diploma program, units of study, consultations, workshops, and a tutoring service. (303) 670-8180

Connecticut

Emanuel Homestead (289 Barlow Cemetery Road, Woodstock CT 06281): A Christian home-education resource center. Provides a ministry to women at home, their husbands and children, home-school curriculum recommendations; organizational, homemaking, homesteading idea exchanges. (203) 974-2415

District of Columbia

National Committee for Citizens in Education (900 Second Street Northeast, Suite 8, Washington DC 20002): Offers many publications related to parental involvement in the education of children and parents' rights, primarily with regards to public schools. (800) 638-9675

National Home Study Council (1601 Eighteenth Street Northwest, Washington DC 20009): An organization which advocates for quality correspondence or distance education, serves as a clearinghouse of information about the home-study field, and sponsors a nationally recognized accrediting agency for home-study schools. (202) 234-5100

Georgia

Perimeter Christian School (5701 Spalding Drive, Norcross GA 30092): A home satellite program with monthly consultations, standardized testing, curriculum assistance, record keeping, access to athletic teams, field days, library, teaching resources. (404)662-8134

Illinois

Christian Liberty Academy Satellite Schools (502 West Euclid Avenue, Arlington Heights IL 60004): Provides a nationally normed standardized achievement test, scoring, and reports for home schoolers.

Constitutional Rights Foundation (407 South Dearborn, Suite 1700, Chicago IL 60615): Offers a quarterly newsletter, curricular materials, and publications of interest to education-law educators.

Family Resource Coalition (200 South Michigan Avenue, Suite 1420, Chicago IL 60604-2404): Activities, conferences, monitoring and lobbying policy makers and promoting the development of prevention-oriented, community-based programs to strengthen families.

Maine

Homeschool Associates (116 Third Avenue, Auburn ME 04210): A broad-based service organization that facilitates home-school conferences, publishes two newspapers: "At Home in New England" for northeastern home schoolers and "Home Educator's Family Times"

MA-MI

for Michigan families, maintains a curriculum store in Auburn with a toll free order line, purchases used textbooks for reuse, outfits a bookmobile, provides standardized testing and transcript and diploma services, advocates for home schoolers before school and government officials, writes public policy statements, executes an "educator-buy" program with Apple Computer for members of the Associates, issues positive home-school press releases, publishes communications for state organizations, promotes home schooling through radio and TV ads, designs curriculums, offers expertise with home schooling the special education home student, facilitates networking. (207) 777-1700

Massachusetts

Holt Associates Inc. (2269 Massachusetts Avenue, Cambridge MA 02140): Offers information dissemination, networking throughout the nation, many publications of interest to home educators (John Holt's Book and Music Store catalog), and Quadro construction toys. Publishes *Growing Without Schooling*, a well-known national, home-schoolers' newsletter. (617)864-3100

National Center for Fair and Open Testing (342 Broadway, Cambridge MA 02139): An advocacy organization working to end the overuse and misuses of standardized, multiple-choice testing and make certain that the evaluation of students and workers is fair, open, accurate, accountable and educationally sound. Publishes, among other publications, a quarterly newsletter, the "FairTest Examiner" and a booklet titled, "Standardized Tests and Our Children: A Guide to Testing Reform," which explains testing terms and parent's rights and makes suggestions for reform. (617) 864-4810

Michigan

Clonlara School (1289 Jewett, Ann Arbor MI 48104): Clonlara is both a campus school and a home-based education program. Offers a newsletter, curriculum programs, family tuition, state math and communication skills guidebooks, home-school start-up assistance (including help dealing with "officials"), monthly record sheets, networking, pen pals, instructional videotapes and audiotapes, certificated teachers, standardized testing, class time schedules, student interest surveys, report cards, transcripts, diplomas, networking, teacher education workshops, seminars, conferences. (313) 769-4515

The Michigan Center for Career and Technical Education (133 East Erickson Hall, Lansing MI 48824-1034): Offers copies of the state's "Model Core Curriculum Outcomes" for five dollars each, or three dollars each for twenty-five or more. (800) 292-1606

Minnesota

Catholic Home-School Newsletter (688 Eleventh Avenue Northwest, New Brighton MN 55112): Offers an annually updated resource newsletter which lists and annotates resources and catalogs both particular to Catholic home schoolers and others for any home schoolers. (612) 636-5761

National Association for Gifted Children (4175 Lovell Road, Suite 140, Circle Pines MN 55014): Disseminates information to parents, public officials, and schools; serves as a public advocate of the gifted; promotes research and development related to gifted education; assists the development of gifted education support organizations. Offers an information network, encouragement and assistance to gifted education support groups, research and development journal, newsletter including parent ideas, legislative monitoring, annual convention and institute, a "Private Schools for the Gifted Directory," a catalog of materials of interest to parents of gifted children. (612) 784-3475

T.E.A.C.H.(4350 Lakeland Avenue North, Robbinsdale MN 55422): Offers an independent, Christian-oriented home-school program for preschool through grade twelve, consultations and supervision by certified teachers, curriculum assistance, materials and aids for instruction, publications of interest to home teachers, workshops, conferences, curriculum/materials fair, record-keeping service, local support group training and assistance, meetings and idea exchanges, newsletter, student socializing opportunities, field trips, networking, achievement testing, legislative monitoring and action. Serves as an accrediting association able to give home educators a certificate of accreditation upon meeting certain criteria. (612) 535-5514

Minnesota Statewide Testing Program (UCCS/Office of Measurement Services, University of Minnesota, 2520 Broadway Drive, Room 130, St. Paul MN 55113-5100): Provides nationally standardized achievement tests (and other tests) and a scoring and reporting service for home schoolers. Ask for the "Home School Service" order form.

Missouri

Parents' Rights Organization (12571 Northwinds Drive, St. Louis MO 63146): Promotes and defends parents' right to establish private and independent schools for their children. Offers information and publications for home schoolers, educational conference hosting, speakers, advisory services to groups attempting to implement initiatives to free tax monies for support of private schools. (314) 434-4171

MT-NY

Montana

"The Grapevine" (1702 Highway 83 North, Seeley Lake MT 59868): Newsletter providing statewide home-school news and networking through relevant articles, teaching information, group listings, reviews.

Homeschool Resource (P.O. Box 121, Red Lodge MT 59068): Free browsing room including publications about how to start home schooling; where to find curriculums, laws, and qualifications; lending library; support group information; information clearinghouse for used materials. Also classes in Spalding's *Writing Road to Reading.*

Nevada

Parent Activists Committed to Education (P.O. Box 13587, Las Vegas NV 89112): An organization dedicated to the repeal of the compulsory attendance law; first, in Nevada, then across the nation. PACE advises parents about how to avoid government entanglement and exercise their right to control their children's educations. (702) 457-1509

New Mexico

National Association for the Legal Support of Alternative Schools (P.O. Box 2823, Santa Fe NM 87501): A national information and legal service center designed to research, coordinate, and support legal actions involving non-public educational alternatives.

National Coalition of Alternative Community Schools (P.O. Box 15036, Santa Fe NM 87506): A coalition of schools, groups, and individuals committed to participant control, whereby students, parents, and staff create and implement their own learning programs. Includes networking, advocacy, annual conference. (505) 474-4312

Santa Fe Community School (P.O. Box 2241, Santa Fe NM 87501): A state-recognized, alternative school which also provides assistance to home schoolers — home-school planning, development, and supervisory assistance, record keeping, a children's exchange newsletter.

New York

Alliance for Parental Involvement in Education (P.O. Box 59, East Chatham NY 12060-0059): Nonprofit national organization that encourages parents to become involved in their children's educations — in public, or private, or home school. Provides information about educational options, family rights in education, educational trends, and resources. ALLPIE aids person-to-person networking, publishes a newsletter and a book and resources catalog with many home-school related items, provides a mail order lending library, and conducts annual family conferences and workshops including home-school topics. The ALLPIE newsletter contains a special insert concerning home-school issues related to New York State. (518) 392-6900

Alternative Education Resource Organization (417 Roslyn Road, Roslyn Heights NY 11577): Helps people who want to change education to a more empowering and holistic form and those individuals and groups who want to start new community schools, public and private, or to change existing schools. AERO provides information to people interested in home schooling or in finding private or public alternative schools, publishes a newsletter which provides networking news from various realms of alternative and holistic education, and offers videos and speaking and consulting services. (516) 621-2195

The Christian Homesteading Movement (RD 2-HS, Oxford NY 13830): Workshops that support home-education ideals and help fathers and mothers learn ways to stay at home full-time with their children.

International Arts and Culture Association (206 Glen Street, Fifth Floor, Glens Falls NY 12801): An art exchange program for American elementary and middle school-level children who wish to exchange artwork with children in thirty-two other nations.

Longview Publishing (RD 1 Box 172, East Chatham NY 12060): Offers for sale Seth Rockmuller's book *School Law in New York State: A Manual for Parents.*

North Country School (Camp Treetops, P.O. Box 187, Lake Placid NY 12946-0187): A private school which offers a special series of enrichment programs integrating varied subject areas for home schoolers in a natural and farm setting. (518) 523-9329

North Dakota

Division of Independent Study (P.O. Box 5036, 1510 Twelfth Avenue North, State University Station, Fargo ND 58105): Correspondence courses for grades 9-12 curriculums, including the on-line computer services of the Home Education Resource Network. (701) 239-7282

Ohio

Cassidy and Nells Publishing (P.O. Box 24133, Dayton OH 45424): Offers for sale a 104-page book titled "Home-Education Regulations: Answers for Ohio Parents." (800) 453-6114

Oregon

Christian Life Workshops (P.O. Box 2250, Gresham OR 97030): Offers home-school workshops and publications. (800) 225-5259

PA

Homeschool Associates (9025 Southwest 50th, Portland OR 97219): Achievement testing by a certified teacher in a home environment; introductory home-school workshops; math and writing workshops; seminars; tutoring. (503) 244-9677

The Learning Connection (P.O. Box 1091 #196, Grants Pass OR 97526): A K-12 private school and a weekly call-in talk-radio show on KOPE 103.5 FM, both called "The Learning Connection." The radio show provides information on home education, parenting, learning styles, adoption issues, and lifelong learning. School personnel provide person-to-person support/encouragement, legal information, meetings and idea exchanges, in-state networking, materials exchanges, consultations, legislative monitoring, informal home-teacher training, record keeping service, legal assistance, home school-to-school district liaison. (503) 476-5686

National Home Education Research Institute (Attn: Brian Ray, %Western Baptist College, 5000 Deer Park Drive Southeast, Salem OR 97301): Executes educational research focusing on home education and relevant to home education, educates the public about home education, publishes results of research involving home schoolers in a newsletter, "Home School Researcher," and provides home educators with information which will assist them in teaching. (503) 375-7018

Pennsylvania

Buxmont Christian Educational Institute (146 West Broad Street, Telford PA 18969): Offers academic transcripts, diplomas, testing, evaluators, curriculum catalogs, consultations, meetings, student activities.

Learning Disabilities Association of America (4156 Library Road, Pittsburgh PA 15234): Offers publications related to the education and lives of children with learning disabilities.

Open Connections (312 Bryn Mawr Avenue, Bryn Mawr PA 19010): A nonprofit educational organization whose purpose is to promote self-directed learning and flexible thinking in children and their families. Offers a Family Resource Center with an assortment of programs and workshops for parents and for children, publications regarding self-directed learning and flexible thinking, speeches and slide presentations, family consultations. (215) 527-1504

Seton Home Study (P.O. Box 396, Front Royal VA 22630): Provides a nationally normed standardized achievement test, test prep materials, scoring, and reports for home schoolers.

Upattinas Educational Resource Center (429 Greenridge Road, Glenmoore PA 19343): Private school that offers classes and activities to home schoolers, including travel opportunities. Acts as a resource center for home-schooling families and other independent learners.

South Carolina

Testing and Evaluation Service (Bob Jones University Press, Greenville SC 29614): Provides a nationally normed standardized test, practice tests, scoring and reports for home schoolers. Tests must be given by a certified teacher, a four-year college graduate, or a teacher from a conventional school.

South Carolina Association of Independent Home Schools (P.O. Box 2104, Irmo SC 29063-2104): Parents may home teach under the auspices of this organization in lieu of *individually* meeting requirements outlined by law. (803) 732-8680

Texas

Texas Home School Coalition (P.O. Box 6982, Lubbock TX 79493): A political action committee which publishes the *Texas Home School Alert* and monitors activities of the Texas Legislature, the Texas Education Agency and other government institutions which may have an impact on home schoolers' rights. (806) 797-4927

Virginia

Council for Exceptional Children (1920 Association Drive, Reston VA 22091): Offers publications and bibliographies related to the education of exceptional children, both handicapped and gifted, including the professional journals *Exceptional Children* and *Teaching Exceptional Children.* (800) 845-6232

Home School Legal Defense Association (P.O. Box 159, Paeonian Springs, VA 22129): An information and legal service center whose purpose is to research, coordinate, and support legal actions involving nonpublic education; also to help others locate, evaluate, and/or create alternatives to traditional schooling. Offers legal insurance, the "Home School Court Report" newsletter, support and help as noted above, networking, publications. (703) 338-5600

National Center for Home Education (P.O. Box 149, Paeonian Springs VA 22129): A branch of HSLDA (above). Assists state home-school organizations by providing a network for cooperation/communication, state and federal legislative information and monitoring, and the promotion of legislation favorable to home schoolers. (703) 338-5600

Rutherford Institute (P.O. Box 7482, Charlottesville VA 22906-7482): A legal (not religious) organization that protects the freedom of religious expression. Free legal service, home-school consultations, monthly action newsletter, and quarterly journal. Also offers other publications of interest to home educators, including the *Home Education Reporter* — a state-by-state analysis of compulsory education laws and relevant court rulings. (703) 369-0100

WA

Washington

Hewitt Research Foundation (P.O. Box 9, Washougal WA 98671): Offers nondoctrinal, nonsectarian, Christ-centered learning programs and materials for preschool through grade twelve. Placement assessments, information, procurement of your child's public school records, progress evaluations, parent-teacher counseling, transcripts, parent-administered standardized tests for grades 3-8, children's activity newsletter, programs for children with special needs, and the Hewitt Educational Resources catalog. (206)835-8708 or (800) 348-1750

Home Education Press (P.O. Box 1083, Tonasket WA 98855): Offers a variety of publications for home educators and parents in general, including *Home Education Magazine*, a well-known national magazine for home-school parents which includes informative articles related to all aspects of home teaching, resource lists and reviews, support group lists, children's pages, legal newsbits, and more.(509) 486-1351

The Moore Foundation (P.O. Box 1, Camas WA 98607): Publishes the *Moore Report International* newsletter, which includes home-school-related research and ideas; provides enrollment with individualized curriculum in the Moore Academy for K-12 students, including diplomas and programs for special needs students. The Moore's (Dorothy and Raymond) conduct home-school research and serve as advisors and speakers to home-school groups.

National Challenged Homeschoolers Associated Network (5383 Alpine Road Southeast, Olalla WA 98359): A Christian-oriented national support system for home-schooling families with "challenged" or special needs children. Offers support, a resource guide, newsletter, family networking, family directory, lending library. (206) 857-4257

❊❊❊

Section **6**

Readings
and
Resources

225

Readings

The following list of readings includes those mentioned earlier in this book and also others useful to home educators. Some are philosophical or theoretical in nature — concentrating on home education as a schooling concept. Many are more practical — presenting learning activities, lesson formats, children's book titles, experiments, checklists, and so on. A few include commentaries on public education. This and the other lists in this section, are not intended to be definitive, and although the titles noted are recommended, they are not necessarily recommended above all other possible titles. You will find here, however, many of the books considered by home schoolers to be key readings. Most will be available in public libraries or through interlibrary loan, and you'll find several in home-school organization lending libraries. All should be available, too, either directly through the publisher or through mainstream, Christian, or home-school bookstores and catalogues.

Please note that publisher's addresses are given only the first time each appears in this list of readings.

"A, B, C, or F; Test Your Child's School." *Parents Magazine*, November 1987, p. 138-142. (On informing yourself about a public school.)

Anthony, Susan C. *Facts Plus: An Almanac of Essential Information.* Instructional Resources Company. (A reference book covering basic facts, concepts, statistics, etc., in most subject areas. Also, *Facts Plus Activity Book*, a teacher's guide to activities that help kids learn to use reference books.)

Arbuthnot, May Hill, et. al. *The Arbuthnot Anthology of Children's Literature,* 1976. Scott, Foresman & Co., 1900 East Lake Avenue., Glenview IL 60025. (Children's tales and poetry.)

Armstrong, Thomas. *In Their Own Way,* 1987. Jeremy P. Tarcher, Inc.; 9110 Sunset Boulevard, Los Angeles CA 90069. (An explanation of learning styles and how to nurture and motivate learners whatever their "style.")

"Barbe Reading Skills Check List." Prentice-Hall, Prentice-Hall Building, Sylvan Avenue., Englewood Cliffs NJ 07632. (K-6 reading skills listed by grade level. Useful for developing a reading curriculum and for designing ongoing assessments of student progress.)

Barrata-Lorton, Mary. *Math Their Way*, 1976. Addison-Wesley, 2725 Sand Hill Road, Menlo Park CA. (A manipulative, activity-centered math program for early childhood and primary education.)

Bauer, Marion Dane. *What's Your Story? A Young Person's Guide to Writing Fiction*, 1992. Clarion Books, 215 Park Avenue South, New York NY 10003. (Step-by-step guidance to writing short stories, for junior high to senior high home schoolers.)

Boardman, Bob. *Red Hot Peppers: The Skookum Jumprope Book of Games, Rhymes, and Fancy Footwork*, 1993. Sasquatch Books, 1931 Second Avenue, Seattle WA 98101. (A book full of fun-and-fitness traditional and new jumprope activities for ages 7-12.)

Boyd, Margaret. *Craft Supply Source Book*, New Second Edition, 1989. Betterway Publications, P.O. Box 219, Crozet VA 22932. (Lists over 2500 catalogues that offer art and craft supplies.)

Brown, Tom, Jr. and Judy Brown. *Tom Brown's Field Guide to Nature and Survival for Children*, 1989. Berkley Publishing, 200 Madison Avenue, New York NY 10016. (On teaching children to observe and identify animals and plants, stalk and track, find water and food in nature, keep from getting lost in the wilderness, take safety measures, and use first aid.)

Buscaglia, Leo. *Living, Loving & Learning*, 1982. Ballantine, 400 Hahn Road, Westminster MD 21157. (Segments emphasizing the importance of warmth and love in teaching.)

The Cambridge Annotated Study Bible, New Revised Standard Version, 1993. Cambridge University Press, 40 West 20th Street, New York NY 10011-4211. (Includes study notes, concordance, tables of chronology and measures, and parallel gospels.)

Carlson, Laurie. *EcoArt: Earth Friendly Art and Craft Experiences for 3 to 9 Year Olds*. Williamson Publishing, Church Hill Road, Charlotte VT 05445. (Using natural, recyclable, and reusable materials for creative art and craft projects.)

Cassidy, John and The Exploratorium. *The Exploratorium*. Klutz Press, 2121 Staunton Court, Palo Alto CA 94306. (A guide plus kit, with equipment, for science-related discovery learning.)

Churbuck, David C. "The Ultimate School Choice: No School at All." *Forbes Magazine*, October 11, 1993, p. 144-150. (On reasons for opting to home school and on uses of computer software and networks for home schooling.)

Coles, Gerald. *The Learning Mystique: A Critical Look at Learning Disabilities*, 1987. Pantheon, 201 East 50th Street, New York NY 10022. (A careful dismantling of the "learning disabled" category so heavily used by our public schools.)

Colfax, David and Micki Colfax. *Homeschooling for Excellence, 1987.* Mountain House Press, Box 246, Booneville CA 95415. (Homeschooling philosophies and experiences of the Colfax family whose sons were offered admittance to Harvard, Princeton, and Yale after years of home schooling.)

Collins, Marva and Civia Tamarkin. *Marva Collins' Way,* 1982. J.P. Tarcher Inc., 9110 Sunset Boulevard, Los Angeles CA 90069. (The teaching techniques of the highly successful educator Marva Collins. Includes much on the teaching of phonics.)

"Consumer Information Catalog." Consumer Information Catalog, P.O. Box 100, Pueblo CO 81009. (Lists over 200 free and low-cost publications on various subjects including consumer education.)

Copperman, Paul. *Taking Books to Heart: How to Develop a Love of Reading in Your Child,* 1986. Addison-Wesley. (For parents of children 2 to 9. Clear explanations of basal readers, beginning reading instruction, comprehension instruction, and thorough descriptions of at-home reading sessions. Includes activities and book lists.)

Cox, J., N. Daniel and B.D. Boston. *Educating Able Learners,* 1985. University of Texas Press, Austin, TX. (Educating the gifted/ talented.)

Cummings, Rhoda and Cleborne Maddux. *Parenting the Learning Disabled: A Realistic Approach..* Charles C. Thomas Publishing, 2600 South First Street, Springfield IL 62717. (Parenting skills for parents of learning-disabled children.)

Dobson, James C. *Parenting Isn't for Cowards.* 1988, Word Books, 4800 West Waco Drive, Waco TX 76703. (Parenting skills.)

The Doubleday Illustrated Children's Bible, Retold by Sandol Stoddard, 1983. Doubleday & Co., 501 Franklin Avenue, Garden City NY 11530. (Useful for Christian education and sessions in the Bible as literature.)

Duffy, Cathy. *Christian Home Educator's Curriculum Manual-Elementary Grades,* 1992. Home Run Enterprises, 12531 Aristocrat Avenue, Garden Grove CA 92641. (A guide to establishing an elementary-grades, Christian home curriculum.)

Duffy, Cathy. *Christian Home Educator's Curriculum Manual- Junior/ Senior High,* 1992. Home Run Enterprises. (Guide to establishing a junior/senior high level, Christian home curriculum.)

Elbow, Peter. *Writing Without Teachers,* 1973. Oxford University Press, Inc., 200 Madison Avenue, New York NY 10016. (A guide to teaching and facilitating the writing process. You may want to be your children's writing classmate with a teacher-less writing "class.")

Elbow, Peter. *Writing With Power:Techniques for Mastering the Writing Process*, 1981. Oxford University Press. (Written for the secondary or college student, but useable by the parent educator teaching writing at any level. Also an introduction to the writing process.)

Elkind, David. *The Hurried Child: Growing Up Too Fast Too Soon*, 1981. Addison-Wesley. (About the stresses caused by hurrying the growth and education of children.)

Elkind, David. *Miseducation: Preschoolers at Risk*, 1987. Knopf, 400 Hahn Road, Westminster MD 21157. (Negative effects of enrolling children in preschools and attempting to create superlearners.)

"The Evidence Continues to Grow, Parent Involvement Improves Student Achievement." National Committee for Citizens in Education, 10840 Little Patuxent Parkway, Suite 301, Columbia MD 21044. (An annotated bibliography of available studies that document the effects of parent involvement in children's educations.)

Fluegelman, Andrew, editor.*The New Games Book.* Doubleday. (Cooperative games.)

Freeman, Judy. *Books Kids Will Sit Still For: A Guide to Using Children's Literature for Librarians, Teachers, and Parents*, 1984. The Alleyside Press, P.O. Box 889, Hagerstown, MD 21741. (An annotated list of 1200 read-aloud children's books and chapters on the use of children's literature for improved reading comprehension.)

Friedman, Anita Cross. *My Own Fun: Creative Learning Activities for Home and School.* Chicago Review Press, 814 North Franklin, Chicago Il 60610. (Varied home-learning activities for ages 6-12.)

Gates, Frieda. *Easy to Make North American Indian Crafts*, 1981. Harvey House. (Explains the making and uses of Indian artifacts and shows children how to make facsimiles with easy-to-find materials. Included are "extra easy" methods for the youngest kids.)

Gelner, Judy, *College Admissions: A Guide for Homeschoolers*, 1988. Poppyseed Press, P.O. Box 85, Sedalia CO 80135. (Information about procedures, records, testing, and financial aid when a home-schooled student applies for college admission.)

Gibbs, Jeanne. *Tribes: A Process for Social Development and Cooperative Learning*, 1987. Center Source Publications, 305 Tesconi Circle, Santa Rosa CA 95401. (A book full of small-to-large group activities that foster cooperation and self-esteem.)

Gorder, Cheryl. *Home Schools: An Alternative*, 1985. Blue Bird Publications, 1713 East Broadway #306, Tempe AZ 85282. (Getting started.)

Gordon, Edward. "Home Tutoring Programs Gain Respectability." *Phi Delta Kappan,* February 1983, p. 398-399. (A report on home schooling in the United States.)

Graubard, Allen. *Free the Children*, 1972. Random House, 201 East 50th Street, New York NY 10022. (An analysis of the free schools movement and school reform literature.)

Guterson, David. *Family Matters: Why Homeschooling Makes Sense*, 1992. Harcourt Brace Jovanovich, 6277 Sea Harbor Drive, Orlando FL 32887. (An examination of schooling, wherever it occurs and the tremendous importance of *family* and of *individual fulfillment*.

The HarperCollins Study Bible, New Revised Standard Version, 1993. HarperCollins, 1160 Battery Street, San Francisco CA 94111. (A Bible for scholars, with study notes and explanations.)

Harris, Gregg. *The Christian Home School*, 1988. Christian Life Workshops, P.O. Box 2250, Gresham OR 97030. (The Christian home-school perspective, answers to common home-school questions, and how to start a Christian home school.)

Hegener, Mark and Helen, editors. *Alternatives in Education*, 1992. Home Education Press, P.O. Box 1083, Tonasket WA 98855. (An anthology of articles exploring and explaining the various educational options outside the public and traditional private school systems in the United States.)

Hegener, Mark and Helen, editors. *Home School Reader*, 1988. Home Education Press. (An anthology of articles on various aspects and issues of home schooling.)

Henderson, Anne. "Parents Are a School's Best Friends," *Phi Delta Kappan*, October 1988. (On parent-participatory education.)

Hendrickson, Borg. *How to Write a Low Cost/No Cost Curriculum for Your Home-School Child*, 1990. Mountain Meadow Press, P.O. Box 318, Sitka AK 99835-0318. (Step-by-step guide to writing your own curriculum based upon your own educational philosophies and custom-tailored to meet your child's interests and needs.)

Hoffman, Jane. *The Backyard Scientist*. P.O. Box 16966, Irvine CA 92713. (Experiential hands-on science activities.)

Holt, John. *How Children Learn*, 1971. Dell Publishing. (How children learn and how teachers and parents should nurture them.)

Holt, John. *Teach Your Own*, 1981. Delacorte Press, 245 East 47th Street, New York NY 10017. (Home-school reasons, explanations and experiences, with comments from many experienced home schoolers.)

Holt, John, *What Do I Do Monday?*, 1970. Dutton, 2 Park Avenue, New York, NY 10016. (Philosophies for teaching and specifics on teaching math and writing.)

"Home Education; Is It Working?" 1986. Texas Home School Coalition, P.O. Box 835105, Richardson TX 75083. (A booklet citing positive home-school research.)

Hubbs, Don. *Home Education Resource Guide.* Blue Bird Publishing. (A directory of home-education resource materials.)

Hughes, Thomas. "Home Education: A Bibliography." University of Colorado. Boulder CO 80302 (Bibliography.)

Hunt, Tamara and Nancy Renfro. *Puppetry in Early Childhood Education.* Nancy Renfro Studios (Guide to making and teaching with puppets.)

The Illustrated Children's Bible, 1982. Retold by David Christie-Murry. Grosset & Dunlap, 51 Madison Avenue., New York NY 10010. (Useful for Christian education and sessions in the Bible as literature.)

"I'm Not Stupid," 1987. Association for Children and Adults with Learning Disabilities, 4156 Library Road, Pittsburgh PA 15200. (A video about the learning disabled.)

Judy, Stephen N. and Susan J. Judy. *An Introduction to the Teaching of Writing*, 1981. John Wiley & Sons, 605 Third Avenue, New York NY 10158. (A sound introduction.)

Julicher, Kathleen. *Experiences in Chemistry for Small Schools.* Castle Heights Press, 5866 Hunter Road, Enon OH 45323. (Complete home lab guide for high schoolers.)

Kaseman, M. Larry and Susan D. Kaseman. *Taking Charge Through HomeSchooling:Personal and Political Empowerment*, 1990. Koshkonong Press, 2545 Koshkonong Road, Stoughton WI 53589. (On opting to home school, aware of the "opposition," and feeling empowered as you proceed.)

Kaufman, Felice. *Your Gifted Child and You*, 1983. Council for Exceptional Children, Dept. CS88M, 1920 Association Drive, Reston VA 22091-1589. (On fostering creativity and helping gifted children develop their interests at home.)

Klicka, Christopher. *The Right Choice;: The Incredible Failure of Public Education and the Rising Hope of Home Schooling*, 1992. Noble Publishing, P.O. Box 2250, Gresham OR 97030. (On reasons and rights of Christian home-schooling parents. Includes some resources.)

Kline, Peter. *The Everyday Genius: Restoring Children's Natural Joy of Learning*, Great Ocean Publishers, 1823 North Lincoln Street, Arlington VA 22207. (On joyful family relationships and learning.)

Koch, Kenneth. *Rose, where did you get that red? Teaching Great Poetry to Children*, 1973. Random House. (A useful guide for teaching poetry to children.)

Koch, Kenneth. *Wishes, Lies, and Dreams: Teaching Children to Write Poetry.* Harper & Row, 10 East 53rd Street, New York NY 10022. (An easily used guide to teaching children how to write poetry.)

Kohl, MaryAnn and Cindy Gainer. *Good Earth Art: Environmental Art for Kids*. Bright Ring Publishers. (Art activities using natural and recycled materials, for ages 1-10.)

Kohl, MaryAnn and Jean Potter. *ScienceArts: Discovering Science Through Art Activities*. Bright Ring Publishers. (Art activities that also involve science concepts.)

Kohn, Alfie."Home Schooling." *Atlantic Monthly*, April 1988, p.20- 25. (An overview of home schooling in the United States.)

Kohn, Alfie. *No Contest: The Case Against Competition*, 1992. Houghton Mifflin, 215 Park Avenue South, New York NY 10003. (About cooperation vs. competition.)

Kohn, Alfie. *Punished by Rewards: The Trouble with Gold Stars, Incentive Plans, A's, Praise, and Other Bribes*, 1993. Houghton Mifflin. (On the longterm negative effects of extrinsic motivation.)

Larrick, Nancy. *A Parent's Guide to Children's Reading*, 1983. Doubleday. (On reading instruction.)

Laughy, Linwood. *Getting the Best Bite of the Apple*, 1993. Mountain Meadow Press, P.O. Box 318, Sitka AK 99835-0318. (A useful guide to the *whys* and *hows* of remaining in control of your child's education should your child be enrolled in public school. Also helpful for home schoolers who deal with public school officials in any way.)

Leistico, Agnes. *I Learn Better by Teaching Myself*, 1989. School of Home Learning, P.O. Box 92, Escondido CA 92025. (An introduction to child-directed, interest-initiated learning.)

Leonard, George B. *Education and Ecstasy*, 1987. North Atlantic Books, 2320 Lake Street, Berkeley CA 94704. (Describes what public education is and what education could be and poses the question: Do we really need or want public schools?)

Lines, Patricia M. "An Overview of Home Instruction." *Phi Delta Kappan*, March 1987, p. 510-517. (About the home-school movement.)

Lipson, Eden Ross. *The New York Times Parent's Guide to Best Books for Children*, 1988. Times Books, 201 East 50th Street, New York NY 10022. (A preschool through high school best-books bibliography.)

Llewellyn, Grace. *The Teenage Liberation Handbook: How to Quit School and Get a Real Life and Education*, 1991. Lowry House, P.O. Box 1014, Eugene OR 97440-1014. (Tells teenagers why and how to free themselves from institutional schooling and how to start and to get a *real* education. Also includes first-person accounts of the lives/educations of unschooled teens.)

Love, Robert. *How to Start Your Own School*, 1973. Macmillan, 866 Third Avenue, New York NY 10022. (A description of how Robert

Love and others began and maintained a nonpublic school, with advice for parents who wish to do the same.)

Macfarlan, A. and P. *Handbook of American Indian Games*, 1985. Dover Publications, 31 East Second Street, Mineola NY 11501. (Traditional Native American games, teaching skills of survival, cooperation, observation, animal behaviors, and the *how* of playing.)

McLean, Mollie and Anne Wiseman. *Adventures of the Greek Heroes.* Houghton-Mifflin, 2 Park Street, Boston MA 02108. (Greek myths retold for children.)

Medveseek, Chris. "Everybody Wins." *Parents Magazine*, April 1988, p. 121-124. (An article which discusses examples of cooperative games.)

Merrow, John. *Learning Disabilities: The Hidden Handicapped.* National Committee for Citizens in Education. (Video on learning disabilities for parents whose child appears to be learning disabled.)

Miles, Bernard. *Favorite Tales from Shakespeare*, 1977. Rand McNally, 8255 Central Park Avenue, Skokie IL 60076. (An illustrated anthology for children.)

Mintz, Jerry. "National Directory of Alternative Schools." The National Coalition of Alternative Community Schools, 58 Schoolhouse Road, Summertown TN 38483. (A directory.)

Moffett, James and Betty Jane Wagner. *Student-Centered Language Arts and Reading, K-13: A Handbook for Teachers,*1983. Houghton Mifflin. (A comprehensive description of a K-13 language and reading curriculum, including activities.)

Moore, Raymond and Dorothy Moore. *Home Grown Kids: A Practical Handbook for Teaching Your Children at Home*, 1984. Word Books. (Home-school rationale and how-to; lists of resources.)

Moore, Raymond and Dorothy Moore. *Home School Burnout*, 1988. Wolgemuth & Hyatt Publishers. Available from The Moore Foundation, P.O. Box 1, Camas, WA 98607. (Home-teacher burnout)

Moore, Raymond and Dorothy Moore. *Home-Spun Schools,* 1982. Word Books. (On the benefits of being schooled at home.)

Moore, Raymond. *Home-Style Teaching*, 1984. Word Books. (On home instruction.)

Moore, Raymond. *School Can Wait*, 1979. Brigham Young University Press, Provo, UT 84601 (On the importance of the home in nurturing children and on school readiness.)

Moore, Raymond. "What Educators Should Know About Home Schools," Family Research Council of America, 515 Second Street, Northeast Capitol Hill, Washington D.C. 20002. Also available from Hewitt Research Foundation, P.O. Box 9, Washougal, WA 98671. (Booklet on home schooling, educational authority, recommendations to public educators about home schools.)

Naturescope. National Wildlife Federation, 1412 Sixteenth Street Northwest, Washington DC 10036-2266. (A series of teaching guides for nature/science education—very useful for home teaching. Ask for a catalog of all available issues.)

Ocone, Lynn and Eve Pranis. *The National Garden Association Guide to Kids' Gardening: A Complete Guide for Teachers, Parents, and Youth Leaders,* 1990. John Wiley and Sons, 605 Third Avenue, New York NY 10158. (Gardening projects for small groups of children.)

O'Mahony, Kieran. *Geography and Education..* EduCare Press. (On teaching geography.)

O'Mahony, Kieran. *The Dictionary of Geographical Literacy: The Complete Geography Reference,* 1993. EduCare Press, P.O. Box 31511, Seattle WA 98103. (A children's and parents' dictionary of over 2000 geographical concepts, ideas, and places.)

O'Mahony, Kieran. *Geographical Literacy,* 1992. EduCare Press. (Explanations, hands-on activities, and exercises for geography lessons.)

Orlick, Terry. *The Cooperative Sports and Games Book* and *The Second Cooperative Sports and Games Book.* Pantheon. (Cooperative games.)

Our Nation at Risk: Imperative for Educational Reform, 1983. National Commission on Excellence in Education. (A report on the state of public education in the U.S.)

Palder, Edward L. *The Catalog of Catalogs; The Complete Mail-Order Directory,* 1993 (an annual). Woodbine House, 5615 Fishers Lane, Rockville MD 20852. (Listings of over 12,000 catalogs, many of which have materials useful with home-school learning activities.)

"Parents Can Understand Testing." 1980. National Committee for Citizens in Education. (A booklet on test interpretation.)

Pederson, Anne and Peggy O'Mara. *Schooling at Home: Parents, Kids, and Learning,* 1990. John Muir Publications, P.O. Box 613, Santa Fe NM 87504. (A collection of articles related to home schooling.)

Pride, Bill and Mary Pride. *Pride's Guide to Educational Software,* 1993. Crossway Books, 1300 Crescent Street, Wheaton Il 60187. (Reviews of over 750 software programs, preschool—early college, all subjects.)

Pride, Mary. *The Big Books of Home Learning,* Great Christian Books, 1319 Newport Gap Pike, Wilmington DE 19804. (Home-school resources guides—Volume 1: Getting Started; Volume 2: Preschool and Elementary; Volume 3: Teen and Adult; Volume 4: Afterschooling.)

Ray, Brian. "Home Centered Learning Annotated Bibliography." Brian Ray, National Home Education Research Institute, % Western Baptist College, 5000 Deer Park Drive Southeast, Salem OR 97301. (A bibliography.)

"Reading Beyond the Basals," Perfection Form Co., 1000 North Second Avenue, Logan IA 51546. (A series of booklets full of reading comprehension activities to accompany selected children's literature.)

Recyclopedia: Games, Science Equipment, and Crafts Made from Recycled Materials, 1976. Houghton-Mifflin. (A fine guide, developed by the Boston Children's Museum.)

Reed, Donn. *The Home School Source Book,* 1991. Brook Farm Books, P.O. Box 246, Bridgewater ME 04735. (A catalog and directory of home-school learning materials and supplies.)

Roth, Robert A. "Emergency Certificates, Misassignment of Teachers, and Other 'Dirty Little Secrets'." *Phi Delta Kappan,* June 1986, p.725-727. (Truths about public education, especially teacher certification and course assignments.)

Rowland, Howard S. *No More School,* 1975. Dutton. (Story of a family's year of adventurous home schooling in Spain.)

Rupp, Rebecca. *Good Stuff: Learning Tools for All Ages,* 1994. Home Education Press. (A home-school resource guide covering most subject areas and many new resources, and includes recommended, grade-level-appropriate children's literature.)

Rupp, Rebecca. "Teach Your Children Well", *Harrowsmith Country Life,* October 1993. Harrowsmith Country Life, P.O. Box 1000, Charlotte VT 05445-9984. (Well-written, detailed article on the day-to-day life of a home-schooling family.)

Russell, William F. *Classics to Read Aloud to Your Children,* 1984. Crown, 225 Park Avenue South, New York NY 10003. (An anthology of excerpts from world classics.)

Sabin, William A. *The Gregg Reference Manual,* 1977. McGraw-Hill Book Company, 1221 Avenue of the Americas, New York NY 10020. (Comprehensive guide to the mechanics of English usage. Useful as a reference during writing and language lessons.)

Schooling at Home. Mothering Magazine, P.O. Box 1690, Santa Fe NM 87501. (Articles by key persons in the home-schooling movement.)

Simic, Marjorie R. and others. *The Curious Learner: Help Your Child Develop Academic and Creative Skills,* 1992. Grayson-Bernard Publishers, P.O. Box 5247, Bloomington IN 47407. (On encouraging your child to ask questions, take learning risks, be curious, and get excited about learning in each subject area. Includes subject-related resources.)

Smith, Frank. *Insult to Intelligence*, 1986, Arbor House, 105 Madison Avenue, New York NY 10016. (On the negative effects of drilling, testing, and grading.)

Spalding, Romalda Bishop and Walter T. Spalding. *The Writing Road to Reading*, 1969. Quill, 105 Madison Avenue, New York NY 10016. (An easy-to-use guide to teaching phonics, spelling, reading.)

Stenmark, Jean Kerr and others. *Family Math.* Family Math, Lawrence Hall of Science, University of California, Berkeley CA 94720. (A bookful of hands-on math activities with a section listing typical grade level math curricula, sample lesson plans, and resource lists of math materials.)

Stillman, Peter R. *Families Writing.* Writer's Digest Books, 9933 Alliance Road, Cincinnati OH 45242. (A book full of family-style writing activities. Includes a list of related books for writing students.)

The Teen Study Bible, New International Version, 1993. Zondervan, 5300 Patterson Avenue Southeast, Grand Rapids MI 49530. (Study Bible for ages 12-16.)

Terzian, Alexandra M. *The Kids' Multicultural Art Book: Art and Craft Experiences from Around the World.* Williamson Publishing. (Ceremonial, cultural art experiences.)

"Tips for Teaching the Marginal Learner," 1986. Appalachia Education Lab, P.O. Box 1348, Charleston WV 25325 (Teaching "slow" learners.)

Wade, Theodore E and others. *The Home School Manual*, 1986. Gazelle Publications, 1906 Niles-Buchanen Road, Niles MI 49120. (Home-school how-to.)

Wallace, Nancy. *Better Than School: One Family's Declaration of Independence*, 1983. Lawson Publishing. (An account of a family's home-schooling experiences, with recommendations for other parents.)

Wallace, Nancy. *Child's Work: Taking Children's Choices Seriously*, 1990. Holt Associates, 2269 Massachusetts Avenue, Cambridge MA 02140 (On allowing and supporting children's own educational explorations, proclivities, and directions.)

Weaver, Roy, et. al. "Home Tutorials vs. Public Schools in Los Angeles." *Phi Delta Kappan*, Dec. 1980, p. 254-255. (Home-tutorial results.)

"What Works: Research About Teaching and Learning," 1986. U.S. Department of Education, 1200 Nineteenth Street Northwest, Washington DC 20208. (Effective teaching and effective schools research results in easy-to-understand format.)

Whitehead, John and Alexis Irene Crow. *Home Education: Rights and Reasons*, 1993. Crossway Books, 1300 Crescent Street, Wheaton Il 60187. (An examination of home education in relation to ethical and United States constitutional issues; that is, in terms of home-schoolers' reasons and rights.)

Whitehead, John and Wendell Bird. *Home Education and Constitutional Liberties,* 1984. Goodnews Publishers. (Historical and legal arguments for home schooling.)

Williams, Jane. *How to Stock a Quality Home Library Inexpensively.* Bluestocking Press/Educational Spectrums, P.O. Box 1014, Placerville CA 95667. (On selecting, locating, and securing books.)

Williams, Jane. *Who Reads What When: Literature Selections for Children Ages Three Through Thirteen.* Bluestocking Press. (Lists over 500 children's books, indexed by age, author, and title.)

Williams, Jane. *Young Thinkers Bookshelf: Books to Encourage Independent and Critical Thinking.* Bluestocking Press. (On book selection for a graduated reading program, indexed by subjects: literature, history, law, economics, communications, education, critical thinking — 300 books to stimulate creative and intuitive thought, reasoning skills, self-directed growth, and character development.)

The Word in Life Study Bible, 1993. Thomas Nelson, Nelson Place at Elm Hill Pike, Nashville TN 37214. (Includes fact boxes, maps, and study notes.)

Periodicals for Children

A number of excellent magazines are available for children today. Perhaps your children would like to help you select those that are most appealing to them and that might be useful as supplements to their studies. While some of the listed periodicals are available on newsstands, others are not. You may want to look at a sample copy — try the children's room of a large library — before entering a subscription.

American Girl (8400 Fairway Place, P.O. Box 620986, Middleton WI 53562-0986) Magazine that celebrates the lives and traditions of American girls yesterday and today, including fiction about historical and contemporary figures, nonfiction stories and articles, book excerpts, games, activities, puzzles, and contests, and sometimes includes a punch-out paper doll (of an actual subscriber to the magazine) and clothes on card stock, for ages 7-12.

Boomerang (P.O. Box 261, LaHonda Ca 94020) An audio-magazine of news for children presented in 70-minute issues, covering history, science, economics, current events, music, humor, and interviews.

Calliope (7 School Street, Peterborough NH 03458) Carefully researched articles, stories, activities, and departments focusing on word origins, archaeology, maps, time lines, current events, art from major international museums and archaeological sites, photos and original illustrations, and resource lists, all related to world history, for ages 9-16.

Chicadee Magazine (56 The Esplanade, Suite 306, Toronto, Ontario M5E 1A7, Canada) Invites hands-on learning, including stories, games, puzzles, crafts, personal experience and wildlife, for ages 3-9.

Child Life (1100 Waterway Boulevard, P.O. Box 567, Indianapolis IN 46206) Stories, photo features, puzzles, activities that teach good health habits, history, adventure, humor, and mystery, for ages 9-11.

The Children's Album (1320 Galaxy Way, Concord CA 94520) Children's writing techniques, crafts, children's literature, and writings by children, for ages 8-14.

Children's Digest (1100 Waterway Boulevard, P.O. Box 567, Indianapolis IN 46202) Suspenseful and humorous stories related to good health, articles on exercise, sports, nutrition, health, history, biography, safety, reviews, recipes, crafts, puzzles, for preteens.

Children's Playmate Magazine (1100 Waterway Boulevard, P.O. Box 567, Indianapolis IN 46206) Science, cultures, humor, holidays, health, nutrition, safety, and exercise, for ages 6-8.

Clubhouse (464 West Ferry, Box 15, Berrien Springs MI 49103) Personal experiences, natural food recipes, self-esteem, for ages 9-14.

Cobblestone (7 School Street, Peterborough NH 03458) Highly regarded magazine which emphasizes American history with firsthand accounts, lively biographies, poems, maps, games, puzzles, cartoons, songs, recipes, contests, resource lists, historic photos and illustrations, for grades 4-9.

Creative Kids (P.O. Box 637, Holmes PA 19043) For and by gifted and talented children.

Cricket (P.O. Box 300, Peru IL 61354) A magazine full of stories, poems, folklore, nonfiction, and activities by topnotch writers and artists that encourage reading, for ages 9-14. Also sponsors writing and art contests with publication of winners' work.

Current Events (245 Longhill Road, Middletown CT 06457) Current events news for junior/senior high school students.

Current Health (60 Revere Drive, Northbrook IL 60062-1563) Health education, for grades 4-7.

Current Science (245 Longhill Road, Middletown CT 06457) Science news for junior/senior high students.

Discovery Crew Science Club News (Discovery Crew, %Knickerbocker Publishing, P.O. Box 113, Fiskdale MA 01518) Science news for members of the club, ages 6-11.

The Dolphin Log (The Cousteau Society, 8440 Santa Monica Boulevard, Los Angeles CA 90069) An educational magazine for children ages 7-15, including marine biology, ecology, the environment, natural history, and water-related stories and personal experiences. Family membership also includes a parent magazine.

Faces, The Magazine About People (7 School Street, Peterborough NH 03458) Articles, legends, projects, puzzles, recipes, maps, photo essays, and more, that emphasize world cultures; the lifestyles, beliefs, and customs of other peoples; civilization; geography; economics; religions; politics; anthropology, for grades 4-9. Won the Parents' Choice Award in 1986 and 1987.

Highlights for Children (2301 West Fifth Avenue, Columbus OH 43215) History, science, sports, biography, crafts, poetry, stories, ages 2-12.

Home Schooled Kids (96 Acorn Street, Millis MA 02054) A newsletter consisting of stories, letters, poems, book reviews, interviews, etc., written by home-schooled kids.

Hopscotch for Girls (The Bluffton News, P.O. Box 164, Bluffton OH 45817 -0164) Fiction, puzzles, game pages, crafts, features about girls of past and present, creative science experiments, animal features.

Humpty Dumpty (1100 Waterway Boulevard, P.O. Box 567, Indianapolis IN 46202) Stories and poems, puzzles and other activities, that teach good health habits, for ages 4-6.

Jack and Jill (1100 Waterway Boulevard, P.O. Box 567, Indianapolis IN 46202) Articles on health, safety, exercise and nutrition, adventure, humor, puzzles and craft projects, for ages 7-10.

Kid City (One Lincoln Square Plaza, Third Floor, New York NY 10023) Adventure, fantasy, history, humor, mystery, westerns, ages 6-10. Formerly *Electric Company Magazine.*

KidsArt News (P.O. Box 274, Mt. Shasta CA 96067) Ideas, activities, and information for art education for children of all ages.

Kids Discover (170 Fifth Avenue, New York NY 10010) Each issue of this magazine focuses on one topic, including illustration and photograph features, learning activities, thought-provoking questions to stimulate parent-child discussions, and lists of books for further reading about the topic, for ages 5-12.

Kid Sports (1101 Wilson Boulevard, Suite 1800, Arlington VA 22209) Instructional sports advice from professionals, for ages 8-14.

Ladybug (P.O. Box 300, Peru IL 61354) A magazine including illustrated nonfiction features, fiction, poetry, songs, activities, for ages 2-7, plus inserted pages of hints for parents to use with little learners and lists of suggested books to read with children.

Merlyn's Pen, The National Magazine of Student Writing (P.O. Box 1058, East Greenwich RI 02818-9936) A magazine of student writings for and by grades 7-10 students. Opportunities to submit writings for publication in the magazine and an art contest.

Merlyn's Pen Senior Edition, The National Magazine of Student Writing (P.O. Box 1058, East Greewich RI 02818-9936) A magazine of student writings for and by grades 9-12 students. Opportunities to submit writings for publication and an art contest.

Mickey Mouse Magazine (300 Madison Avenue, New York NY 10017) Games, puzzles, stories, parents' pages, for preschoolers to age 6.

National Geographic World (National Geographic Society, 1145 Seventeenth Street Northwest, Washington DC 20036) Nature, conservation, science, geography, history, sports, outdoor adventure, and children's activities, for ages 8-13.

National Wildlife (1400 Sixteenth Street, Washington DC 20078-6420) A nature magazine for older children and adults.

Nature's Friend Magazine (P.O. Box 73, Goshen IN 46526) A nature and science magazine — stories and projects with a Creation perspective.

New Moon (P.O. Box 3587, Duluth MN 55803-3587) A magazine for girls featuring *real* girl talk and information; readers' letters, dreams, views, complaints; advice column; articles on girls' issues, girls around the world, and women in history.

Odyssey (7 School Street, Peterborough NH 03458) Theme-related feature articles covering all the physical sciences, photos and illustrations, projects, experiments, mind teasers, sky charts and observation activities, reader forums on timely topics, writing and art contests, poems, legends.

Oh! Zone (Project Oh! Zone, 420 East Hewitt Avenue, Marquette MI 49855) Sixty to seventy percent student written; a journal for young people which includes environmental news, art, opinion, poetry, fiction, essays, and interviews.

Outside Kids (Welsh Publishing, 300 Madison Avenue, New York NY 10017) Outdoor activities, environmental issues, and sports.)

OWL (56 The Esplanade, Suite 306, Toronto, Ontario, M5E 1A7 Canada) How-to, personal experience, science, and nature, for ages 3-12.

Plays:The Drama Magazine for Young People (120 Boylston Street, Boston MA 02116) A magazine for grades 3-8 children and their parents who are looking for play production ideas and scripts.

Ranger Rick (National Wildlife Federation, 1400 Sixteenth Street Northwest, Washington DC 20078-6420) A reading, science, crafts, and nature magazine for elementary level children.

Scienceland (501 Fifth Avenue, New York NY 10017) Focus on science for ages 6-11.

Sesame Street Magazine (One Lincoln Square Plaza, Third Floor, New York NY 10023) Games, puzzles, stories, and parents' guide to learning skills, for ages 2-6.

Skipping Stones (P.O. Box 3939, Eugene OR 97403-0939) Photo-articles, activity pages, and poetry which encourage cooperation, creativity, celebration of cultures and languages, environmental stewardship.

Snoopy Magazine (300 Madison Avenue, New York NY 10017) Games, puzzles, stories, mini-articles, parents' pages, for preschoolers.

Spark! (P.O. Box 5027, Harlan IA 51593-2527) Nutures creativity, literary, and artistic growth in children by featuring art and writing projects, for ages 6-12.

Spider (P.O. Box 300, Peru IL 61354) A magazine of fiction, nonfiction, poetry, activities, and opportunities to submit writing and artwork for possible publication, for ages 6-9.

Stone Soup: The Magazine by Children (Children's Art Foundation, P.O. Box 83, Santa Cruz CA 95063-0083) A literary journal written by children, includes fiction, poetry, and artwork by mid-elementary to junior high children that can serve as models of creative writing.

3-2-1 Contact (One Lincoln Square Plaza, New York NY 10023) Profiles, photo features, educational games focusing on science, ages 8-14.

Treasure Trove (Hewitt Research Foundation, P.O. Box 9, Washougal WA 98671-0009) A children's activities and ideas publication, with some brief parent articles.

Turtle Magazine (1100 Waterway Boulevard, P.O. Box 567, Indianapolis IN 46202) Fantasy, humor, and health-related stories, for ages 2-5.

Weekly Reader (245 Long Hill Road, Middletown CT 06457) Children's newspaper of current events, features, science.

Wee Wisdom (Unity Village MO 64065) Nature, self-image, projects and activities to encourage an appreciation of life, for ages 12 and under.

Young Author's Magazine (3015 Woodsvale Boulevard, Lincoln NE 68502-5053) How-to, profile, personal experience, adventure, fantasy, humor, mystery, poetry by young writers, for upper elementary to junior high children. Also offers a home-study course on novel writing for children.

Your Big Backyard (1400 Sixteenth Street Northwest, Washington DC 20036-2266) A reading, science, crafts, nature magazine for preschoolers and primary level children.

Zoobooks (P.O. Box 85271, San Diego CA 92138) Illustrated science magazine for elementary level children.

Periodicals for Parent Educators

Some of the following periodicals are written specifically for home teachers. Others are written mainly for public school teachers, but are quite useable for home teachers able to adapt whole classroom activities to a single child or a few children. This is often not difficult. Many of the teaching ideas presented in these periodicals are innovative and creative. By reading the annotations for each publication below, you can select those that may be most useful to you.

Anthro Notes (ATTN: P.A. Kaupp, Anthropology Outreach and Public Information Office, Department of Anthropology, NHB 363 MRC 112, Smithsonian Institution, Washington DC 20560) A bulletin for teachers with subject-specific background articles, activities and teaching ideas, and recommended books. Published three times a year by the National Museum of Natural History.

Arts & Activities (Suite 200, 591 Camino de la Reina, San Diego CA 92108) Learning activities for art education, materials and publications reviews, advertisers' directory, clip and save art prints.

BackHome (P.O. Box 370, Mountain Home NC 28758) Practical, how-to articles, family projects for self-reliant, independent family living.

Basic Education (Council for Basic Education, 1319 F Street Northwest, Suite 900, Washington DC 20004) Journal providing updates on education issues and promoting basic education for all children.

Book Links (50 East Huron Street, Chicago IL 60611) Magazine focusing on uses of children's books in children's learning, including annotated subject-related groupings of K-8 children's books, teaching ideas, thematic units of learning, and author studies.

The Catholic Home Educator (P.O. Box 420225, San Diego CA 92142) A quarterly newsletter for Catholic home schoolers featuring articles related to child rearing and education, Catholic traditions, book reviews, personal accounts, and a question/answer column.

Childhood Education (Association for Childhood Education International, 11141 Georgia Avenue, Suite 200, Wheaton MD 20902) An award-winning magazine with articles on innovative educational practices that can be used in home teaching plus educator's and children's book, film, and magazine reviews.

Childhood (Route 2 Box 2675, Westford VT 05494) A newsletter related to Waldorf education, including practical teaching activities and resources useful to home schoolers.

Children's Video Report (145 West 96th Street, New York NY 10025) Reviews for parents and teachers looking for good children's videos.

Christian Parenting Today (P.O. Box 850, Sisters OR 97759-0850) Magazine whose articles cover parenting issues of all sorts—child care, the development of values and self-esteem in children, educating the young, discipline, and more.

Classroom Computer Learning (2451 East River Road, Dayton OH 45439) Computer education teaching methods and information.

The Computing Teacher (ISTE, University of Oregon, 1787 Agate Street, Eugene OR 97405) Computer education teaching methods.

The Drinking Gourd (P.O. Box 2557, Redmond WA 98073) Multicultural home-education magazine that explores and celebrates diversity.

Exceptional Parent (1170 Commonwealth Avenue, Third Floor, Boston MA 02134) Magazine which covers issues of concern to parents of disabled children; practical guidance to those interested in the development of disabled people.

Family Life (1290 Avenue of the Americas, New York NY 10104) Mainstream magazine focusing on all aspects of family life.

Feed My Sheep (909 N. Ranney Street, Craig CO 81621-2433) A national newsletter for Lutheran home schoolers.

First Teacher (P.O. Box 180, Wilmington NC 28401) Activity ideas for those who work with toddlers.

Gifted Children Monthly (P.O. Box 10149, Des Moines IA 50340) Award-winning magazine for parents of gifted/talented children—strategies, product reviews, practical information, children's pullout section.

Gifted Child Quarterly (National Association for Gifted Children, 4175 Lovell Road, Suite 140, Circle Pines MN 55014) Magazine of practical ideas for applying research-based methods of teaching children.

The Gifted Child Today (P.O. Box 637, Holmes PA 19043) Magazine with activities and information for gifted, creative, talented learners.

Good Apple Newspaper (P.O. Box 299, Carthage IL 62321) Learning activities for grades 2-8 in various subject areas, including holidays.

Growing Without Schooling (2269 Massachusetts Avenue, Cambridge MA 02140) Magazine including informative letters from readers, articles, directory of readers, legal information, and more.

Holistic Education Review (P.O. Box 1476, Greenfield MA 01302) Journal providing information on varied aspects of holistic learning, both theoretical and practical, including home schooling.

Home Business Advisor (NextStep Publications, 1485 Third Street, Astoria OR 97103) Newsletter aimed at helping parents achieve success in home-business endeavors while home with children.

Home Education Magazine (P.O. Box 1083, Tonasket WA 98855) Magazine offering well-written, helpful articles on methods of teaching (all subjects) at home and on the full range of home-school issues, activity pages for children, resource reviews, and more.

Homefires (180 El Camino Real, Suite 10, Millbrae CA 94030) Publication focusing on home-education ideas, including a resources guide, directory, historical/biographical calendar, family movie reviews, articles about family adventures, multicultural events, and pages for and by children (short stories, poems, art, science/craft activities).

Home Schooling at Its Best (175 Gladys Avenue, #7, Mountain View CA 94043) Periodical including teaching ideas and learning activities.

Home School Researcher (Dr. Brian Ray, National Home Education Research Institute, %Western Baptist College, 5000 Deer Park Drive Southeast, Salem OR 97301) Publication aimed at reviewing home-school research and sharing ideas, articles, etc., related to home-school research. (503) 754-4151 or 754-2511 or 838-1248

Homeschooling Today (P.O. Box 1425, Melrose FL 32666) Christian-oriented magazine of practical teaching ideas covering varied subject areas.

Instructor (555 Broadway, New York NY 10012) Magazine covering teaching methods and activities in various subject areas.

Journal of Reading (International Reading Association, 800 Barksdale Road, P.O. Box 8139, Newark DE 19714-8139) Journal including secondary reading instruction methods.

Learning (1111 Bethlehem Pike, Springhouse PA 19477) Magazine covering teaching tips and learning activities.

Lollipops (P.O. Box 299, Carthage IL 62321-0299) Learning activities in varied subject areas for preschool and primary education.

The Moore Report International (P.O. Box 1, Camas WA 98607) Newsletter on family issues including home-school research and ideas.

Mother Earth News (P.O. Box 70, Hendersonville NC 28791) Popular magazine covering home crafts, how-to, home business, etc.

Mothering (P.O. Box 1690, Santa Fe NM 87504) Parenting magazine whose aim is to empower parents to make informed choices for the welfare of their children and which publishes articles on many aspects of parenting including home schooling.

National Coalition News (P.O. Box 15036, Santa Fe NM 87506) Newsletter of the National Coalition of Alternative Community Schools including information regarding the activities of the Coalition and regarding schooling alternatives and issues.

"Notable 1993 Children's Trade Books in the Field of Social Studies" (CBC, 568 Broadway, Suite 404, New York NY 10012) An annual list of some of the best books for children that cover social studies subjects. Send a 75¢-stamped, self-addressed, 6"x9" envelope.

"Outstanding Science Trade Books for Children in 1993" (CBC, 568 Broadway, Suite 404, New York NY 10012) An annual list of some of the best books for children that cover science subjects. Send a 75¢-stamped, self-addressed, 6"x9" envelope.

Parenting (P.O. Box 52424, Boulder CO 80321-2424) Mainstream magazine covering varied aspects of parenting—child health, travel, child care programs, nutrition, etc.

Parents Magazine (685 Third Avenue, New York NY 10017) Mainstream magazine including many aspects of parenting, such as childbirth, infant care, mothers in multiple roles, child discipline, post-infant to age thirteen child care, and child issues of all sorts.)

Practical Homeschooling (%Home Life, P.O. Box 1250, Fenton MO 63026-1850) Magazine for Christian home educators.

The Reading Edge (P.O. Box 3, Crownsville MD 21032) Reviews of current children's books to facilitate selection by parents.

The Reading Teacher (International Reading Association, 800 Barksdale Road, P.O. Box 8139, Newark DE 19714-8139) Journal for teachers of reading which includes elementary reading teaching methods.

School Arts (Printers Building, 50 Portland Street, Worcester MA 01608) Learning activities for art education; art materials; school and college summer program announcements; new art products news. Separately: a booklet of criteria for purchasing school art supplies called "Selection, Testing and Specifications Guide."

School Shop (416 Longshore Drive, Box 8623, Ann Arbor MI 48107) Shop activities and projects that could be undertaken by individual home students working alone or with an adult tutor.

Shining Star (P.O. Box 299, Carthage IL 62321-0299) Reproducible activities and ideas for Christian home schoolers.

Shop Talk (5737 64th Street, Lubbock TX 79424) Newsletter that includes home-school ideas and parenting ideas through articles written by its parent readers.

Softworlds for Children (P.O. Box 219, Edmonds WA 98020) A buyer's guide which reviews MacIntosh computer software for children.

Teaching Exceptional Children (Council on Exceptional Children, 1920 Association Drive, Reston VA 22091-1589) Magazine with practical instructional methods, materials, and techniques for working with children who have disabilities or who are gifted.

The Teaching Home (P.O. Box 20219, Portland OR 97220-0219) Magazine covering many Christian home-school topics, resource descriptions, good articles on teaching methods, and includes newsletter insets from several of the states—perhaps yours.

Thinking Families, The Magazine for Parents with Children in Elementary School (605 Worchester Road, Towson MD 21204) Lists of resources and short articles useful to home-school parents. Listed are such resources as travel books, children's fiction and nonfiction, educational events for children, and other publications that help parents help children learn at home.

WonderScience (American Chemical Society, 1155 Sixteenth Street Northwest, Washington DC 20036) Magazine of hands-on physical science experiments, activities, and information for parents to use with elementary age students, published October to May.

Young Children (National Association for the Education of Young Children, 1509 Sixteenth Street Northwest, Washington DC 20036-1426) Magazine with informational articles and teaching ideas for teachers of preschoolers through third graders.

Home-School Curriculum Suppliers

Below is a sampling of suppliers of full curriculums. You'll want to read "Curriculum and Materials" in Section Three before ordering any curriculums. Then, consider carefully the content of each subject area, potential teaching methods and student learning styles, and the philosophies behind any of the curriculums you might purchase. Remember, too, that, as facilitated by my book *How to Write a Low Cost/No Cost Curriculum for Your Home-School Child*, it is quite possible, and in many cases beneficial, to design your own curriculum; i.e., to not purchase a commercial curriculum for *total* use. However, in designing your own curriculum a purchased one can effectively serve as a reference, or in some cases even a mainstay, as long as you remain in control of your overall curriculum. Or perhaps you'll decide to integrate ideas from several curriculums into your own. Please note that because home schoolers' needs vary so greatly, it is not possible to offer recommendations regarding the following curriculum suppliers, but many are among those heavily used by home-schoolers. Also note that many home-school support organizations offer assistance with curriculum development.

May I further recommend, as you consider curriculum, that, if you have a precocious youngster or a high school home student, you contact colleges and universities in your area or state (and even out of state) regarding independent study courses offered by mail. Most state universities offer such courses and sometimes courses numerous enough to nearly fill out a high school home-schooler's full curriculum. Just a few are listed below that were brought to my attention, but you are likely to find others. Also, in some cases, high school students are ready to attend regular college courses — junior colleges and community colleges often allow such enrollments. At times, too, younger students with special talents (in art or music, for example) may make special arrangements to take courses at local colleges or participate in special groups (drama troupes or musicians' groups, for example). In proposing such possibilities, the best approach to a local college may be a personal one. Make an appointment to visit with an admissions administrator or with an instructor in the field of your child's interest.

Most of the other suppliers listed below should be contacted by mail with a request for information regarding their services, curriculum aids and prices.

A Beka Book Publications (P.O. Box 18000, Pensacola FL 32523-9160) Traditional approach, textbook oriented, Christian and patriotic, grades K-12. Curriculum guides and materials. Correspondence courses and courses on video available. (800) 874-2352

ACE School of Tomorrow (Home School Department, P.O. Box 1438, Lewisville TX 75067-1438) Christian curriculums, skills mastery approach, diagnostic placement tests, self instructional materials, videos, computer products, grades K-12. (800) 925-7777

Addison-Wesley (2725 Sand Hill Road, Menlo Park CA 94025) The *Math Their Way* beginning math curriculum and materials.

Alpha Omega Publications (P.O. Box 3153, Tempe AZ 85280) Mastery learning and programmed learning approaches, Christian, grades K-12. Curriculums, materials and satellite programs for Christian schools are available. (800) 821-4443

Alta Vista Homeschool Curriculum Office (P.O. Box 55535, Seattle WA 98155) Bible-based integrated unit studies, interdenominational, grades K-7 multi-age. (800) 544-1397

Alyeska Central School, *"Alaska's Centralized Correspondence School"* (3141 Channel Drive #100, Juneau AK 99801-7897): A fully accredited public correspondence school that offers a complete K-12 curriculum in all subject areas, issues a high school diploma, provides free enrollment with materials-return (for Alaskans), and certified teacher assistance. (907) 465-2835

Associated Christian Schools (P.O. Box 981, Largo FL 34649) Preschool through grade 12 Christian curriculums and materials, achievement test scoring and record keeping.

Association of Christian Schools International (P.O. Box 4097, Whittier CA 90607) Christian curriculums, focus on character development. Also *Encyclopedia of Biblical Truths* by Ruth Haycock. (310) 694-4791

Bea's Spelling, Penmanship, and Creative Writing Program (P.O. Box 50284, Billings MT 59105) Grades 1-9 learning packages, including spelling, penmanship, creative writing, and teacher's guides.

Bob Jones University Press (Greenville SC 29614) Conventional approach, textbook oriented, Christian, grades K-12. Curriculums, materials, teacher workshops, and achievement testing.

Bradrick Family Enterprises (P. O. Box 2240, Port Orchard WA 98366) A grades 1-12, Bible-based English language and composition curriculum adaptable to single or multi-level tutoring written by Susan Bradrick, titled *Understanding Writing*.

Brigham Young University (Independent Study, 206 Harman Building, Provo UT 83602) High school and college correspondence courses in an array of subject areas; also parenting courses. (801) 378-2868

Calvert School (105 Tuscany Road, Baltimore MD 21210) Grades K-8 curriculums and materials, advisory teacher service, transcripts.

Center for Educational Guidance (P.O. Box 445, North San Juan CA 95960) Holistic curriculums; cooperative game days; parenting/ teaching workshops; outdoor education programs for individuals, groups and families; Ropes Course; family counseling service; resources and literature on child development. (916) 292-3623

Center for Independent Study Through Correspondence (University of Missouri, 136 Clark Hall, Columbia MO 65211) Grades 9-12 correspondence courses. (314) 882-2491

Christian Liberty Academy Satellite Schools (502 West Euclid Avenue, Arlington Heights IL 60004) Grades K-12 correspondence curriculums and materials, record keeping, testing and copies of the Iowa Standardized Achievement Test. (708) 259-8736

Christian Light Education (P.O. Box 1212, Harrisonburg VA 22801) Mennonite, core curriculum, grades K-12, diplomas. (703) 434-0750

Circle Christian School (4644 Adanson Street, Orlando FL 32804) Curriculum packages and other support.

Clonlara School (1289 Jewett, Ann Arbor MI 48104) Private school that offers help in designing/operating a home-school program, counseling and guidance, transcripts, diplomas, and "The Learning Edge" newsletter; preschool through grade 12. (313) 769-4515

Correspondence Study Office (University of Idaho Campus, Moscow ID 83844-3225) Grades 9-12 correspondence courses in a wide array of subject areas. (208) 885-6641

Covenant Home Curriculum (17700 West Capitol Drive, Brookfield WI 53045) Grades K-12 correspondence curriculums and materials, Christian and secular options.

Davis Publications Inc. (50 Portland Street, Worcester MA 01608) Grades K-12 art curriculums and materials.

Division of Independent Study (P.O. Box 5036, State University Station, Fargo ND 58105) Grades 8-12 complete correspondence curriculum. (701) 237-7182.

Extended Studies (Indiana University, Owen Hall, Bloomington IN 47405-5201) Full curriculum of grades 9-12 correspondence courses. Nationwide: (800) 334-1011; in Indiana: (800) 342-5410; in Bloomington and outside the toll-free area: (812) 855-5792

Franklin Learning Resources (122 Burrs Road, Mt. Holly NJ 08060) A language, writing, and research skills curriculum involving the use of Franklin electronic reference books.

Freedom Christian Academy (Route 15 Box 150, Denton TX 76201-9507) Grades K-12 correspondence curriculums and materials.

Front Row Experience (540 Discovery Bay Boulevard, Byron CA 94514) Curriculum guides for movement education, special education, educational games, perceptual-motor development. (800) 524-9091

Hewitt Research Foundation (P.O. Box 9, Washougal WA 98671-0009) Christ-centered learning programs and materials for preschool through grade twelve. (206) 835-8708

HCL (P.O. Box 4643, Whittier CA 90607) A private school and administrative unit. Curriculum guides, record keeping, materials references, networking, consultations. (310) 696-4696

High School Correspondence Courses (University of California Extension, 2223 Fulton Street, Berkeley CA 94720) Grades 9-12 correspondence courses in a wide array of subject areas. (510) 642-4124

Home Education Services (728 South Winnetka Avenue, Dallas TX 75208) Essential elements of grade-level home-school curriculums for Texans; current research in education; consultations. (214) 941-6048

Home Study Alternative School (P.O. Box 10356, Newport Beach CA 92658) K-8 correspondence curriculums.

Independent Study Department (University of Oklahoma, 1700 Asp Avenue, Room B-1, Norman OK 73037) Fully accredited high school diploma program. Complete grades 9-12 curriculum with over 125 courses in core and elective subjects. (402) 472-1926

Independent Study High School (University of Nebraska-Lincoln, 269 NCCE, Lincoln NE 68583-9800) Grades 9-12 correspondence courses in various subject areas. (402) 472-1926

International Institute (N6128 Sawyer Lake Road, White Lake WI 54491) Grades K-8 correspondence courses, parent advisory service. (715) 484-5002

Keys to Learning International (1411 Oak Street, South Pasadena CA 91030) Grades K-12 curriculums in all basic academic subjects. (818) 441-0020

KONOS (P.O. Box 1534, Richardson TX 75083) Multilevel curriculum which emphasizes the development of Christian character, using a hands-on approach; K-8.

Life Span Learning Programs (Utah State University, Independent Study, Life Span Learning Programs, Logan UT 84322-5000) Grades 9-12 correspondence courses in a wide array of subject areas. (801) 750-2014 or (800) 233-2137

McGuffey Academy International (2213 Spur Trail, Grapevine TX 76050) Grades K-12 home-school curriculums in core subjects, business, Bible, art, and home economics; diagnostic and achievement testing; record keeping; telephone counseling; report cards; high school transcripts; diplomas. (817) 481-7008

Marin HomeLink (220 Redwood Highway, Suite 353, Mill Valley CA 94941) Grades K-12 curriculum on CD-ROM.

The Montgomery Institute (P.O. Box 532, Boise ID 83701) A private enterprise umbrella school with Christian emphasis. Provides consultations and home-school program development, activity days, legislative and other information, bookstore, workshops. (208) 888-2315

Moore Academy (Moore Foundation, P.O. Box 1, Camas WA 98607) Individualized K-12 curriculums (including Christian), diplomas, satellite student programs for those who need to demonstrate accountability, and programs for special needs children.

Mountain Meadow Press (P.O. Box 318, Sitka AK 99835-0318) Grades K-12, easy-to-use, step-by-step workbook-style guide to creating a curriculum based upon your own educational philosophies and custom-tailored to meet your child's educational needs and interests, by Borg Hendrickson, titled *How to Write a Low Cost/No Cost Curriculum for Your Home-School Child*. Also K-12, Dr. Linwood Laughy's guide for parents who have enrolled a child in public school and want to maintain as much control as possible over that child's education, titled *Getting the Best Bite of the Apple*.

The Music Place (for Kids) (2132 Forest Oak Drive, Akron OH 44312) A progressive music program.

National Writing Institute (7946 Wright Road, Niles MI 49120) Preschool through grade 12 basic, expository, creative, and research writing programs, beginning with oral language experiences for preschoolers — all designed especially for home schools. Includes lists of learning objectives, teaching/learning directions, and progress records.

North Dakota Department of Public Instruction (Division of Independent Study, 600 East Boulevard 9th Floor, Bismarck ND 58505-0440) Correspondence courses for a grades 9-12 curriculum.

Oak Meadow School (P.O. Box 712, Blacksburg VA 24063) Grades K-12 curriculums, experienced teacher advisors, student progress evaluations, teacher training. (703) 552-3263

Phoenix Special Programs (3132 West Clarendon, Phoenix AZ 85017) Grades 7-12 correspondence courses, diploma. (800) 426-4952

Reading Instruction Support Programs (RISP) (Self Investment Unlimited, 13097 South 42nd Vicksburg MI 49097) Phonics-based reading programs, preschool through adult, at-home screening assessments, consulting service for those in the programs. (616) 778-3395

Riggs Institute (4185 SW 102nd Avenue, Beaverton OR 97005) *The Writing Road to Reading*, a multi-sensory method which integrates listening, speaking, writing, spelling, reading comprehension, vocabulary, penmanship, grammar and thinking skills from an intensive phonetic spelling base; teacher training tapes and teacher's manual. (503) 646-9459

Rockwood Christian Ministries (P.O. Box 972, Fenton MO 63026) Christian curriculums. (314) 843-2811

Rod and Staff Publishers (Highway 172, Crockett KY 41413) Traditional approach, Christian, grades 1-9 curriculums and materials.

Seton Home Study School (1350 Progress Drive, Front Royal VA 22630) Grades K-12 curriculums, correspondence courses and materials, integrated with lessons in Catholicism. Transcripts, achievement testing, consultations. (703) 636-9990

Southeast Academy (P.O. Box MM, 137 Main Street, Saltville VA 24370) Grades K-12 correspondence courses. (703) 496-7777 or 496-7791

Summit Christian Academy (P.O. Box 802041, Dallas TX 75380) Grades 1-12 correspondence curriculums, teacher training, placement testing, supplemental materials.

The Sycamore Tree (2179 Meyer Place, Costa Mesa CA 92627) Grades K-12 correspondence curriculums, Christian and secular options; standardized testing. (714) 650-4466

Teaching Guides (P.O. Box 270, Honaunau HI 96726) Preschool through age 12 home curriculum guides.

The Waldorf Institute (260 Hungry Hollow Road, Spring Valley NY 10977) A network of Waldorf schools; an array of teacher training courses primarily for Waldorf education but also of interest to home educators. (914) 425-0055 or FAX (914) 425-1413

Teaching Materials, Aids
and Information Suppliers

Remember to design or select your curriculum and to decide how much control you want over your curriculum before you shop for materials with which to teach your curriculum. Textbooks and other learning materials *are not* curriculum. They *do not teach* curriculum. Your curriculum, as explained in Section Three, is your list of subject areas to be covered with accompanying rosters of learning goals in each subject area. Textbooks and other learning materials are aids to your children's learning and progression through the curriculum and they are aids to you as *you teach* the curriculum to your children and as they learn and/or teach themselves. You, as teacher, control the curriculum and the textbooks and other materials; *they have no control over you* ...unless, of course, you give them control.

There are so many school materials and aids suppliers that listing them all here would be prohibitive. The following, therefore, is just a smattering of those available to you, but with these you should be able to locate suppliers who offer some of what you are looking for in learning or teaching materials and aids. Check with experienced home schoolers in your area, or even individual public school teachers at the grade levels you will teach, for suggestions and hands-on materials you can review. Visit a local computer store for educational software compatible with your computer, if you have one. Hundreds of educational computer programs are now available. Many large towns and cities also have school supply houses or stores which stock a multitude of items useful to teachers, parents, and parent teachers. Browse, too, through the children's section of a public library for titles and publishers of children's literature you may want to use. Return to Section Five in this book to find home-school organizations in your region that sponsor home-school curriculum and materials fairs that you might attend. Refer back, too, to question 9 in Section One for more materials ideas.

Lastly, remember that *you* can be an incredible resource of ideas for materials and aids, as well as for curriculums and settings for your children's home-school lessons. Also, I must emphasize again the importance of searching for materials that truly suit your style of teaching and philosophies and your children's styles and stages of learning. I also want to emphasize the importance of not relying too heavily on commercial materials rather than invented or environmental or human resources. As you begin teaching at home, you'll find yourself becoming more and more adept at creating your own materials based upon the learning needs and styles of your children and also at piecing together materials from more than one source.

> [Note: All of the suppliers listed here have responded positively to a survey asking if they supply materials to home-schooling families. However, when contacting the larger of the following sources, it may be beneficial to use a school name, even if yours is a one-family school, or a support group name indicating that several home schoolers will share catalogs and information. Suppliers may be happier to send free catalogs if they anticipate multiple sales.]

A Beka Book Publications (P.O. Box 18000, Pensacola FL 32523-9160) Preschool through grade 12 Christian textbooks.

Addison-Wesley Publishing (2725 Sand Hill Road, Menlo Park CA 94025) The *Mathematics Their Way* materials, manipulative math guides, other materials, textbooks, software in several subject areas.

ALLPIE (P.O. Box 59, East Chatham NY 12060-0059) Publications and services which emphasize the importance of family in education, including home schooling. Publishes a newsletter, "Options in Learning;" and offers a catalog of books and other resources about and for teaching in general and for home schooling. Also maintains a mail order lending library.

American Christian History Institute (P.O. Box 648, Palo Cedro CA 96073) Curricular materials, Principle Approach, including *A Guide to American Christian Education for the Home and School*, Guyot's *Physical Geography* map outlines, and more.

American Library Association (Customer Service, 50 East Huron Street, Chicago IL 60611) Posters, bookmarks, reading logs, lists of books for various age groups and related to various topics (such as an annotated list of Caldecott and Newbery Award titles), and books related to literature, libraries, and storytelling.

American Montessori Society (150 Fifth Avenue, New York NY 10011) Teacher training and many publications related to child development and education.

American Science and Surplus (3605 Howard Street, Skokie IL 60076) Surplus educational and other supplies.

American Textbook Committee (Route 1 Box 13, Wadley AL 36276) Textbooks with a Christian perspective, particularly for history, economics, and government subject areas.

Ampersand Press (8040 Northeast Day Road W, #S-A, Bainbridge Island WA 98110) Game activities for science education.

Amsco School Publications (315 Hudson Street, New York NY 10013) Textbooks and workbooks in all high school subjects, including *Vocabulary for the High School Student, Vocabulary for the College Bound, Integrated Mathematics,* and others.

Animal Town Game Company (P.O. Box 485, Healdsburg CA 95448) Cooperative and noncompetitive board games, puzzles, educational playthings, outdoor and group playthings, children's books, books on parenting and cooperation, rubber stamp sets, old time radio and nature tapes, science and nature kits.

Appalachian Mountain Club (5 Joy Street, Boston MA 02108) Books on the outdoors, ecology, environment, nature, recreation, history.

ARCsoft Publishers (P.O. Box 179, Hebron MD 21830) Technical books, including space science, personal computers, and hobby electronics, especially for beginners.

Aristoplay Ltd. (P.O. Box 7529, Ann Arbor MI 48107-7529) Cooperative learning games with focuses on geography, history, art, music, and other subjects.

Audio Forum (Jeffrey Norton Publishers, 96 Broad Street, Guilford CT 06437) Audio cassette foreign language courses with texts and tape transcripts, including all commonly taught languages and others; and video travel guides and foreign language movie videos.

August House (P.O. Box 3223, Little Rock AR 72203-3223) Storytelling, folklore and fiction, books and tapes.

Bellerophon Books (36 Anacapa Street, Santa Barbara CA 93101) Educational coloring books, cutout books, art/history activity books.

Betterway Publications Inc. (1507 Dana Avenue, Cincinnati OH 45207) Books about parenting, going to school by mail, home-based businesses, home activities, and juvenile books.

Binford & Mort Publishing (1202 Northwest 17th Avenue, Portland OR 97209) Books about Northwest history, biography, nature, recreation, reference, travel.

Binney & Smith (1100 Church Lane, P.O. Box 431, Easton PA 18042) Art supplies and a booklet-guide to criteria for selecting and purchasing art supplies.

Bluestocking Press (P.O. Box 1014, Placerville CA 95667-1014) Materials specializing in American history, economics, law, government, performing arts, classical music, critical thinking, and more.

Bookstuff (P.O. Box 13773, Portland OR 97213) Educational materials for thinking and problem solving, pre- through primary school ages.

Borenson & Associates (P.O. Box 3328, Allentown PA 18106) The Hands-On Equations Learning System for teaching algebra to grade school students.

Don Bosco Multimedia (475 North Avenue, Box T, New Rochelle NY 10802-0845) Books and textbooks for Christian education.

Bradshaw Publishers (P.O. Box 277, Bryn Mawr CA 92318) Biblical early readers for home-school use.

Bright Ideas (135 Indian Hill, Carlisle MA 01741) Educational software from various software publishers, supplemented by child development chart which shows developmental milestones in the areas of language, cognitive, creative, social and physical development. (Distributed via home sales consultants.)

Brite (801) 487-5890) Music education resources. (Distributed via home sales representatives.)

Builder Books (P.O. Box 5291, Lynnwood WA 98046) Materials for various subject areas; books for parent educators and Christian character building.

BYLS Press (6617 North Mozart, Chicago IL 60645) How-to books for teachers; children's books, baking, and Jewish holidays.

California State Department of Education (P.O. Box 944272, Sacramento CA 94244-2720) Catalog of publications and curriculum frameworks such as the "History-Social Studies Framework."

CAMS Cleanline Books (P.O. Box 842, Elbe Wa 98330) Books for kids and parents, selected as "clean" reading.

Career Publishing (910 North Main Street, Box 5486, Orange CA 92613-5486) High school textbooks.

Carolina Biological Supply (2700 York Road, Burlington NC 27215) Science supplies and nonfiction books for K-12 students.

Carstens Publications (Hobby Book Division, P.O. Box 700, Newton NJ 07860) Books on model railroading, toy trains, model aviation.

Castle Heights Press (5866 Hunter Road, Enon OH 45323) Science lab kits and manuals, high school level, Christian oriented.

Caxton Printers (312 Main Street, Caldwell ID 83605) Serves as a textbook depository where home schoolers may purchase textbooks.

Census Bureau Education Program (Data User Services Division, Washington DC 20233-8300) Teacher-ready, K-12 activities and lesson suggestions involving skills related to varied subject areas, some including student worksheets, stemming from the 1990 national census with content focuses in mathematics, science, and social studies (especially geography, but also economics, agriculture, ethnic groups, population trends, geography, and others; and Census Bureau history and processes). Most are single-copy free. Also offers other census-originated publications and reports, computer disks and CD-ROMs, and maps; the almost 1000-page *1992 Statistical Abstract of the United States* with a grades 5-12 teaching supplement; and a list of each state's census data center.

Center for the Study of Parent Involvement (John F. Kennedy University, Graduate School of Professional Psychology, 370 Camino Pablo, Orinda CA 94563) A national clearinghouse and training and technical assistance center for public school parents and educators. The center's activities foster and support home-to-school partnerships through research, training, consultations, information dissemination, conferences, and publications related to parent involvement.

Chaselle, Inc. (Early Childhood School Materials, 9645 Gerwig Lane, Columbia MD 21046) Toys and teaching materials and aids for infants through elementary and special education.

Children's Music Network (P.O. Box 2473, Hobe Sound FL 33455-2473) An organization that supports the creation and dissemination of children's songs which encourage cooperation, self-esteem, cultural diversity, respect for our environment, and an understanding of non-violence and justice.

Children's Small Press (719 North Fourth Avenue, Ann Arbor MI 48104) Children's fiction and nonfiction and books on parenting, dealing with children's issues, and home schooling.

Chinaberry Book Service (2780 Via Orange Way, #B, Spring Valley CA 91978) Books of interest to parents, children's literature, videos, audio cassettes, toys, unusual books.

Christian Education Music Publishers (P.O. Box 62, Thorton IL 60476-0062) K-4 music supplies, teachers' guides, student workbooks.

Christian Liberty Press (502 West Euclid Avenue, Arlington Heights IL 60004) Full line of textbooks.

Christian Life Workshops (P.O. Box 2250, Gresham OR 97030) Workshops for parents on home-centered education, covering academics and family ministry from a biblical viewpoint. Also, books for home educators.

Christian Teaching Materials (P.O. Box 639, 14275 Elm Avenue, Glenpool OK 74033-0639) Books, tapes, games, and other materials for teaching keyboarding, geography, science, arts/crafts, economics, foreign languages, English language skills, social studies, home economics, math, music, and books about home schooling.

Cliffs Notes (P.O. Box 80728, Lincoln NE 68501) Self-help study aids for junior high and up, teaching portfolios for literature lessons, textbooks, software for test preparation and course reviews.

Cobblestone Publishing (7 School Street, Peterborough NH 03458-1454) Student magazines covering science, cultures, and American and world history; educational books; activity books; teacher's manuals and resource materials.

Communication Skill Builders (3830 East Bellevue, P.O. Box 42050, Tucson AZ 85733) Speech-language therapy materials. Publications include educational materials, assessments, tests, audio and videotapes, software, and other practical materials.

Computer Aided Teaching Concepts (20380 Excelsior Boulevard, Excelsior MN 55331) Apple Computer software for math education.

Conservation Pioneers (Missouri Department of Conservation, Education Section, Box 180, Jefferson City MO 65102-0180) An environmental involvement and learning program for children.

Consumer Reports Books (101 Truman Avenue, Yonkers NY 10703) How-to books for children.

David C. Cook Publishers (850 North Grove Avenue, Elgin IL 60120) Christian education materials.

Cornell Laboratory of Ornithology (159 Sapsucker Woods Road, Ithaca NY 14850) Project Feeder Watch, an ongoing bird survey program (winter months) through which families monitor birds visiting feeders and receive a biannual newsletter with feeding tips, survey results, and articles about birds, etc.

Council for Exceptional Children (1920 Association Drive, Reston VA 22091) Books, magazines, and videos for teachers of handicapped and/or gifted students, including the research journal *Exceptional Children,* the quarterly abstract journal *Exceptional Child Education Resources,* and the magazine of instructional methods, materials, and techniques for working with exceptional children titled *Teaching Exceptional Children.*

George C. Cram Company (P.O. Box 426, Indianapolis, IN 46206) Materials for geography education.

Creation ex nihilo (P.O. Box 710039, Santee CA 92072) A creation-science magazine.

Creative Educational Surplus (9801 James Circle, Suite C, Bloomington MN 55431-2919) Surplus materials for art, creative play, math, science, and a variety of other goods.

Creative Learning Association (RR #4 Box 330, Charleston IL 61920) Computer literacy learning kits in the TLC for Growing Minds series.

Creative Learning Systems (16510 Via Esprillo, San Diego CA 92127) Technological toys, software, and more.

Crossway Books (1300 Crescent Street, Wheaton, IL 60187) Christian books; home-schooling titles, such as Mary Pride's *Big Books*.

Cuisenaire Company of America (P.O. Box 5026, White Plains NY 10602-5026) Supplies for math education.

Davenport Publishers (26313 Purissima Road, Los Altos Hills CA 94022) Children's and young adults' color and read books and novels.

Davis Publications Inc. (50 Portland Street, Worcester MA 01608) K-12 art education materials.

D.E.A.F. (801 Cedar, Rolla MO 65401) Educational materials for deaf children, networking, picnics, and information on sign language learning opportunities.

T. S. Denison Company (9601 Newton Avenue South, Minneapolis, MN 55431) Early childhood teaching aids and elementary resources.

Dept. 611X Consumer Information Center (Pueblo CO 81009) Free 58-page booklet, "Helping Your Child Learn Science," with basic science information and experiments to do with 3-10 year olds.

The Discovery Channel and The Learning Channel (1-800-321-1832) Free educator's guide to these television channels.

The Drinking Gourd (P.O. Box 2557, Redmond WA 98073) Multicultural educational materials.

Edmund Scientific (101 East Gloucester Pike, Barrington NJ 08007-1380) Supplies for science education.

EduCare Press (P.O. Box 31511, Seattle WA 98103) Materials for geography education.

Educational Development Corporation (P.O. Box 470663, Tulsa OK 74147) Educational children's books, various subject areas.

Educational Insights (19560 South Rancho Way, Dominguez Hills CA 90220) Games, supplies, activity kits, various subject areas.

Education Services (8825 Blue Mountain Drive, Golden CO 80403) Ruth Beechick books, including *You Can Teach Your Child Successfully*, a Christian intermediate and junior high curriculum covering reading, writing, math, history, science, health, music, art, Bible.

Educators Publishing Service (75 Moulton Street, Cambridge MA 02138-1104) Preschool through grade 12 curriculum materials and textbooks, including those for the learning disabled. Over 500 language arts titles, involving literature-based activities using children's books, phonics and beginning reading, vocabulary builders; Kim Marshall Series—reading, English, vocabulary, and math; spelling, grammar, and reasoning skills materials.

Engine-Uity, Ltd. (P.O. Box 9610, Phoenix AZ 85068) Primary level learning kits and independent study packets with teachers' guides —in language, literature-based reading, and integrated curricula. Intermediate and secondary level learning kits for math, science, literature-based reading, and social studies areas.

Enslow Publishers (Box 777, Bloy Street & Ramsey Avenue, Hillside NJ 07205) Books on science and social issues for children.

ERIC/REC—the ERIC Clearinghouse on Reading, English, and Communication (Indiana University, 2805 East Tenth Street, Suite #150, Bloomington IN 47408-9908) Books, booklets, and videos for parents and teachers on various aspects of reading, English, communication education, English as a second language, and on fostering student success, including the booklet "101 Ideas to Help Your Child Learn to Read and Write."

ESP Inc. (7163 123nd Circle North, Largo FL 34643) K-7 workbooks.

Eureka! (Lawrence Hall of Science, University of California, Berkeley CA 94720) Multi-level science learning kits, videos and films, games, teacher's guides, including *Family Math* and many indoor and outdoor science activity modules. Ask for the Eureka! catalog. The Lawrence Hall of Science also offers classes, workshops, films, and lectures for the public, all described in *The LHS Quarterly*.

Evangelistic and Faith Enterprises (Route 2, Poplar Creek Road, Oliver Springs TN 37840) Testing, record keeping, consultations.

Family Learning Center (Route 2 Box 264, Hawthorne Fl 32640) Grades 1-12 language arts textbooks.

Family Literacy Center (Indiana University, 2805 East Tenth Street, Suite 150, Bloomington IN 47408-2698) Offers "Parents and Children Together," a series of books and audio cassettes for children ages 4-10 and their parents. The series includes books and cassettes regarding self-esteem, motivation, discipline and learning, library use, at-home math, summer reading, computers, making history come alive, parents as models, fine arts appreciation, and many more topics, and other book suggestions.

Family Math (Lawrence Hall of Science, University of California, Berkeley, CA 94720) Publishes Jean Kerr Stenmark's *Family Math Book*, a book full of hands-on math activities with a section listing typical grade level math curricula. Offers seminars for parents who want to learn how to teach math at home.

Family Pastimes (RR 4, Perth, Ontario, Canada, K7H 3C6) Cooperative games and books.

Fitness at Home—A Physical Fitness Program for Home Schools (1084 Yale Farm Road, Romulus NY 14541) Parent manuals and student physical training program for ages 6-17, including scripture passages for memorization.

Focus Video (138 Main Street, Montpelier VT 05602) Educational videos, including the award-winning *Fire & Rescue* and *Road Construction Ahead.*

Franklin Learning Resources (122 Burrs Road, Mt. Holly NJ 08060) Electronic reference "books" to aid language, spelling, and writing education, an electronic encyclopedia, and electronic bilingual English speaking dictionaries.

Garden Way Publishing (Schoolhouse Road, Pownal VT 05261) How-to books on gardening, animals, crafts, country living and businesses.

Gazelle Publications (1906 Niles-Buchanen Road, Niles MI 49120) Publications of interest to and for use by home educators, including *The Home School Manual* by Ted Wade.

Thomas Geale Publishers (P.O. Box 370540, Montara CA 94307) K-8 curricular programs to teach thinking.

Gentle Wind (P.O. Box 3103, Albany NY 12203) Music and story tapes.

Gifted Child Today Inc. (Prufrock Press, P.O. Box 8813, Waco TX 76714-8813) Curriculum materials and aids for gifted, creative, and talented learners.

Gifted Education Press (10201 Yuma Court, P.O. Box 1586, Manassas VA 22110) Books about how to educate gifted children, including teaching procedures, methods, and curriculum.

Globe Fearon Educational Publishing (P.O. Box 2649, Columbus OH 43216) Textbooks.

Good Apple, Inc. (P.O. Box 299, Carthage IL 62321) Teaching materials for various subject areas, preschool through junior high, including religious education, books, posters, and more.

Grayson-Bernard Publishers (223 South Pete Ellis Drive, Suite 12, P.O. Box 5247, Bloomington IN 47407) Books for families and educators, including home educators, on several academic subject areas and on learning *per se.*

Greathall Productions (P.O. Box 813, Benicia CA 94510) Storytapes for children, several award-winning.

Greenhaven Press (P.O. Box 289009, San Diego CA 92198-9009) Juvenile books, reference books, textbooks—animals, business and economics, history, nature, philosophy, politics, psychology, religion, sociology, for grades 3-8.

Grey Owl Indian Crafts (P.O. Box 468, Jamaica NY 11434) Native American arts and crafts supplies, historical/cultural books, videos, audiocassettes, musical instruments.

Gryphon House (3706 Otis Street, Box 275, Mount Rainier MD 20712) How-to books and creative educational activities for home teachers of preschoolers and kindergartners.

Hammond Inc. (515 Valley Street, Maplewood NJ 07040) Map skills materials.

Hands On History (201 Constance Drive, New Lenox Il 60451) Books of historical fiction and kits which include activities, props and books that enable children to learn history through reading and meaningful, experiential play, for all ages.

Harcourt Brace Jovanovich (525 B Street, Suite 1900, San Diego CA 92101) Textbooks.

Burt Harrison & Company (P.O. Box 732, Weston MA 02193-0732) Materials for math and science education.

Harvest House Publishers (1075 Arrowsmith, Eugene OR 97402) Juvenile books, reference books, textbooks.

Hear and Learn Publications (603 Southeast Morrison Road, Vancouver WA 98664) Book and folk music tape packages with historical themes, including *Musical Memories of Laura Ingalls Wilder*.

Hearthsong, A Catalog for Families (170 Professional Center Drive, Rohnert Park CA 94928-2149) Art and craft supplies, kits, games, toys and books.

Highsmith Company (P.O. Box 800, Fort Atkinson WI 53538-0800) Catalogue of books by and about people of color for children of all ages.

John Holt's Book and Music Store (2269 Massachusetts Avenue, Cambridge MA 02140) Books of interest to parent educators and texts, materials and publications for use in home schools; the books of home-school proponent John Holt.

Holt, Rhinehart and Winston (6277 Sea Harbor Drive, Orlando FL 32887) Textbooks.

Home Bound Books (3455 Old Hardin Road, #21, Billings MT 59101) Curriculum and resource materials.

The Home School (3131 Smokey Point Drive, Arlington WA 98223) A wide selection of textbooks, workbooks, children's literature, etc., for use in home schools, including Christian.

Homeschool Associates (116 Third Avenue, Auburn ME 04210) Publishes "At Home in New England" a Northeast home-school newspaper, and "Home Educator's Family Times," a Michigan home-school newspaper. Maintains a curriculum store of new and used books (and purchases used books for recycling) with a telephone order line accessible from NH, VT, MA, CT, RI, NY, NJ, PA, DE, MD, VA, MI,

NC, WV. Provides standardized testing and transcript and diploma services, curriculum design and special education assistance.

The Homeschool Seller (P.O. Box 19, Cherry Valley MA 01611-3148) An advertising publication in which home schoolers run classified ads for used curricular materials.

Home School Supply House (P.O. Box F, Fountain Green UT 84632) Textbooks, science kits, art supplies, children's literature, directory of home-school newsletters.

Homestead Publishing (P.O. Box 193, Moose WY 83102) Natural history and nature books for children, young adult stories of western history, and college textbooks.

Honey Tree Educational Services (1484 Woodville Road, Mansfield OH 44903) Materials for home education.

Houghton Mifflin (222 Berkeley Street, Boston MA 02116-3764) Textbooks.

C J Huff Books (371 Beach Street, Aurora IL 60505-2867) Home instructional guides and textbooks, Christian biographies, other nonfiction and fiction children's books, videos and audiotapes.

Humanics Learning (P.O. Box 7400, 1482 Mecaslin Street Northwest, Atlanta GA 30309) Resource books for teachers.

Incentive Publications (3835 Cleghorn Avenue., Nashville TN 37215) Resource books for teachers, grades K-8, on literature, reading, writing, thinking, multicultural, science, math, self-awareness, art.

Insect Lore (P.O. Box 1535, Shafter CA 93263) Science and nature activity kits, supplies, videos.

Institute for Creation Research (P.O. Box 2666, El Cajon CA 92021-0666) Materials and workshops on science education.

International Linguistics Corporation (3505 East Red Bridge, Kansas City MO 64137) Complete French, German, Russian, and Spanish courses on cassette tapes with accompanying books of pictures.

International Reading Association (800 Barksdale Road, P.O. Box 8139, Newark DE 19714-8139) Resource books and booklets related to teaching K-12 reading. Journals for teachers of reading.

Jamestown Publishers (P.O. Box 9168, Providence RI 02940) Textbooks and teaching booklets for reading, literature, study skills, K-12.

Kar-Ben Copies (6800 Tildenwood Lane, Rockville MD 20852) Jewish children's literature and nonfiction.

Key Curriculum Press (P.O. Box 2304, Berkeley CA 94702) Materials for math education; computer software.

Keys to Learning International (1411 Oak Street, South Pasadena CA 91030) Materials, workshops, newsletter, field trips.

KidsArt (P.O. Box 274, Mt. Shasta CA 96067) Art education supplies.

Kids First Catalog (Facets Multimedia, 1517 West Fullerton, Chicago IL 60614) A catalog of videos that promote positive social values (several are award winners) for 5-12 year old viewers.

Klutz Press (2121 Staunton Court, Palo Alto CA 94306) A variety of educational and game books and kits with tools and equipment for carrying out the learning activities in the books.

The Knowledge Tree (19169 East Molly Avenue, Parker CO 80134) A varied selection of books and kits for children and teens about learning and participating actively in life and books for parents about helping children learn and participate, including many titles of potential use to home schoolers.

Lakeshore Learning Materials (P.O. Box 6261, Carson CA 90749) Infant, preschool, elementary, special education curriculum materials.

Landmark Distributors (P.O. Box 849, Fillmore CA 93016) Texts and workbooks for varied subjects and grades, literature guides, time-lines and reference materials, audio/video resources, Saxon math materials, poetry books, how-to books in varied subjects, children's classics and historical books.

Larson Publications (4936 Route 414, Burdett NY 14818) Books and audio tapes of interest to home schoolers.

Laser Learning Technologies (120 Lakeside Avenue, Suite 240, Seattle WA 98122-6552) CD-Rom and laser disk educational products in most subject areas.

Learning Publications (5351 Gulf Drive, Holmes Beach FL 34217) Reference books for teachers, books to help parents of children with reading problems and special needs, art activity books.

Learning Things (P.O. Box 436, Arlington MA 02174) Math, science, and other learning aids.

Lee's Books for Young Readers (P.O. Box 111, O'Neil Professional Building, Wellington TX 79095) Nonfiction historical books for junior high reluctant readers.

Leonardo Press (P.O. Box 1326, Camden ME 04843) Sequential materials for spelling instruction, language and arithmetic lessons, and other related publications, including "The Spelling Newsletter."

Let's Be Frank Products (1850 Union Drive, Lakewood CO 80215) "Jumpstart: How to Become Your Child's Best Reading Teacher," a 28-minute video with parent-teacher's guide.

Lippincott (227 East Washington Square, Philadelphia PA 19106) Phonics and other subject area textbooks.

Longman Publishing Group (10 Bank Street, White Plains NY 10606) Textbooks and supplementary materials in foreign languages, social studies, and English/language arts; levels K-12.

McGraw-Hill Book Co. (1221 Avenue of the Americas, New York NY 10020) Textbooks and curriculum materials; achievement tests.

Master Books (4730 Barnes Road, Colorado Springs CO 80917) Creation science materials, including educational books, videos, and computer games.

Mennonite Central Committee (21 South Twelfth Street, P.O. Box 500, Akron PA 17501-0500) Educational audio visuals, including free-loan videos, and other materials on a wide-range of topics, for children and adults.

Merlin's Learning Store (40 Main Street, Kalispell MT 59901) Geography, science, and nature learning supplies and materials.

Merlyn's Pen (P.O. Box 1058, East Greenwich RI 02818) Publishes "Merlyn's Pen," a magazine of writings written by grades 7-10 youngsters, and a second magazine *Merlyn's Pen Senior Edition* written by grades 9-12 students. Both include two inserts, "The Activity Guide," for teachers to use with students who read the magazine, and "Teachers' Marketplace." Also included, Merlyn's Pen Art Contest and opportunities for students to submit writings of various kinds for publication in the magazine.

Michael Olaf (P.O. Box 1162, Arcata CA 95521) Books, toys and other supplies for teaching various subjects the Montessori way, and books for parents about education and parenting.

The Mind's Eye (P.O. Box 1060, Petaluma CA 94953) Children's literature, classical music and games, audio and videotapes.

Modern Curriculum Press (13900 Prospect Road, Cleveland OH 44136) Textbooks and workbooks.

Moore Foundation (P.O. Box 1, Camas WA 98607) Home-school curricular materials, including Christian.

Morrow & Company (1350 Avenue of the Americas, New York NY 10019) Children's books, textbooks.

Mortensen More Than Math (Academic Excellence Institute, Financial Freedom Report Inc., 2450 East Main, Ft. Union Boulevard., Salt Lake City UT 84121) Math manipulative program with books and manuals for preschool through high school.

Mother's Bookshelf (P.O. Box 70, Hendersonville NC 28791) How-to and self-help books.

Mott Media (1000 East Huron Street, Milford MI 48381) Educational materials, including *McGuffey Readers* and *Ray's Arithmetics*, accompanying workbooks, Sowers Series Biographies. Also home of Evangelical Book Club and Homeschooling Book Club.

Museum of Science—Boston (1-800-729-3000) Science-by-Mail science learning activities kits and pen pals, for use by small groups of home-school students. Covers various science subjects.

Music for Little People (P.O. Box 1460, Redway CA 95560) Music-inspired products, cassettes, CDs, videos, musical instruments for music education, children's books, arts and crafts kits.

N.A.M. Enterprises (P.O. Box 67, Keene TX 76059) Books, games, and other supplies for instruction in nature and science, history, music, and physical education; Christian biographies.

NASA (Education Division, National Aeronautics and Space Administration, Washington DC 20546) Free science publications, including activity booklets and kits and teacher's guides.

National Association for Gifted Children (4175 Lovell Road, Suite 140, Circle Pines MN 55014) Offers *Gifted Child Quarterly* magazine and other services to teachers and parents of gifted students.

National Association for the Education of Young Children (1509 Sixteenth Street NW, Washington DC 20036-1426) Information and publications regarding the education of preschoolers through third graders. Magazine for teachers and parents, *Young Children.*

National Association of Independent Schools (1620 L Street Northwest, Washington DC 20036) An organization which advocates for, networks, and informs independent day schools, boarding schools, and combination schools, and publishes, among other publications, a directory of its 900 member independent schools.

National Council of Teachers of Mathematics (Dept. BHG2, 1906 Association Drive, Reston VA 22091) Two free booklets: "Family Math Awareness Activities" and "Help Your Child Learn Math," and other publications related to math education.

National Gallery of Art (Department of Education Resources, Extension Programs Section, Fourth and Constitution Avenue NW, Washington DC 20565) Filmstrip packets (filmstrips and texts, some with teaching booklets and prints), films, and videocassettes showcasing great works of American and other art to foster art appreciation and teach art history and technique. All for by-mail free loan to individuals, families, and groups in the United States.

National Geographic Society (Seventeenth & M Streets NW, Washington DC 20036) Educational magazines, *National Geographic,* and for children, *National Geographic World,* and other publications, educational videos, filmstrips, learning kits, books, software/multimedia, maps, globes, and posters.

National Home Study Council (1601 Eighteenth Street NW, Washington DC 20009) Professional development program for home-study educators, magazine, publications. Also publishes a directory of home study schools accredited by NHSC.

National Wildlife Federation (1400 Sixteenth Street NW, Washington DC 20036) *Ranger Rick, Your Big Backyard, National Wildlife,* nature magazines for children, Gardening with Wildlife Kit, and hands-on experiential home-teaching manuals for all levels on nature/science subjects—ask for *NatureScope* manuals catalog and other nature-related materials catalog.

National Women's History Project (7738 Bell Road, Windsor CA 95492) Curriculums, books, posters, videos and other learning materials for teaching about women in American history. Originators of annual National Women's History Month.

National Writing Institute (7946 Wright Road, Niles MI 49120) Writing and reading learning resource materials.

Nature Company (P.O. Box 188, Florence KY 41022) Nature games, books, globes, kits and equipment for nature-watching and learning, and other nature-related items.

Nystrom Atlases (3333 Elston Avenue, Chicago IL 60618) Maps, globes, atlases, social studies learning programs, and science, health and environmental instructional materials.

Old Fashioned Products (Route 2 Box 2091, Ellijay GA 30540) Math games and manipulatives kits.

Open Court Publishing Co. (P.O. Box 599, Peru IL 61354-0599) Reading/language arts (K-6) and mathematics (K-8) textbooks and aids. Also the children's magazines *Ladybug, Spider,* and *Cricket.*

Pacific Science Center (200 Second Avenue North, Seattle WA 98109-4895) A wide variety of science resources.

Parenting Press, Inc. (11065 Fifth Avenue NE, #F, Seattle WA 98125) Children's books that deal with problem solving, decision-making, safety, self-esteem, and cooperative living.

Perfection Learning Corporation (1000 North Second Avenue, Logan IA 51546) Teaching materials including "Reading Beyond the Basals" teaching guides for use with children's literature; a wide selection of children's books.

Peterson's (P.O. Box 2123, Princeton NJ 08543-2123) Guides and other books, including independent-study, college prep and college-related guides, and careers-without-college guides.

Priority Parenting Publications (P.O. Box 1793, Warsaw IN 46581-1793) Publishes "Priority Parenting," a newsletter for alternative parents who believe in *natural* child rearing, and other publications covering topics related to parenting but that may be considered out of the mainstream, such as home schooling.

Professor Phonics (S.U.A. Phonics Department, 1339 East McMillan Street, Cincinnati OH 45206-2180) Instructional manuals and student learning materials for intensive phonics, spelling, reading.

Random House (201 East Fiftieth Street, New York, NY 10022) Dictionaries and other reference books, historical and geographical videos and games, globes, atlases (including *Atlas of the Bible*), maps, electronic books, foreign language tapes .

Read Productions (11801-5A 28th Street North, St. Petersburg FL) Publishes a small newsletter of home-school articles and ads, "Christian Home Education News."

Resources for the Gifted (P.O. Box 15667, Phoenix, AZ 85060) Materials for gifted education.

Revels, Inc. (One Kendall Square, Building 600, Cambridge MA 02139) Children's records and books.

The Riggs Institute (4185 Southwest 102nd Avenue, Beaverton OR 97005) *Writing Road to Reading* with teacher's manual, phonogram cards, self-training tapes, lesson plans, and other resources.

S & S Arts and Crafts (P.O. Box 513, Colchester CT 06415) Varied arts and crafts materials.

Sax Arts and Crafts (P.O. Box 51710, New Berlin WI 53151) Varied arts and crafts materials.

Frank Schaffer Publications (23740 Hawthorne Boulevard, Torrance CA 90505) A complete line of teaching aids, including workbooks, charts, floor puzzles, and other resource materials.

Scholastic, Inc. (P.O. Box 7501, 2931 East McCarty Street, Jefferson City MO 65102) Textbooks, software, book clubs, magazines.

School Zone Publishing (P.O. Box 777, Grand Haven MI 49417) A parent-teacher catalog; materials and aids.

Scientific American Frontiers (Frontiers School Program, 105 Terry Drive, Suite 120, Newtown PA 18940) Free teaching materials to accompany the PBS-TV series "Scientific American Frontiers." Also, off-air taping rights to viewers so they can tape each segment in the series to collect their own science video library.

Scott, Foresman & Company (1900 East Lake Avenue, Glenview IL 60025) Textbooks; educational software.

Self-Help for Kids (Free Spirit Publishing, 400 First Avenue North, Suite 616, Minneapolis MN 55401-1730) Books and posters that foster self esteem, personal growth, and address child and teen issues.

Shekinah Curriculum Cellar (P.O. Box 2254, Costa Mesa CA 92628) Home-school materials and aids, including Christian.

Sierra Student Coalition (730 Polk Street, San Francisco CA 94109) Student organization devoted to environmental responsibility.

Silver Burdett Ginn (4350 Equity Drive, P.O. Box 2649, Columbus OH 43216) Textbooks.

Smart Stuff & Good Ideas (56 Ludlow Street, New York NY 10002) Educational tools and games.

Social Studies School Service (P.O. Box 802, 10200 Jefferson Boulevard, Culver City CA 90232) Materials on history, home economics, geography, government.

Story-Stone (Another Place, Route 123, Greenville NH 03048) Story tapes.

StoryTime Creations (Boulder CO) Publishes StoryTime Cards, an interactive, imaginative storytelling card sets designed to stimulate storytelling among children and parents.

Sun Media (1095 25th Street SE, Suite 107, Salem OR 97301) Resources for parents and teachers working with children who have Attention Deficit Disorder and Attention Deficit Hyperactivity Disorder; resources regarding other parenting and teaching issues, problems, and skills, including resources specifically for home-schooled children.

Superintendent of Documents (P.O. Box 371954, Pittsburgh PA 15250-7954) A 12-poster set of solar system posters (ask for stock #033-000-01120-2 for $2.25).

Sycamore Tree (2179 Meyer Place, Costa Mesa CA 92627) A wide variety of instructional materials for all subject areas, including Christian; complete school services including newsletter, testing, record keeping, high school diploma.

Timberdoodle (East 1510 Spencer Lake Road, Shelton WA 98584) Books and hands-on learning materials that encourage critical thinking, including several with a Christian focus.

TOPS Learning Systems (10970 South Mulino Road, Canby OR 97013) Task cards, activity sheets, and an activity newsletter with experiments for hands-on science education.

Toys to Grow On (P.O. Box 17, Long Beach CA 90801) Educational toys.

Transtech (Creative Learning Systems, 16510 Via Esprillo, San Diego CA 92127-1708) Books, kits, software, videos, posters, and more for science and technology education.

Trivium Pursuit (RR 2 Box 169, New Boston IL 61272) Materials for teaching Latin and Greek and thinking skills, and materials for adults related to Christian education.

Upbeat (163 Joralemon Street, Suite 1250, Brooklyn NY 11201) Children's literature and subject-related videos and books.

U.S. Geological Survey (Books and Open-File Reports Section, Federal Center, Box 25425, Denver CO 80225) General interest publications of the U.S. Geological Survey, publications regarding volcanos, earthquakes, and other topics. Ask for a catalog.

Video Tutor Inc. (2109 Herbertsville Road, Point Pleasant NJ 08742) Educational videos in a variety of subjects.

WGBH, Educational Print and Outreach (125 Western Avenue, Boston MA 02134) Teaching guide with activities to encourage geographic awareness of North America.

B.L. Winch & Associates/Jalmar Press (Business Office, 2675 Skypark Drive, Unit 204, Torrance CA 90505) Parenting and teaching materials for conflict resolution, self-concept, values, problem solving, decision-making, stress management for children and parents, drug and alcohol abuse prevention, wholebrain and lifelong learning, gender equity; for working with children ages 3 and up.

World Book Educational Products (Station 7, 101 Northwest Point Boulevard, Elk Grove Village IL 60007-9632) Learning sets and materials in various subject areas; encyclopedia set.

Young Astronauts Council (P.O. Box 65432, Washington DC 20036) Youth chapters across the nation engaging in science activities.

The Young Naturalist Foundation (56 The Esplanade, Suite 306, Toronto, Ontario M5E 1A7, Canada) Environmental magazines *Chicadee* and *OWL*, books, computer games, annual awards program.

Zaner-Bloser (P.O. Box 16764, Columbus OH 43216-6764) Handwriting workbooks.

Zephyr Press (P.O. Box 66006, Tucson AZ 85728-6006) An array of informative lesson/activity books and audiotapes covering several subject areas, designed to address varied learning styles and to focus on success.

✳✳

Appendix **A**

Teaching Methods/ Approaches

Teaching Methods/Approaches

American home schools, parochial and other private schools, and public schools incorporate a wide variety of teaching methods or approaches, some more commonly used than others. You may need at least a cursory understanding of these methods during discussions with school officials and with other home schoolers, throughout your search for and analysis of curriculums and materials, and during your reading of home-schooling literature. Thus the aim here is definition and familiarization. Should you decide to try methods or approaches listed here, seek further information about them.

The methods listed below and others can be blended for combined use in many ways. Also, one approach may be used for one subject and another approach for another subject, and different subjects may be taught with differing combinations of methods. Teachers (like you) are free to create their own methods and styles of teaching any given subject. In most instances, I have briefly commented on the adaptability of each approach to a home school setting.

Teachers select teaching methods according to student learning styles, ages, needs; the form and content of the subject to be taught; the teacher's own teaching style; the availability of suitable materials and resources; and other considerations. Home educators have the double advantage of close observation of individual student learning styles and the flexibility to apply when appropriate any of the possible teaching methods.

Following the descriptions of nineteen approaches that may be used in any curricular area are fourteen methods particular to the teaching of reading.

General Instruction Methods/Approaches

1. activity-centered learning In activity-centered learning children engage in manipulative, experiential, physically active learning activities. In public school classrooms learning centers may be set up or special equipment used for such activities. At home you can more easily take children to the real setting — such as a forest, a pond, a garden, a tool shed, a kitchen — for activity-centered lessons. These lessons don't always involve an entire setting; they may simply involve materials or items for activity, such as pattern blocks and measuring implements for activity-centered math lessons.

2. learning center approach   In the same manner that highways, trails, lakes, and rivers constructed in a sandbox by an aspiring 5-year-old trucker make a playing (and learning) center, learning centers in school can be used for experiential, exploratory, activity-centered learning. A learning center is a space designed to stimulate learning through various activities made possible by the design and contents of the center. The child selects the activities in which he wishes to participate. In a public or private school classroom, for example, a nature learning center might include such items as an aquarium, a terrarium, crosscuts of small logs and branches, a nature filmstrip on a small screen for individual use, nature books for children, a large diagram of the structure of a tree with magnetic labels for the parts, a forest-scene puzzle, a live rabbit, a nature-related worksheet, books on cassette tape available for listening with earphones, and so on. Learning centers may be combined with and correlated to other more direct methods. At home school you can also construct learning centers. However, as with activity-centered learning above, at home school *real* settings can also easily and effectively be used as learning centers.

3. mastery learning   With this approach instruction involves the identification (through testing) of those parts of an instructional unit that a student did not learn, reteaching this material through peer-tutoring or programmed learning or some other means not usually the same as the initial teaching, and finally assessing learning through testing that pits the learner against criteria of mastery rather than against her fellow students. The home teacher may design or purchase ready-made mastery learning materials.

4. programmed learning   With programmed learning the student functions in great part on his own, materials in hand. The materials include questions the student answers and a correction column or an answer card which he then checks to determine whether or not his responses are correct. The student is thus given immediate corrective or affirmative feedback. If he does well, he may go on to the next lesson. If he does poorly, he repeats the lesson or completes a reteaching lesson. In effect, the textbook is the teacher and lessons primarily involve literal recall and rote memorization. Several text series are available which use the programmed learning approach exclusively. Such a set of materials would be essential were a home teacher planning to use this approach.

5. computer-assisted instruction (CAI)   Instruction is presented to students with the aid of a computer. Computer-assisted instruction may involve visual presentations, interactive exercises, creativity activities, and even sophisticated simulations of real-life situations such as operating a plane's flight instruments. CAI is usually supplementary to instruction by a teacher. Obviously, a home teacher would need to have the necessary computer equipment on hand, a knowledge of how to use that equipment, and access to educational software.

6. competency-based instruction   With this approach learning is determined through demonstrations of a student's skills or knowledge, as opposed to being measured by the amount of time spent exposed to instruction. Having completed a unit of study within an allotted period of time would not constitute completion unless the needed skills had been gained. Likewise, having completed a year of third grade would not necessarily qualify a student for classification as a fourth grader unless competency of expected third grade skills had been demonstrated. This approach is not commonly applied in public schools or even most private schools, but a home teacher could easily base her instruction upon student-demonstrated competencies.

7. outcomes-based instruction Outcomes-based instruction focuses teaching and learning on targeted definitions of what students will learn (desired outcomes), which will be measured by actual performance (rather than by "artificial" means, such as a test). Application and integrated use of skills and knowledge are the "tests" of outcomes-based learning. All students are expected to be able to reach the outcomes. When a student has difficulty, the teacher, who has been analyzing the student's progress throughout the learning sequence, tries alternative instructional approaches, providing the student with multiple routes to learning, until the student succeeds at a predetermined performance level.

8. direct instruction   Direct instruction is formally said to occur when the teacher states the learner objective, gives small bits of instruction, models the skills involved, and then asks for student response…then more instruction and more response, and so on throughout the lesson. Direct instruction can be practiced by the teacher in any subject area and with any materials other than programmed materials. Some teaching materials, typically for language arts and reading, identify their teaching approach as "direct instruction." With these materials unison response is usually requested so that no one student leads or prompts the response. In this way, theoretically, each student must remain alert to the instruction and the teacher can quickly determine if one student has missed an item. Then reteaching can be immediately applied. The term *direct instruction* may also be used to refer simply to lessons in which there is much student-teacher interaction.

9. traditional An approach described as "traditional" would include the basics in subject matter and be text-based and teacher-directed rather than child-directed, activity-centered, or innovative. Traditional materials are available to home teachers.

10. unit study approach With this approach lessons are grouped into broad units of study, each followed by tests or other assessments to determine skills and knowledge gained throughout the entire unit. Through this method students are able, for example, to view happenings or concepts in chronological order, time-based units, or in large subcategories of a given subject. For instance, history units might be segmented by centuries or decades or major historical events. This is a commonly used approach and involves the use of other approaches or teaching methods as well. A home teacher may either locate materials arranged in units of study or design her own units of study by drawing from various sources and including various resources and activities.

11. child-directed learning (*aka* child-centered learning) Lessons that are child-directed proceed in directions established by the child as his next step, his next interest, his next challenge, his next enthusiasm. Lesson formats and learning situations and opportunities may be designed by the teacher but in an unimposing fashion and with the student's input. Lesson objectives are based upon the child's current keenest interests or needs within a curricular area. The child-directed learning method is typically most used with preschool and primary grade children. This approach is particularly possible for home schoolers, since the home teacher doesn't instruct large numbers of students with widely varying interests. Purchased as well as self-made materials can be used — as necessitated by the child-established goals of the lessons.

12. integrated curriculum The teacher who uses the integrated subject approach will draw from several curricular areas at once to teach any unit of study. For example, a history unit on the American Civil War might include Civil War poetry and song, military statistics, dioramas of the housing of Civil War soldiers, the literature of slavery, the economic impact of the war, the writing by students of letters between fictitious cousins living on opposite sides of the Mason-Dixon line, the enactment of a Civil War drama, the singing of spirituals, a video of "Red Badge of Courage," as well as the reading of the Civil War section of the history text. Thus the curricular areas of literature, mathematics, architecture, social history, economics, creative writing, drama, music, and visual arts are blended or integrated in order to teach the *history* lesson.

The theory behind the integrated approach is that in order to fully understand any one segment of study, such as the Civil War, a student needs to view the whole scene, understand the full scope of influencing factors, develop a sense for the ambiance of the entire situation, and recognize how many variables fitted together to create the situation. The integrated approach also allows for input involving both creative and logical thinking and all of the physical senses, thus enhancing the possibility that students with varying learning styles will learn. Brain research further shows that integrated learning facilitates understanding and longterm memory by supporting the brain's natural inclination to seek patterns and relationships in information. The integrated approach to teaching is easily adaptable to home teaching. With a little practice, the home teacher can learn to design most lessons in an integrated fashion.

13. diagnostic/prescriptive learning With this approach a child is given a pretest to determine his deficiencies and strengths before a particular unit of study, then he is taught whatever he appears to need in order to acquire the deficient skills and finally he is given a post-test. In other words, instruction is designed (prescribed) according to the results of the pretest (diagnosis). The student does not spend time working on skills he has already mastered. Thus instruction is individualized to meet a student's particular needs. A parent could construct pre- and post-tests for any upcoming home-school lesson if she chose to use the diagnostic/prescriptive method. Also, many commercial materials are designed with this approach built in.

14. individualized instruction When a teacher individualizes his instruction, he determines the learning needs of each student and designs instruction to meet those specific needs. Students with similar needs may be grouped for instruction. Thus individualized instruction does not require one-on-one teaching. At home, individualized instruction can be accomplished much more easily than in a full classroom setting. As you begin to home school, you will find yourself increasingly tuned in to your children's learning needs and at the same time more and more able to design instruction to meet their individual needs.

15. cooperative learning Group-centered, cooperative learning focuses learners' attention on the goal they will jointly try to reach or task they will try to complete. The teacher functions on the periphery as consultant and facilitator, not as conductor of the process. Students within the group are responsible for their own process and progress towards the learning goal. Since all members are reaching for the same goal, cooperation, not competition, occurs. All members contribute; all are included in the process. Many parents and educators believe that cooperative learning fosters self-responsibility within the context of a cooperative social milieu, individual social development that will carry over into life in general, and increased self-esteem resulting from mutual support within the group.

16. manipulative learning Instruction that allows for manipulative learning includes much handling, exploring, and manipulating of real objects by students. Manipulative learning is underused in our public schools partly because of the number of pupils in typical classes and the unavailability in the classroom of many real objects, but can easily become an integral part of home learning. Manipulative learning is useful, for example, in early math instruction, for experiments in science instruction, and for developing experiences upon which the writing and reading of stories can be based. This approach is especially suited for younger learners because their foremost means of learning is manipulation.

17. principle approach The principle approach usually involves lessons which are based upon biblical precepts and perspectives. Study and activities involve research, reasoning, relating, and the recording (writing) of biblical principles and truths as applied to lesson topics. The principle approach lends itself to an integrated subject area approach as well, for the learner's research may include a blend of correlated information and resources, including, as its core, the Bible. The Christian home schooler may choose this as her primary method of instruction, particularly with study areas such as history, science, personal development, government, international relations, and so on.

18. thematic lessons Lessons or units of study may be centered around a significant concept, abstraction, or theme. An integrated subject area approach may be taken with respect to the theme. For example, were a thematic unit centered on love, the unit might include love poetry, biographies of persons whose lives were based upon the extension of loving acts of brotherhood towards others, love as the river of Christian expression and motivation, histories involving significant events stemming from love/hate motives, stories exploring family relationships, the writing of personal essays on the subject of love, a stage play with a love theme, special recognition of those people in a child's life whom he loves, crafts based upon symbols of love, and so on. The home teacher can handily create study units centering on themes and involving varying activities and resources.

19. the writing process Composition assignments in public schools have traditionally been oriented towards the end product, the final form of the composition. Students were shown what a paragraph, essay, poem, short story, or other form was and then were asked to write one. The process a student used was not taught. Today the process of writing has become as important as the product in writing instruction. When the writing process is taught, learners begin with the thinking that must occur before one can write — often, brainstorming. During this stage ideas may fly in many directions related to the central topic, but are then gradually given form by the identification of the writer's audience and his purpose for telling that audience what he wants to tell them. Then "rough" writing takes place and may involve free-writing — uncensored and nonstop writing of one's spontaneous thoughts about a topic. Next the student revises. Rough work is read, oftentimes aloud to other students for feedback, and then it is reread, perhaps several times. With each reading the student may ask for help from listeners who may offer straightforward reactions to what the student has written — what pleases, what is clear, what is awkward or confusing, what is thorough, what needs further detail, what is out of order, what needs to be more concrete, and so on. Following these reactions, the writer returns to his writing, pencil in hand, to consider the reactions and to revise as he wishes. Once revision has been fairly well completed so that a final copy is close at hand, editing occurs. Editing involves checking and improving the mechanical aspects of writing — punctuation, spelling, grammar, layout, neatness, and so on. Then the student is ready, if required, to write a final copy for submission to the teacher who as soon as possible provides feedback. Use of the writing process (in various subject areas) has been shown to improve learners' writing skills.

Home educators and learners can become writing partners in the writing process by helping each other think — cooperative brainstorming, if you will — and by being listeners who offer feedback to each other's writings. Use of the writing process can become integral to every subject area in which a learner writes.

Reading Instruction Methods/Approaches

A reading instruction program includes several components. Learning to read begins, for example, with unwritten language. Thus the first component in a child's reading development is oral — listening, then speaking. When a teacher first begins to formally teach reading to a youngster, oral language activities of various sorts precede and later are intermixed with activities involving written letters, words, and sentences. Second, written symbols — letters — are presented for identification and decoding. Letter identification, letter-sound associations (phonics), sounds affected by letter positions in words, blended letter sounds, word-part families of sounds, and whole-word reading (sight reading) — all are forms of decoding and should be basic elements of beginning reading instruction.

While oral language experiences constitute the first component of a child's reading program, and decoding activities the second, reading comprehension; i.e., understanding, is the focus of the third component. Oral language activities often aim to stimulate comprehension of oral words and sentences, and some aid comprehension of written material. However, all of the above symbol-related activities only teach the decoding of letters and words; none teaches reading comprehension. Decoding alone is not reading — in full. Nor does comprehension alone enable the reading of written symbols. Decoding facilitates comprehension. Comprehension, in turn, makes decoding worthwhile and meaningful. Therefore, beginning reading instruction involves both decoding and comprehension. As the learner advances in reading ability, his skill as a facile decoder improves so that decoding lessons become less needed. However, comprehension activities remain important.

A fourth component of reading instruction is fluency, which involves the speed and flow of a child's reading. Skillful decoding and good comprehension enhance the development of reading fluency.

Controversy exists in the United States regarding the best methods of teaching beginning reading. Three approaches, in particular, are currently at the center of conflicting views: the sight word approach (which critics call "the look-say method"), intensive phonics instruction, and the whole-language approach which has most recently appeared on the scene. The best and most effective resolution of the conflict regarding these three methods is simply to recognize that none of the three needs to be used exclusive of the others. While phonics instruction is research supported and should be included as part of any beginning reading program, phonics by itself does not constitute an entire reading program. Oral language experiences, comprehension activities, and fluency development should also be included. Likewise, any use of the sight word approach should be in combination with other methods — including phonics. Used alone, the sight word approach is slow and restrictive. Finally, while the whole-language approach places much emphasis on comprehension and the wholeness of language versus language parts, it is, nevertheless, inherently a combined approach. Any description of its components will show you that word attack, including phonics, vocabulary development, fluency, comprehension, story schema, language experience, and so on, are all involved, plus oral language and writing activities — and sight word reading, as well as phonics instruction, can be and typically is integrated into a whole-language reading program.

In other words, polarized views towards these three or any other reading instruction method are unnecessary. If you feel intensive phonics is the best early reading instruction method, fine. However, that conviction need not leave you fearful or disdainful of other methods. Your phonics lessons will teach the decoding (unlocking symbols) component, but you can select other approaches to focus on comprehension and fluency. Study them all and develop a blend of methods that works well for you and your children.

One consideration that may influence your selection of methods is your children's individual learning styles. For example, if you have a child who does not learn well aurally (through sound), phonics instruction may be more difficult for him than for other children. Then you can look for alternative methods to supplement phonics instruction. Perhaps that child is a strong visual learner, able to mentally "photograph" word configurations. For him, sight word instruction may be a helpful side dish to his phonics lessons.

As you read the following explanations of reading instruction methods, therefore, try to think in terms of possible combinations and of methods most suited to your children's styles of learning and stages in reading development. Recognize, too, that nearly all seventeen of the above nineteen general instruction methods may apply to reading instruction. A reading program, for example, may be a direct instruction program. Activity-centered exercises or a learning center may help build background knowledge for readings. Unit study in reading could be segmented by forms of literature — poetry, short stories, novels, essays — or by themes. Diagnostic/prescriptive or mastery learning methods may be applied to reading instruction. Reading selections and activities could be based upon the principle approach. Computer activities can assist you with reading instruction. Likewise, many of the reading methods below could facilitate reading done in connection with any subject area, not just during reading instruction. For example, activities involving language experience, word attack, comprehension, vocabulary, sustained silent reading, and whole-language could be valuable to reading required in any content area — social studies, science, home economics, health, and others. So look for ways to combine approaches.

1. oral language methods Listening and talking are prerequisites to reading and writing. Therefore, at the primary level reading instruction includes oral language activities, such as listening to directions that require a physical response, listening to and discussing children's books read aloud, storytelling, listening to puppet shows, conversing about topics related to readings, performing skits or plays, talking on the telephone or CB radio, choral reading, recognizing and reciting rhymed words or lines, oral use of key vocabulary in upcoming readings, sharing personal anecdotes, listening to taped stories, responding to informal questions, listening to and reciting poetry, and many other oral language activities.

While oral language activities are vital at the primary level, they only partially diminish in importance as children become more advanced readers. At the intermediate level and beyond, storytelling, play performances, choral readings, background discussions for upcoming readings, vocabulary practice, and lots of conversation are particularly beneficial to students' reading achievement. At the secondary level, in all subject areas, much conversation involving topics about which students soon will be reading and oral practice with vocabulary which will appear in upcoming readings are valuable to most students and often crucial to the poorer readers.

Despite their importance, oral language methods are not often built into commercial learning materials, especially for intermediate and older children. However, beginning with the suggested activities above, you can design and conduct even casually many oral language experiences for your children.

2. sight word approach With this approach an instructor teaches single whole words until quick sight recognition is achieved by the student. The words taught are those that appear in the *readers* (story texts) that are used for actual reading. Typically the teacher introduces each word by writing it in view of the student, reading it aloud, and then having the student read it aloud and write it himself. Independent activities follow which involve responses to and applications of the learned word. Through repeated exposure, the student memorizes the word and then practices reading it in the context of a story. Eventually the student builds a *sight vocabulary* (a body of words he recognizes instantly).

The sight word approach may be used particularly as a supplement for learners who do not easily learn to read using another approach such as phonics, for learners who are especially oriented to visual learning, or as one of a combination of methods. Sight-reading materials can be purchased by the home teacher, or she can learn the method itself and select words to include in graduated levels of difficulty and/or that can be applied in the reading of selected children's literature. There are also available basic lists of sight words for sequential levels of learning.

3. phonics With an approach known as *intensive phonics*, the teacher teaches the letter sounds one-by-one and then teaches how they are blended to form words. Students learn to *sound out* words (read by letter sounds). Typically, if intensive phonics is the method, students are first taught beginning consonant sounds, then ending consonant sounds, then vowel sounds, several combined-letter sounds, and the rules for blending sounds. As they learn the letter sounds they are given practice in blending the sounds to read simple one-syllable words, then brief sentences, then two-syllable words and slightly longer sentences, and so on.

If *whole language* is the overall approach (See #11), the above carefully sequential, step-by-step, skill-by-skill process is not used. While focus may be given to each individual letter-sound, the students meet them in whole words, sentences, and stories, for the most part. The context of the words, sentences, paragraphs, and stories in which the letter-sounds appear support the decoding of the letter-sounds. For example, the words in italics in the following sentence help you "decode" the underlined word, from which letters are missing in order to help you recognize how context supports your efforts to figure out that word: *After asking Mom for permission, Tommy ran to the A-frame h___ on the corner where Colin lived.* Context (and the beginning letter-sound *h*) tells you the word is "house." Without the sentence, you would have to *sound out* the word in order to recognize what it was. *Sounding out* is a phonics skill which helps the reader decode, particularly when good context clues are missing. Home teachers using the whole language approach will primarily use whole pieces of literature in which their children's efforts to decode, using phonics, will be supported by the context. These teachers will further include a blend of speaking, listening, reading, and writing (including phonetic and *invented* spelling) in their children's reading lessons.

The more work a student does with letter-sounding to read words, the closer he gets to instant recognition of whole words; i.e., sight recognition. Eventually he develops a sight vocabulary for which he no longer needs to use the phonics method he has learned. To read unfamiliar words, however, he can continue to rely on phonics. A home teacher wishing to use the intensive phonics approach would be wise to purchase phonics-based reading materials in order to determine an appropriate sequence of instruction and to ensure the inclusion of all phonic elements. Many such materials are available. Materials which integrate other methods with the intensive phonics method also exist. Whole language home educators rely heavily on children's library books, and on magazines, newspapers, letters, posters, cereal boxes, and so on—various whole pieces of literature.

Research supports the teaching of phonics to beginning readers. If teaching intensive phonics, instruction has its best effect when it is at the center of a multi-faceted, overall reading program and is not taught as an isolated subject. Intensive phonics instruction should be completed with reasonable rapidity — by the end of the child's first year of reading instruction, if possible, or his second.

4. linguistics Like phonics, linguistics uses letter sounds. However, with the linguistics approach the teacher teaches groups of letter sounds that frequently appear together to form *word families* (sets of words in which the same sequence of sounds appears, such as *-end* in lend, send, mend; or *-og* in dog, log, frog). Students learn to instantly recognize the letter-group sound and to heed the initial letter in order to read new words.

The ability to rhyme is an important prerequisite to linguistic learning; thus rhyming is often taught first — orally, with no print in sight. The linguistic method is frequently integrated into a phonics approach for the teaching of reading. As with other methods, eventually the student develops a sight vocabulary of tens, then hundreds, and then thousands of words. Unfamiliar words can still be attacked linguistically. Home educators wishing to use this method may want to locate specifically linguistic materials; however, activities involving linguistics may be and usually are woven into other approaches.

5. language experience approach When this approach is used, the child's own language becomes the basis for instruction. He dictates to a teacher or aide, or talks into a tape recorder, or learns to type his own words into a computer. He will later see his words, phrases, sentences, and stories in print (provided by the teacher or aide) and learn to read them. He may also learn to read stories, rhymes and songs that were previously auditorily familiar to him. The theory behind the language experience approach is that a learner learns best by beginning with what he himself experiences and knows. He learns to read his own expressions about his own experiences and his own knowledge before learning to read about the experiences and knowledge of others in the words of others.

While watching his words being translated into symbols, he learns the link between spoken and written language. He may be given the experience of *writing* the words himself by tracing with colored pencil or crayon over the teacher's writing. When his composition is read back to him, the spoken/written link is reinforced, comprehension is again engendered, and the child may do his first reading of his own discourse.

His own language, then, becomes a vehicle for instruction and is typically not corrected in writing or reading unless meaning is hampered. In other words, reading errors are accepted unless the meaning of the text is altered by the error. If, for example, a child has been reading about a boy named Bill but when the child sees the word *Bill* on the page, she says *boy*, no correction would be offered by the teacher because the meaning of the passage had not been changed. In fact, it is apparent that the meaning is clearly understood by the child. If, on the other hand, the child says *bag* instead of *Bill*, the meaning of the passage would be changed and the child would need correction. It is apparent in this latter case that the child does not comprehend the meaning of the passage or he would not *read* a word that doesn't make sense in the passage.

This approach is used mostly with primary students. Public school classroom management and organization often make this approach difficult to include, but such instruction could easily become a daily occurrence at home school and requires no special training or even special materials on the part of the home instructor — just a clear understanding of the process and the many various applications of it to lesson activities. Also, it blends well with other approaches as part of an overall reading program.

6. word attack in context Some approaches to teaching reading primarily involve sounding out symbols — letters and punctuation — on a page, such as intensive phonics. Such decoding comprises a reader's basic processes for *word attack*; i.e., means of figuring out unfamiliar words. However, there are additional means of word attack having to do with the *context* (sentence or composition) within which an unfamiliar word appears. These means involve reading comprehension; i.e., an *understanding* of the meaning of the words and sentences.

The *Bill-boy-bag* illustration above is one example. The child must comprehend the passage in which the word *Bill* appears in order to decode that word accurately or with a logical substitution such as *boy*. Through word attack instruction the teacher encourages the child to heed clues that occur in the passage or context. Use of these *context clues* depends upon the reader's comprehension of the passage and can be used to figure out unfamiliar words. Perhaps, for example, the sentence in which the word Bill appeared included references to a boy's basketball game and masculine pronouns such as *his* and *him.* Obviously, a girl would not be named and a bag would not be involved in the meaning of that sentence. The context clues would limit the reader's choices for decoding the word *Bill.* Materials are available which include the teaching of such word attack techniques to youngsters, but the home teacher who simply learns more about the techniques could help a child learn to use them with any reading that he does.

7. comprehension activities The goal of reading comprehension activities is the child's *understanding* of the meaning of a written passage. Unfortunately, many teachers tend to emphasize decoding activities while neglecting comprehension activities. You won't make that error if you keep in mind that the ultimate goal of **all** reading is comprehension. Virtually no reading lessons should occur without comprehension activities. Otherwise the beginner may believe that decoding symbols equals *reading, in toto,* whereas in actuality decoding is merely one reading task, a route to comprehension. Reading, in the whole, must result in understanding...*meaning*...comprehension.

When a child is first learning to read, comprehension activities are oral. Oral comprehension is the natural prerequisite to the comprehension of written material, as noted in number *1* above. Oral comprehension activities should be one component of a reading comprehension program.

Oral story reading and storytelling, for example, can encourage students' recognition of language patterns and of what is called "story schema." Story schema are the parts of a story that we can expect will be present, such as a setting, an event from which conflict evolves, a sequence of events that build suspense and develop the plot, a climactic event, and an ending that unwinds any leftover complications in the story and usually leaves the reader with a sense of closure. Recognition and expectation of these common story parts aids comprehension.

Once the learner has been introduced to the written word and begins to recognize the connection between spoken (read aloud) and written words, comprehension of written material begins. At this point the home teacher can introduce comprehension activities for use with written materials. The context clue activities noted above are examples. The teacher can also teach comprehension by working on vocabulary in preparation for a reading; exploring the youngster's prior knowledge of the content of an upcoming reading selection; providing non-reading experiences to expand that prior knowledge; working towards understanding abstractions and key concepts that will appear in a reading; focusing on differences between literal and figurative meaning; encouraging critical thinking and comprehension before, during, and after a reading; involving the child in interpretive activities which stem from a reading; conversing about the topic of a reading, and so on. Another effective comprehension activity is called "prediction." Based upon what has already happened in a reading, the learner anticipates what will happen next. Comprehension is emphasized because prediction is impossible without comprehension of what occurred in the story before the learner is asked to predict upcoming events.

Few reading materials include a wide enough array of comprehension activities, but through familiarity with methods such as those noted here, the home teacher can ensure the inclusion of these activities in reading instruction.

8. vocabulary development Vocabulary development is an important factor in reading comprehension. Vocabulary instruction may stem either from lists of words that are related to each other in meaning — unusual color words, nature words, words describing character traits, for example — or from lists of key words from upcoming readings. While both help expand a child's overall vocabulary, the latter is vital to his immediate need to comprehend what he reads. Prereading activities should almost always include vocabulary instruction, or at the least an informal, oral exploration of the child's familiarity with key words in the reading which will allow the teacher to determine whether or not vocabulary instruction is needed.

With primary level children, vocabulary instruction may be entirely oral. With intermediate and older children, it should include listening, speaking, reading, and writing activities with an emphasis on vocabulary word *use*. As a result of such activities, a student should eventually internalize the words — own them, in effect.

Perhaps the best benefit of home-taught vocabulary lessons is the ease with which you and your children can orally practice the words. At home oral practice can begin informally, before actual vocabulary lessons, and continue endlessly in everyday conversation to ensure internalization.

9. sustained silent reading Much attention has recently been paid to the naturalness of silent reading in addition to the traditional reading aloud that has been done for years in schools. As a result, many schools now include periods of sustained silent reading. The period of sustained time is typically fifteen to thirty minutes. Surprisingly, even the youngest of children whose attention span would ordinarily average seven minutes can "read" silently for about fifteen minutes, especially if allowed more than one book for each session. Students benefit from the sessions in several ways: First, they experience *real* reading, rather than a reading lesson during this time. Second, reading for pleasure or for recreation is encouraged. Third, students are able to self-select the reading materials that interest them most. Fourth, a daily reading habit is engendered.

Fifth, since everyone present reads during the SSR time, the teacher and any aides model reading behavior. Finally, because the SSR time is typically followed by a brief and informal sharing time during which students and teacher discuss what they have read, the focus remains with comprehension. Later, reading lesson activities may make use of the materials that are read during SSR time. Sustained silent reading time is not a reading lesson, *per se*, but is instead one segment of a child's overall reading instruction and practice. SSR can easily and informally become a part of a home-schooled child's reading education. It never by itself comprises a reading program but is used in combination with other approaches.

10. children's literature With an approach whose core materials are children's literature, decoding and comprehension are taught in connection with library books for children — storybooks primarily but also nonfiction. Some emphasis may be given to the qualities and elements of literature, such as characterization, plot, and conflict and to the building of a literary background in students. Also, of course, the learners would be developing a knowledge and appreciation of the literature of our culture and perhaps of other cultures as well. Unfortunately, many school reading programs neglect the use of children's literature or use it only for supplementary, spare-time reading. At home school children's literature could pervade daily life as well as a reading program.

11. whole-language approach In part child-directed, the whole-language approach involves children in experiment and experience with all sorts of written materials. This approach allows natural discovery of patterns and meanings and shapes and sounds of oral and written language. Comprehension is emphasized. Step-by-step approaches to reading are deemphasized. Included in a whole-language reading program might be combinations of the following: predictable stories (repeated phonics and language-usage patterns or story lines allow for anticipation and prediction), much story reading and shared reading, sustained silent reading, language experience, phonics focus activities, reading writings that are found around us — signs, grocery containers, ads, menus, etc., reading writings that help us do things — recipes, directions, etc., and writings that inform. Whole language instruction involves speaking, listening, reading, and writing.

Proponents of intensive phonics instruction may elect to use several of the whole-language comprehension activities as complements to the intensive phonics approach.

12. content area reading methods Most educators recognize that reading doesn't stop with reading lessons, but extends into all aspects of a student's school day and beyond. For this reason teachers will sometimes "teach" reading comprehension during *content area classes* (history, biology, home economics, government, and other classes aside from reading class or language-related classes). Comprehension activities such as those noted in *7-8* above are used.

Content area reading instruction may be crucial to a student's understanding of the material he is asked to read, particularly if the student is a poor reader. Yet such instruction is not often given in public school content area classes. At home school where the parents and children can engage in experiential activities and critical thinking activities most freely, the home teacher has the opportunity to provide much instruction that will enable her children to comprehend fully their content area readings.

13. fluency training When students work on fluency in reading they are attempting to read efficiently, smoothly, and with relative speed. Training in fluency will involve silent reading and out loud or timed reading which enables the teacher to assess fluency. Such training will include activities that encourage efficient eye movement, regular practice activities, and may be computer-assisted.

14. There is an additional teaching method for reading instruction that is not listed above and which doesn't actually have a professional term attached to it. Strangely, it is often a neglected approach to reading instruction. However, it is a method that should *always* be used, whether in public, private, religious, alternative, or home school, and should be used in combination with any of the other methods. This method is simply ***reading*** — reading to your child, reading with your child, listening with your child to taped readings with book in hand, listening to your child read, sharing reading with other children, encouraging your child to read independently, modeling independent reading — *every* day. Studies tell us that the amount of time a child spends reading is directly reflected in his ability to comprehend what he reads, the size of his vocabulary, his reading fluency, and his achievement in reading. Nothing will help your child learn to read better nor more profoundly generate a marvelous, lifelong love for all kinds of literature than loads of daily reading.

✳✳

Effective Teaching

1. Engaged Time
2. Focus on Learner Goals
3. Teacher-Student Interaction
4. Individual Learner Levels
5. Teacher Expectation
6. Positive Feelings and Congenial Communications
7. Frequent Use of Realia
8. Intrinsic Motivation
9. Conversation
10. Direct Instruction
11. Application, Analysis, Synthesis, Evaluation

Effective Teaching

"**E**ffective teaching practices" has become a catch phrase for the results of a body of educational research conducted in recent years by various persons, groups, and institutions. These results are finally providing public school teachers and administrators with solid hooks upon which to hang "teaching effectiveness" tags. Although the results are only slowly being heeded by school personnel and in many instances are difficult to implement in the full classroom setting, the identified effective teaching practices are valid and reliable. The studies were carried out, not to prove that any given program or methods worked, but rather to watch what teachers were doing *when kids were succeeding* at learning. What their teachers were doing at those times became recognized, through repeated studies, as "effective practices." Although these studies were conducted on classrooms of children, I believe many of the resulting recommended teaching practices lend themselves more easily to home schooling than public schooling.

Effective teaching research addresses the issues of teaching style and efficiency, teaching processes and dynamics, learning atmospheres, interpersonal relationships between teacher and student(s), and instructional management and organization — rather than methods of or approaches to teaching a subject. While I will not attempt here to cover the entire gamut of what are now called "effective teaching practices," I would like to present a few that you may find applicable to your home-school situation. You may also use this information to interject statements that reflect knowledge of effective teaching research into your paperwork and discussions as you seek approval, if necessary, for your home school or undergo a visitation by officials or accumulate records to demonstrate the quality of your home school. Further, of course, should public school officials speak of effectiveness research results, you will have gained bits of knowledge here that will enable you to understand their comments. What then does effective teaching research tell us?

1. Engaged Time

While a teacher's management practices typically apply to a full classroom and school setting, there are components of instructional management that apply to home-school settings. Research on classroom management has demonstrated that in the public school setting precious little time is actually spent on instruction — an average of three to four hours out of a typical six--hour school day. Also, of that three or four hours, the time during which any one student is "engaged" may be as low as one or two hours. This in itself is both startling and revealing, but the most important factor derived from this information is that **a consistent relationship exists between how much students learn and the actual amount of time students are engaged in learning**. In other words, the teacher who manages the instructional day so that student engaged-time is at its maximum is the most effective teacher. This teacher's students learn more.

Because public school teachers have to spend time on routine matters such as taking roll and recording lunch money received, on transitional movement from one activity or one location in the building to another, on discipline and assistance for one student while others wait, and so on, they can increase student engaged-time only to a limited degree. At home school you'll have almost none of such routine, small student numbers nearly eliminate waiting, and transitional movement can itself easily become learning time. In addition, you have an entire day for learning rather than an allotted time period. This enables you to stretch far beyond the typical one to two or three hours of engaged student time, with either formal lessons or informal learning situations, or a blend. You can accomplish *engaged-time* in a single day during perhaps a one-hour sit-down lesson, a one-hour manipulative or experiential period, another sit-down lesson, a casual on-site exploration of a real setting, a session of cooking together in the kitchen (math, health, etc.), a third sit-down lesson, an independent research activity, a joint experiment (science), a music lesson at the neighbor's house, a conversation during snack time (history, current events, children's literature, farming practices), a trip to the library, gardening together...on and on. Your days with your children can become the fullest of all possible learning days — simply, happily, effectively spilling over with engaged-time.

You will soon discover that time-related efficiency is a key factor. In other words, to be effective, actual sit-down lessons mustn't be interrupted by Cousin Julie slipping in for coffee and a chat. An on-site or in-the-field learning session may be fun and casual but should remain focused on the process of gaining experience, skills and knowledge. Time to walk or ride to a piano lesson can be, if you make it, learning time. You might, for instance, use it to discuss the feelings of characters in a story read recently or to encourage your child to retell the story in sequence — both comprehension activities. You'll learn to smoothly move from activity to activity and to manage as much of each day's time as possible for engaged, although at times very informal, learning.

Because the effective management of time can be so freely achieved at home school, without institutional limitations and impositions, the potential for learning at home is extraordinary. As you design or contemplate your children's learning days, remember this first criteria for effective teaching — the effective management of time, which translates to the "maximizing of student *engaged* learning time."

2. Focus on Learner Goals

One aspect of effective time management in teaching involves knowing what it is that the student is trying to learn or achieve. In public schools clearly-stated, specific learner objectives supposedly guide the direction of each lesson and unit of study. As a home teacher, you may be expected to record specific lesson objectives for submittal to officials, or you may be asked to keep a record available. You may be allowed to record general goals instead of specific objectives. Or, if your state allows more freedom to home schoolers, no written objectives or goals may be required.

In any of these cases, the research regarding the importance of **centering lessons on the desired learner goals** is applicable. It is directly applicable for formal lessons — there is little gained by performing an odd assortment of academic activities aimed in no consistent direction. Well, one thing may be gained: confusion. And another: a lack of forward growth. Generally, most of what humans learn they learn sequentially, whether in school or in life. The acquiring of human language serves as an example. As infants we first simply listen to the cadences, pitches, and tones of human sounds. Then we begin to attach emotions and eventually meaning to certain human sounds. Next we attempt to emulate some of the sounds. Eventually we use the sounds as whole sounds with meaning — words. Further along we notice that people spout strings of sound — phrases and sentences, and we begin to understand those strings. In time we too string together word sounds with meaning. Thus, the learning of language progresses and actually never ends all of our lives. The point here is that an obvious sequence of learning occurs. A consistent direction is followed, in this case, naturally.

As in this example, children are often quite able to establish clear and consistent direction for their learning by themselves. The teacher then becomes a facilitator. But facilitation will be best carried out if the teacher-facilitator helps students focus on the final goal of the learning and on the sequence of skills that they are trying to learn in order to reach the goal. Without thinking about it formally, we do help the toddler focus on the goal of his language-learning efforts. We frequently repeat words to him, we tell him to "say daddy" and "say momma," we urge him to respond when we speak, and we talk and talk to him even though we have no idea what he understands, if anything. Helping a student focus on goals is similarly important during more formal learning, even when learning approaches are used that are holistic in nature rather than task-by-task oriented.

This is likewise true if the current learning taking place is experiential, like the building of a shed or the maintenance of a small business or farm; learning goals can be and should be identified by the home teacher. This will enable the teacher and learner to concentrate on steps and skills and knowledge and experiences that lead towards the goal. It's just a matter of saying, "Hmmm. Johnny and Janey seem very interested in growing and selling trees. OK, that means they are going to try to establish and run a tree nursery business. That's the goal. Now what *fields of study* and *sequence of steps* are involved in reaching that goal? What sorts of knowledge and skills must they gain in order to establish their nursery business? And how can I, as home teacher, teach to and facilitate their gaining that knowledge and those skills?" While the skills don't necessarily need to be taught or learned one-by-one, acknowledging your children's need to learn them will provide you with guidelines for helping them reach their goal. You will probably find that working out the details on paper at least in outline form will help you maintain the focus. Johnny and Janey will no doubt want to help you work out the details, maybe even work them out without you! This is just the sort of planning that any business person would carry out before beginning a business venture. However, in the case of you and your children, having less background knowledge will cause you to begin at a more basic step than the experienced business person.

As the project (unit of study) progresses, the goal serves as a guide. You and your children may discover that additions, deletions, and alterations may need to be made as your children learn and move towards their goal. You may find your children eager to jump right into the middle of a project — a naturally holistic approach — and that's fine, but as teacher/facilitator you can informally help them recognize where to begin, with what skills, how to backtrack when mistakes are made because basic skills weren't learned first, how to move ahead when skills have been mastered. All "lessons," all activities, all attempts to proceed will continue to be centered on reaching the identified learning goal, a nursery business. Reliable educational research indicates that learning geared to goals will be the most effective learning.

In addition, because the home teacher is so thoroughly involved in all aspects of the home learner's studies, the home teacher will be cognizant of current goals in all subject areas towards which her students are working. This awareness enables the home teacher to relate literally anything that occurs in the life of the learner to a learning goal. Thus, not only his formal and informal lessons, but nearly all of a home learner's life experiences can be directed, often quite subtly, at learning goals.

3. Teacher-Student Interaction

Throughout the progression of a learning project or other unit of study or single lesson, **the effective teacher is the highly interactive one.** Research studies show that the teacher who is physically and verbally interactive with his students during the learning process enhances his students' learning. He is not overpowering, but is a lively assistant to the learners — exchanging information, generating excitement, monitoring progress, drilling, questioning to stimulate thinking, praising, providing input and feedback, sharing, working alongside, modeling, guiding, focusing and refocusing. Through his direct, active involvement he keeps the learning pace brisk and the learning atmosphere exciting. Nowhere could this happen more assuredly that at home school. With a one-to-one or one-to-few student-teacher ratio and the energy and devotion of a parent teacher, this research-based effectiveness criteria — teacher interaction — can be well met at home school.

4. Individual Learner Levels

The effective teacher establishes **learning goals and objectives appropriate to the individual learner's level.** In other words, having assessed the student's abilities, formally or informally, and continuously monitored progress, the teacher focuses and helps the student focus on the next sequential steps, not on steps for which he has insufficient background or skill. The key is to challenge but not to frustrate. The frequently frustrated learner is likely to become a nonlearner. The challenged but successful learner will more likely become a lover of learning. A learner should consistently experience success at least 75 percent of the time during learning sessions in which the teacher plays an active part. A learner should consistently experience nearly 100 percent success during independent work. In other words, if a child is having a difficult and unsuccessful (less than 75 percent) learning experience with a certain set of activities, he is not equipped to handle those activities. Goals and objectives should be set at a more appropriate level for that child. However, *the expectation that he can and will eventually be successful at the higher level should be maintained*. Also, if a child is achieving 100 percent during interactive learning sessions with the home teacher, that child probably needs goals and objectives adjusted to a higher level.

Keep in mind, too, that sometimes high goals look deceptively difficult. The shed building project is an example. A couple of bright, well-schooled, high school home students who have never constructed any building may not be overwhelmed by the shed building project — it may not be too high a goal — if the students have the skills needed to approach the steps involved in completing the project. If they have the investigative skills necessary, for instance, to complete the initial planning steps, they will be able to successfully proceed, learning skills pretty much sequentially, until they are able to actually build the shed.

Since a home teacher guides nearly every learning experience of her children, she can be more closely in tune with each of her children's mastery levels in any one subject area than a public school teacher could be. Such close monitoring of progress should enable her to effectively and consistently establish learning goals and objectives that are well suited to her learner's skill levels. Experience as a home teacher will soon enable you to recognize your children's levels and to meet the effective teaching criteria of establishing *appropriate* goals and objectives for your children's lessons.

5. Teacher Expectation

Expectation, as mentioned above, also plays a role in effective teaching. Studies have documented that **teacher expectation can lend powerful stimulation to student learning**. In effect, low expectation reaps low achievement and high expectation reaps high achievement. Whether at home school or public school, effective teachers set appropriate goals for their students and then consistently convey an optimistic, confident expectation for student success. This is easier done at home school where classroom management issues don't interfere with a teacher's acceptance of a child and of his abilities. A bright child who is a discipline problem in a full classroom, for example, may be viewed as incapable of good performance by the teacher, which can result in lowered academic expectation or an unwillingness to feel optimistic with regards to that child's academic performance. Similarly, a slower learner who has received negative feedback for his slowness may eventually exhibit self-deprecation and disinterest. These behaviors, in turn, cue the teacher to lower her expectation — unjustifiably. The student perceived as *average*, as a third example, may even be denied opportunities to participate in special interest classes and events or to enroll in college preparatory courses because she isn't *expected* to succeed. Public school teachers often let grade and test records and comments from previous teachers tell them what expectation levels they should have for each of their students. In other words, they have a tendency to rely upon a child's past history in public school to determine the child's ability. Studies show that this reliance is often erroneous. One such study, for example, demonstrated that when a teacher was informed that a group of previously low-performing students was a group of bright students, the teacher's expectations were set high and, lo and behold, the students' performance was high for the first time in their school lives. Public school teachers also tend to think of intelligence itself as comprised only of those verbal-analytical-logical abilities frequently correlated with public school success. Those children whose intellectual abilities are higher in other areas tend to be thought of as less able learners. In contrast, the home teacher is likely to approach the whole notion of teaching his children with much enthusiastic expectation for their achievement.

6. Positive Feelings and Congenial Communications

Along with optimistic expectation, **effective teachers display positive feelings and engage in congenial communications with**

children. In the effective teacher's dealings with children there is an absence of negative behavior. No belittling or berating or needling or hassling or embarrassing of children occurs. Children are trusted, supported and respected. Research has consistently revealed a negative relationship between student learning gains and any teacher behaviors that are derogatory to students. Effective teachers heed that research. A loving parent is much more likely to feel congenial towards her children as they learn than anyone else. Even if you are sometimes frustrated with snags in your children's progress, you are no more frustrated than a public school teacher would be, and probably less so considering your deep, personal desire to see your own children learn. Who more than a caring parent would consistently treat her young learner with trust, support, and respect?

7. Frequent Use of Realia

Effective teaching includes realia (real objects). Manipulatives, demonstrations, experiments, exploration, field trips, resource persons — all sorts of firsthand, sensory, experiential activities — can be continuously integral to learning. This is particularly important in science instruction in which experimentation clarifies what is being learned, but the use of realia is also highly effective and important in other subject areas. Through his own experimentation and exploration a child learns to trust himself as a capable learner, learns to question and innovate, learns with a free flow of enthusiasm, and discovers the benefits of industriousness. The foremost learning mode of young children, in particular, is manipulation, which suggests that much of any young child's learning should involve realia. The inclusion of realia is one of the greatest benefits of home schooling because realia is often so close at hand and because time can be so easily taken to open the home-school door and bring in items and people from the outside world or walk out into that world to learn.

8. Intrinsic Motivation

Students learn best and maintain a love for learning when they are motivated intrinsically (from within themselves). Research tells us that long-term intrinsic motivation is not engendered through extrinsic rewards. In attempts to mold and control student behavior, public school teachers frequently offer tangible, extrinsic rewards (parties, snacks, free time, stickers, grades, etc.). Such extrinsic rewards may result in desirable short-term behaviors. For example, whenever public school teacher Mr. Ross wants students to complete an assignment quickly, he offers bags of popcorn as a reward, and the students respond with fast work. However, as a sideline effect of this reward situation students will gradually become motivated to work fast only when popcorn or some other extrinsic reward is offered. Eventually, extrinsically rewarded students select easier learning tasks, utilize random guessing rather than logic in problem-solving activities, produce more stereotyped and less creative work, and are less likely to return to a task they once found interesting.

Research shows that students will be most motivated when they are consistently allowed to follow their own curiosities and enthusiasms into their learning world and to *feel for themselves* the excitement and joy and pride in learning. Your role is to encourage their excitement, joy, and pride. Give your children and their ideas your respect, invite their interaction with you, solicit their opinions and views, welcome their responses, and design opportunities for them to make decisions. By demonstrating in such ways that you value them, their ideas, and their learning, they, too, will take themselves and their learning seriously. In addition, at home school you can ensure that extrinsic rewards for learning are simply not offered, so that your learners are allowed to become intrinsically, rather than extrinsically, motivated.

9. Conversation

A learner's ability to successfully read, reason and understand are enhanced through much conversation. I once heard a principal counteract a school visitor's complaint about the noise in one classroom with this reply: "Ah, but such a wonderful noise...the noise of learning." If such noise is in actuality conversation or discussion related to the subject matter, then indeed learning is enhanced by that noise. We know, for example, that reading comprehension is increased when students and teacher discuss background knowledge or concepts, issues, and difficult word meanings before a reading, interrupt the reading to express reactions and to predict upcoming events, and after the reading reflect together upon interpretations and applications of what was read. For poor readers, in fact, reading-related discussions may be crucial to their comprehension. The positive effects of such conversations apply to all situations and subject area studies that require reading, reasoning and understanding.

In public schools noise is often toned down to maintain a quiet or studious atmosphere, and, of course, at times this is necessary. But it is not always academically productive. At home school conversation can not only be allowed, but stimulated and guided and participated in by the parent teacher who wants to let it become a learning tool. Research tells us that abundant conversation can, in fact, be a valuable and even vital learning tool.

10. Direct Instruction

Direct instruction increases student learning. Direct instruction occurs when a teacher explains to students exactly what they are expected to learn and when during instruction the teacher demonstrates or models the steps that lead toward achievement of the learning task. In other words, students need to know the goal, focus or direction of a sequence of learning steps before they attempt those steps. Also, demonstration and modeling enable students to more easily visualize their own potential and peak task performance. It seems apparent that home school offers a natural setting for demonstration and modeling and an opportunity to gear these elements to the individual student's next performance level or goal.

11. Application, Analysis, Synthesis, Evaluation

While memorization is an important learning tool because memorized information facilitates the learning of further information, **student achievement is improved when teachers design questions and lesson activities that encourage students to apply, analyze, synthesize, and evaluate** old and new information. Questions don't necessarily need answers and activities don't necessarily need to end in right vs. wrong finality in order to stimulate higher level thinking processes. It is the design of the questions and activities that stimulates thinking. While public school teachers are usually aware of the importance of such stimulation, they often find applying such questions and activities difficult for various reasons. At home, where you can be comfortable with predictions, estimates, wrong answers, varied ideas, contrasting reactions, experimentation, and innovation, you can freely encourage your children to use application, analysis, synthesis, and evaluation. You can also help your youngsters develop the ability to follow their thinking all the way through complex issues, projects, topics, happenings, and to produce involved and thorough responses and results. These abilities are also important to improved learning.

❋❋❋

Become familiar with the above teaching practices. They represent the heart of effective teaching and offer you eleven keys to home-teaching success. Indeed, judging by our review of these results of effective teaching research, home-school teaching has the potential for winning the gold medal in the effectiveness competition. Where indeed could these teaching effectiveness criteria be better met than at home school?

❋❋❋❋❋❋❋❋❋❋❋❋❋❋❋❋❋❋❋❋❋❋❋❋❋❋❋❋❋❋❋❋❋❋❋❋❋❋❋

Appendix **C**

The Lesson

The Lesson

To familiarize you with the structure of what many educators consider a good lesson, I include below what is known as the "5-step lesson format," sometimes referred to as the "7-step format" or the "Madeline Hunter format." From this lesson format a home teacher can derive an acceptable design for written, daily or weekly lesson plans, as demonstrated in the "Lesson Planning" portion of Section Three in this book. An understanding of the following 5-step lesson format should help you to write plans, if you must, that are acceptable to officials, or to write just sketchy plans but be able to discuss how they fit into 5-step lessons, or to recognize what public school officials are talking about should they refer to the 5-step plan or just to lesson plans in general. As we look at the 5-step format now, remember that you are not locked into using it for lessons or for lesson planning, unless required, of course, but that it does offer a viable design for good lessons.

We will again rely on the turtle lesson which was given in Section Three so you can relate the explanations below to the actual plans shown on pages 126 and 127.

5-Step Lesson Plan

Step 1 — Anticipatory Set (Serves as an introduction.)

<u>The teacher engages the students' attention or participation</u> through an attention-getting activity aimed at arousing student interest in the subject of the lesson. Possibly the students themselves will become enthused about an area for study, thus creating a spontaneous anticipatory set.

> Example: To draw attention and arouse interest, the teacher takes the children to watch a turtle in its natural habitat and elicit, as well as offer, numerous open-ended questions. The questions may be recorded for later reference.

<u>The teacher states the learning objective(s)</u> of this lesson.

> Example: "Students, after learning about turtles, you'll be able to identify all of the parts of a turtle's

body and tell how those parts are useful to him. You'll also be able to explain the turtle's life cycle and needs, food, dangers, reptilian characteristics, and habitat."

Then, she links the objective to the activities that will follow. She may have planned these activities herself or in cooperation with her children.

> Example: "To find out about turtle bodies and body functions we will read books, check encyclopedias, watch and listen to a demonstration by a biologist who knows a lot about turtles. We'll also examine turtles ourselves, paint a mural of a turtle in his habitat, and keep track of what we're learning on a large chart we will make."

Step 2 — Instruction

Information is provided from a combination of sources — the teacher, a textbook, an expert, a close examination of the subject (turtle, in this case), a photograph, an experiment, etc.; or information is searched for and found in subject-specific books, reference books such as encyclopedias, children's educational magazines, textbooks, etc.

The teacher may model and assist book-research techniques, firsthand examination of the subject or photograph, listening, questioning, perhaps note taking during expert's presentation, subject-specific story reading if books are storybooks (primary level), and even textbook reading with note taking.

Throughout these instructional activities the teacher frequently asks questions or requests that certain tasks be performed that allow her to determine whether or not students are understanding the information. (Some call this "checking for understanding.") Also, the teacher and students regularly review what they've learned and try to identify what still needs to be learned.

Step 3 — Guided Practice

The teacher engages the students in an activity through which they practice using the knowledge and skills they've gained. She continues to provide information (for clarification now), to assist, and to check for understanding. She may summarize or elicit student summaries of the learned information.

Step 4 — Closure

The teacher engages students in <u>an assessment activity</u>, an activity through which she can determine how much of the learned information can be applied by individual students functioning on their own.

Those students who have difficulty here are given more instruction. Then they will be given another closure or assessment activity. Then they will go to Step 5.

Those who successfully completed the closure activity go immediately to Step 5.

Step 5 — Independent Practice

The <u>students engage in individual projects or activities</u>.

The teacher monitors, offering little or no assistance, checking for students' demonstration of the learned information.

To finish this activity the teacher might orally ask for comments related to the procedures students followed in order to apply the learned information and complete the projects.

Typically such a lesson, which may, incidentally, take a few days to complete, is only one part of a *unit of study* which may take a few weeks to complete. In the case of the turtle, it might be a unit on reptiles, or perhaps in primary grades a unit on animals that carry their homes with them. Also, it is possible that at some later date a test will be given or a project completed that will include the knowledge gained from this lesson as well as other lessons in the unit.

While lessons may be organized in other ways as well as with the 5-step format, and while some home schoolers may not believe lesson plans are necessary at all, many home teachers do find lesson plans useful or do need a plan design that will be acceptable to school officials. You may be one of the latter two, and if so, you may want to rely on the above 5-step lesson format as you write lesson plans.

Glossary

As a home-school parent you are likely to hear from school personnel or read in education-related documents many of the same terms that public school parents hear and read, and find the terms just as baffling. The glossary of terms below will help you understand the more commonly used of these education terms.

Several terms relate specifically to home-education, such as *activity day* and *assurances*. Most, however, refer to education in a broader sense. Subject areas are included, such as *business education* and *language arts* to aid those who are writing home-school curriculums.

ability level The maximum level at which a child is *believed* able to perform successfully, due to general intelligence and previous learning. (see also *expectation*)

absence (from home school) The nonparticipation by a child in any learning activity related to the child's home-school curriculum due to illness or other circumstances. This should not be confused with simply being away from one's home or normal instructional setting on an excursion which involves learning activities.

academic progress The movement by a child through a sequence of learning objectives in a curriculum as demonstrated by mastery of or successful application of the involved skills and concepts.

accountability Teachers' ability to prove through testing that their students have mastered the material outlined in a curriculum, and used by parents, educators and legislators to express a desire for concrete knowledge of what teachers are or are not accomplishing.

accreditation The official recognition of a school or college by an accrediting agency. Such accreditation may or may not denote quality in the program or product, but is, nevertheless, considered essential by many educators.

achievement Mastery of learned skills and knowledge and/or a demonstration of goals reached.

achievement test (see *standardized achievement test*)

ACT American College Testing Service — the college-entrance exam offered by this service, which tests a student's general knowledge and skills in English, math, social studies and natural science.

activity-centered learning (see Appendix A)

activity day The involvement of a home-school student in a recreational and/or learning experience outside of the usual home-school setting, often in conjunction with other home-schoolers.

administrator A person who administers a school or school district, or has particular administrative responsibilities within either, such as a superintendent, a principal, or vice principal.

affidavit A written statement made to an authorized official which has the status of having been made under oath.

age-appropriate curriculum Learning objectives that a student will typically master at a particular age based upon normal intellectual, emotional and physiological development. Example: Children normally do not fully understand the concept of cause and effect until they are beyond the ages of primary students; likewise with the development of sufficient hand-eye coordination to write within narrow lines. What constitutes "normal" may not be normal for your child or dozens of other children, but, nevertheless, age-appropriateness is often expected in home-school curriculums.

alternative education Schooling options other than public schools. Those schools identified by such labels as *private*, *community*, *Christian*, *parochial*, *alternative*, and *home school.*

alternative school A school established by a private group or individual as an alternative to public education. A private school which typically embraces an educational philosophy and instructional methods that differ from those of public education, and which usually maintains low or nonexistent tuition charges. There are also special purpose alternative schools created by and existing within public school systems.

annual calendar A record of the days that a home school will be in session during a given academic year; includes beginning date, vacation days, and closing date as well as in-session days.

annual evaluation A compilation of the data available on what a student has learned during a given home-school year. Such information may take the form of standardized achievement test results, other written work, teacher observations, portfolios of finished work, completed projects, observations by others.

In *special education*, this term refers to a formal assessment of a special education student's progress toward completing the objectives of a specific individual education plan (IEP).

anticipatory set (see Appendix C)

appeal process Steps available to a parent whose home-school program has been denied initial approval. If the original proposal went to a school superintendent, an appeal process may involve the presentation of the proposal to the local school board or committee; if the denial came from the board, an appeal may be possible to the state superintendent of instruction or the governing body of the state department of education. Finally, courts may be involved. The procedures for an appeal process vary by state.

art education Instruction in and practice with colors, depth perception, shapes, size relationships, picture composition, art mediums, art appreciation and history, and so on.

assessment of progress (see *progress assessment*)

assurances Typically a signed agreement which states that a home-schooling parent is complying with all state requirements for home schools.

attendance register/record A dated grid on which are denoted the days during which a school is in session and the days of attendance and absence of each enrolled student.

authentic assessment A progress assessment in which the student completes or demonstrates the learned skills or knowledge *in a real-life context*.

baccalaureate degree (see *bachelor's degree*)

bachelor's degree A degree awarded by a college or university to students who have completed a specific sequence of courses, typically involving eight semesters of academic work.

basic education (basic skills) Core courses or subjects taught in a school, such as reading, language, math, social studies, and science; and basic or common skills within those core subjects, such as addition, subtraction, division, and multiplication in math.

burden of proof The responsibility of a home-schooling parent to maintain and/or provide those records and documents necessary to demonstrate compliance with a given state's statutes and regulations dealing with home schooling.

business education Instruction in the skills associated with office work such as keyboarding, business English, office machines, bookkeeping, accounting, marketing, computers in business, and additional business-related courses. Business education courses may come under the umbrella of "vocational education." At home school experiential entrepreneurship may be the vehicle for business education.

calendar (see *annual calendar*)

career education Instruction about the world of work that typically includes job categories, training requirements, salaries and working conditions, career paths, and career decision-making.

case law Legal decisions rendered in the courts that may set precedents for findings in similar, subsequent cases. Case law resulting from home-school litigation may affect home-schooling procedures within the state where the legal proceedings took place.

certificate of exemption A document which declares a child officially exempt from compulsory attendance in a public school.

certification The formal licensing of an individual to teach or perform other professional duties assigned to school personnel in a given state. Certification may be for various periods of time, and is usually granted with endorsements in specific areas; e.g., elementary, high school science, K-12 counselor, principal, etc.

certified consultant A state-certified teacher who assists a home-schooling parent in performing various aspects of the home-schooling process, such as planning a curriculum and conducting an annual student evaluation. A certified consultant may or may not be required by a state's home-school statutes and regulations.

Chapter 1 A federally funded compensatory program for disadvantaged children designed to help them improve their academic performance; a remedial reading or remedial math program to which low-achieving students are assigned. Chapter 1 regulations require local school districts to offer similar services to any private schools located within school district boundaries.

child-directed learning (see Appendix A)

child study team (CST) A group consisting of a child's teacher(s), principal, parent(s) and special education personnel (teacher, school psychologist, etc.) who make decisions about the instructional program of an exceptional child in a manner specifically prescribed by federal law. (see also *IEP* and *Public Law 94-142)*

children's literature (see Appendix A)

chronological age A child's *actual* age in years and months.

citizenship Part of a school's curriculum, sometimes of an unwritten, informal curriculum, involving the inculcation of particular values in children. Examples: learning to be considerate of other children, to play cooperatively, to respect adults, to contribute to group efforts, to develop a sense of one's role in American society.

class schedule A listing of times during the instructional day during which given subjects will be taught; e.g., 9:00-10:00 reading, 10:00–10:30 arithmetic.

closure (see Appendix C)

competency-based instruction (see Appendix A)

competency testing The testing of students to see if they have achieved minimal skill levels. Sometimes used to screen students for graduation diplomas. (see also *teacher competency test*)

compliance The condition of having met all requirements for state or local school board approval of your home-school plan. Also, continuing to meet those requirements throughout your home-school year.

compulsory education The legal requirement in all states that children of certain ages be enrolled in an approved school program.

computer-assisted instruction (see Appendix A)

computer literacy The ability to understand basic computer terminology and to use a computer in performing rudimentary tasks, such as word processing.

consultant (see *certified consultant*)

consumer education Instruction in the skills and knowledge necessary to be an informed consumer in our economic system. Examples include critical analysis of advertising, understanding consumer credit, and savings and investment alternatives.

content area reading methods (see Appendix A)

cooperative learning (see Appendix A)

core curriculum The basic subjects, including reading, language and math, and in most cases also science and social studies.

correspondence study A learning situation in which teacher and student are physically separated, with an exchange of written interactions (lessons, completed assignments) typically sent through the mail. The student mostly works independently, but in the case of home schoolers may have his at-home teacher assist him. Correspondence study is in a process of change with the advent of video instruction, electronic mail systems, and instruction via live teleconferencing and videoconferencing.

course syllabus (see *syllabus*)

creative writing Writing instruction involving various forms of written composition, such as language experience stories, expository compositions, short stories, poems, and many others. (see also Appendix A)

criterion-referenced test (CRT) An achievement test with results described only in terms of the number of correct responses each student makes. CRT's enable an instructor to determine whether a student has adequately mastered a given set of skills or knowledge. CRT's do not provide for comparison of your child's achievement with others taking the same test.

CST (see *child study team*)

curriculum A description of the content of an instructional program stating what a student is to be taught. Usually in roster or outline form, including broad learning goals and specific learning objectives, and often prefaced by educational philosophies. There can actually be several different curricula at work in an educational setting, ranging from the official curriculum described above, to the classroom curriculum which includes what the teacher actually teaches, to the hidden curriculum which includes lessons taught unconsciously through the actions of teachers and the structure of the learning environment itself.

curriculum fair A conference or other gathering where curriculum and instructional materials are displayed, instructional equipment is demonstrated, and other teaching aids and ideas are presented.

curriculum guide A book or notebook, often prepared by a school district, department of education or publishing company, and which contains outlines of learning objectives that are to be taught in one or more subject areas. (see also *curriculum*)

curriculum mastery The development by a student of a high degree of competence in the skills contained in a given curriculum and of an understanding of the relationships among information in that curriculum that transcends rote learning of facts.

declaration of intent (See *statement of intent*)

department of education The branch of state government that licenses teachers, disburses state funds to school districts, administers federal education programs within a state, and oversees the implementation of state laws governing education.

diagnostic/prescriptive teaching (see Appendix A)

diploma Formal recognition by an educational institution that a student has completed a particular course of study. Such recognition takes two forms: the actual paper document and, more importantly, an official record of program completion in the form of a transcript available in the school's files.

direct instruction (see Appendix A; see also Appendix B)

documentation A written record generally considered as proof to an authority. In the case of home schooling, such items as an attendance register, curriculum outlines, and test results that may constitute proof that a parent is meeting state statutes regulating home instruction.

early childhood education Education provided for preschoolers through third graders. This phrase is often referred to in relationship to the teaching principles specifically atuned to this age group that have been identified and disseminated by the National Association for the Education of Young Children.

education journals Periodical publications that address issues in education as their primary subject matter. Some education journals are scholarly publications for professionals (e.g.: *Harvard Education Review, Reading Research Quarterly, School Psychology*), while others contain information that is, in differing degrees, of interest to both education professionals and parents (e.g.: *Phi Delta Kappan, The Reading Teacher, Instructor*). Some of these offer activities and ideas directly applicable to home teaching.

educationally-deprived child A child who has had fewer than the "normal" pre-school or out-of-school learning experiences and as a result is not as prepared for public school as other children. Socioeconomic class and culture often are factors behind this educational concept.

emergency certificate A temporary license to teach granted to an individual who does not meet the requirements in a given state for a regular certificate. An emergency certificate is usually granted for a limited time period, such as one year.

emotionally-disturbed child A child whose state of emotional health requires special instruction or other services to enable him to achieve an acceptable level of academic progress.

engaged-time (see *on-task time*; see also Appendix B)

enrollee Any student who is regularly attending a given school. In the case of home schooling, your children become enrollees of your home school (or, in some instances, your private school).

entrepreneurship Learning about, developing, and assuming responsibility for a small business.

equivalent instruction A term included in several states' home-schooling statutes to indicate that a home-school curriculum must be closely correlated with the public school curriculum in the respective states. However, the exact meaning of *equivalent instruction* in any one state may be subject to interpretive review during home-school litigation occurring in that state.

ESL English as a second language. Instruction in the English language for students whose first or primary language is not English.

evaluation of students Testing or other observational data-gathering that enables a teacher or other school personnel to determine a child's ability or achievement level. (see also *annual evaluation*)

exceptional child A child who is either gifted or handicapped to the extent that modifications of the school's regular instructional program are necessary for the child to develop educationally to maximum potential.

exemption An officially granted waiver from compulsory attendance in a public school.

expectation The level of academic or other achievement conveyed to a child as acceptable or praiseworthy, or that the teacher *thinks* the child is able to achieve. In either case, because this level of expectation is consciously or unconsciously conveyed to the child, it frequently becomes an unintentionally imposed cap on levels of formal learning. The higher the expectation level conveyed, the higher the cap. (see also Appendix B)

extracurricular School activities offered in addition to instruction in the regular curriculum. (e.g., production of a play, sports activities)

extrinsic reward A reward that is external to an activity but which is provided for engaging in that activity. The reward may be contingent upon the length or quality of the performance. (e.g., a child receives a grade of "A" on a math test or a smiley sticker for following the rules; a class earns a party for everyone's completing an assignment.)

field trip A brief trip, usually a few hours, during which students leave their home-school building to learn in another setting. (see also *activity day*)

fine arts education Instruction in courses such as music, painting, drama, creative writing, dance, and appreciation of art, music and literature.

functional illiteracy (see *illiterate*)

GED The General Education Development exam taken by unenrolled high school aged students or adults who hope to earn a sufficient score to be awarded a high school equivalency diploma by a state department of education.

gifted and talented student A student whose learning ability in one or more academic areas is sufficiently exceptional to require special instruction, or whose talent in a particular field is determined to be such that special training is warranted. Each state and/or school district uses its own criteria for defining this term, such as a minimum score on a specific I.Q. test and demonstrated academic achievement in the top three percent of students.

grade equivalent score (GE) (see "Annual Evaluation" in Section Three)

grade placement End-of-the-year placement of a student in his next year's grade level.

guided practice (see Appendix C)

handicapped child A child who requires special educational services to enable him to reach his educational potential as determined by a child-study team (CST). Further, a child who meets one of several definitions of the handicapped (e.g., mentally retarded, emotionally disturbed, learning disabled).

health education (see *safety/health education*)

home economics Courses involving homemaker skills and sometimes parenting skills, such as cooking, sewing, nutrition awareness, child growth and development and interior home design.

home-bound student A student who is unable for health reasons to attend public school and so is taught at home either by a parent or by a certified educator.

home school plan A statement or notice or declaration of intent or some other form of home-school program proposal or design which explains and describes one's at-home education program. The plan will include any combination of segments required by the laws and procedures of the individual home schooler's state. (see also *statement of intent*)

humanities Courses such as classical literature, languages, fine arts, philosophy, and others which are not considered as *the sciences*.

IEP (see *individual education program*)

illiterate, illiteracy Inability to read or write. Various descriptors suggest degrees of illiteracy. *Functional illiteracy*, for example, indicates that a person is unable to function safely, productively, and with his own welfare assured, because of his inability to read and write.

independent practice (see Appendix C)

independent work Work completed by a student with little or no assistance). (see also *independent practice* in Appendix C)

individual education program A formal, annual statement of a special education student's instructional goals, objectives, and the activities planned to achieve these objectives. The IEP is formulated by a child study team, requires parental approval (with rare exception), and contains means for evaluation of the plan's success. (see also *CST* and *Public Law 94-142*)

individualized instruction (see Appendix A)

industrial arts Courses such as woodworking, auto mechanics and metal work.

instructional level The level at which a student is able to understand new material being presented.

instructional time In-class time during which students actually receive instruction.

integrated subject areas (see Appendix A)

intelligence A student's capacity for learning, understanding, reasoning or thinking critically. A student's score on an I.Q. test. Although mistakenly thought by some educators to be constant and singular, intelligence is variable and multiple.

intermediate Grades four, five, and six.

intrinsic reward A reward that is inherent in engaging in an activity itself. (e.g., A child feels *pleasure* from successfully solving a riddle. A child feels *satisfaction* for having successfully completed a science experiment. A child feels *pride* in having won a race.) (see also Appendix B)

junior high Grades seven and eight, and sometimes nine.

language arts Spelling, grammar, creative writing and related areas. Literature, reading, speech, and drama are also subcategories of language arts, but are sometimes listed separately. Word processing may be included.

language experience approach (see Appendix A)

learning center (see Appendix A)

learning community All the human resources that a child can use in becoming educated, including parents, grandparents, siblings, neighbors, community elders, experts, organization leaders, and peers.

learning disability A malady ascribed to children placed in special education who are not academically successful in school, do not meet the definitions of other special education categories, and whose learning problems are ostensibly not attributable to differences in language or culture.

learning goals The desired, broad outcomes of a child's lessons. Usually specific knowledge and skills are needed in order for a child to achieve his learning goals.(see also Appendix B)

learning objectives Specific skills taught to a student which he needs to master as a step towards a broader learning goal. It is generally thought that each lesson taught should be geared towards one or more identifiable learning objectives.

learning outcomes (see *outcomes-based instruction*)

learning time (see *instructional time*)

lesson plan A teacher's written design for a lesson; usually includes one or more learning objectives. Typically teachers write, in advance, lesson plans in each subject for an entire school week. (see also Appendix C)

linguistics (see Appendix A)

literate, literacy Able to read and write at least at a functional level.

litigation Addressing an unsettled issue in the court system through a legal proceeding.

log A written, dated record of events.

manipulative learning (see Appendix A)

mastery learning (see Appendix A)

mathematics Courses which involve the recognition and manipulation of numbers, from counting through division, fractions, and such secondary courses as algebra, geometry, trigonometry, statistics, probability and measurement, and pre-calculus.

mental age The age of a child stated in terms of his mental capacity, and determined by comparing his knowledge and abilities with the age at which the average child has the same knowledge and abilities. Thus a child with a chronological age of 8.5 might have a mental age of 7.0 or 9.3 or some other mental age.

mentally retarded Children whose general intellectual functioning is in the lowest 2.5 percent of their age group as measured by an I.Q. test and who have been unable to learn expected academic and social skills. It is further necessary that these deficits are not due to cultural or linguistic differences.

mentor Person skilled at a craft or endeavor who coaches and provides instructive feedback to someone who is trying to learn that craft or endeavor.

middle school Typically a school which includes grades six, seven, and eight.

Migrant Education A federally funded compensatory program for children whose parents migrate seasonally due to their jobs. The program is designed to help these students overcome any academic disadvantages and slowed achievement that may be created by their migrancy. Migrant Education programs may in part correlate with Chapter I programs. (see also *Chapter I*)

monitor A person who serves as a noninstructional overseer of the activities of students, such as a teacher's aide or parent volunteer in a public school classroom.

motivation system Means by which a teacher or a school staff attempts to direct or control students' behavior, including learning behavior. In public schools extrinsic reinforcers are typically used, such as smiley stickers (the new gold stars), parties and special events, grades, threats, loss of privileges, and suspension.

Research indicates that intrinsic rewards (felt within the child and inherent within the activity) are more effective motivators for the development of long-term patterns of behavior. (see Appendix B)

music education Instruction involving music for pleasure, recognition of musical instruments, harmony, note-reading, music appreciation and history, and so on.

National Teacher Exam A standardized test of basic English and mathematical skills and of knowledge of the field of education used by some states in the process of teacher certification.

networking The sharing of information about home schooling through informal contact among individuals or groups. Newsletters, support group meetings, one-on-one exchanges, consultations, referrals, shared resources or resource information, and joint activity days and field trips are a few networking activities.

nonpublic education All education programs which do not receive local, state or federal government funds.

normal curve equivalent (NCE) (see *Annual Evaluation* in Section Three)

normed test A standardized test for which there are available past-performance averages which enable a child's test scores to be compared to those of other children who took the same test.

notice of intent (see *statement of intent*)

notice of test selection A statement made by a home-schooling parent to a local school district or state department of education naming the specific standardized achievement test that will be used as part of a student's annual evaluation process.

occupational education (see *vocational education*)

official curriculum Written learning goals and objectives, usually listed by subject area, recommended or mandated by a school district's board of education for teaching in its district.

official policy Policies officially adopted by a district school board.

on-task time In-school time during which a student is actually engaged in learning activities. The amount of engaged or on-task time varies considerably in different classrooms, and studies show a direct relationship between the amount of on-task time and the amount of learning that takes place. (see also Appendix B)

Our Nation at Risk Report prepared by the National Commission on Excellence in Education and presented to the American people in 1983. The report heavily criticized the condition of public education in the United States and fueled the ongoing criticism of public education that had been occurring in the public media.

outcomes-based instruction (see Appendix A)

parent-principal conference A formal meeting between a school's principal and a child's parent(s) for the purpose of resolving a problem that exists in the child's educational program which the parent is unable to resolve at a lower level of the educational hierarchy. In the case of home schooling, a parent-principal conference may involve such matters as a child's participation in some extra-curricular activity or making use of a school resource like the library.

parent rights Legally mandated rights that parents have with respect to the public schools, such as the right to review their children's school records or to have a child evaluated for special education services. Sometimes used in reference to other than legally mandated rights by various parent advocacy groups.

parent-teacher conference A meeting between one or both parents and a child's teacher. Typically an initial parent-teacher conference is scheduled by school personnel at the end of the first quarter of the school year (and sometimes subsequent quarters) for the purpose of presenting an overview of a child's instructional program and indicating the child's progress therein.

parochial school A school operated by a religious organization.

percentile score (see "Annual Evaluation" in Section Three)

performance assessment A progress assessment in which a student demonstrates the skills and knowledge he was attempting to learn. The actual act of performance (not testing) is carried out.

permanent file A complete record of a child's educational progress maintained throughout a child's school years. This file includes yearly grades in all courses, attendance records, and achievement test scores. A copy of a child's permanent file is normally transferred with the child from school to school.

phonics (see Appendix A)

physical education Courses in which students learn about and practice physical exercises, recreational games and sports, teamwork, and sportsmanship.

physical therapist School or other professional personnel who treat children's physical handicaps through special exercises.

placement test A form of achievement test administered to a child in order to help make a decision about which grade level, reading program, or other instructional setting will best suit his educational needs.

policy manual A notebook containing a school district's official policies. (see also *official policy*)

portfolio A file folder containing examples of a student's work and also perhaps of written assessments.

prescriptive teaching (see *diagnostic/prescriptive teaching*)

primary Grades kindergarten, one, two, and three.

principal A school's chief administrative officer who is responsible for the overall operation of the school. This responsibility includes the supervision of all personnel, budget and physical plant management, instructional leadership, and community relations.

principle approach (see Appendix A)

private school A school established and operated by a private group which typically espouses a common educational philosophy and/or value system. A Christian school is one example. In some states, a single-family home school may be a private school.

programmed learning (see Appendix A)

progress assessment An evaluation of a student's progress in a particular educational subject, program or setting. Such an assessment may include formal testing, review of past work, observations and/or interviews, and other means of assessment.

Public Law 94-142 The Education for All Handicapped Children Act passed by Congress in 1975. This legislation was designed to ensure that handicapped students throughout the nation received appropriate educational services. It provides money to states to accomplish this, while requiring states to prove that they are doing so.

quarter One-fourth of a school year. The typical time when schools report to parents the educational progress their children are making in an instructional program. In a few states home schoolers are expected to submit quarterly progress reports.

raw score (see "Annual Evaluation" in Section Three)

readiness A young child's ability to successfully deal with kindergarten and first grade academics and socialization, or any child's ability and inclination to successfully learn to read or to learn other skills at a particular age.

reading Instruction involving learning activities in phonics and other means of word attack, comprehension, literature, fluency, and so on. (see also Appendix A)

reading comprehension (see Appendix A)

reading fluency (see Appendix A)

register (see *attendance register/record*)

religious conflict exemption An official exemption from compulsory attendance in public school granted to a child for religious reasons.

remedial reading Special instruction in reading provided to children who are decidedly below average in reading skills for their age or grade placement. Remedial reading is necessitated by the graded-classroom approach to instruction. Research shows that short term reading gains attributed to remedial reading instruction often wash out over several month's time. Research also indicates that the best remediation may simply be great amounts of reading and listening to stories and literature.

report card An individual report provided by a school to both its students and their parents in an effort to indicate the degree of academic and social success being achieved by the student in question. The grades and other indicators of such achievement can only be correctly interpreted through an understanding of the criteria a given teacher uses while completing the report card.

resource room A classroom where a *special education* teacher provides supplemental instruction primarily to *learning disabled* and other handicapped children. A student's visits to the resource room may be for instruction in one or more subjects (typically reading and math) and often vary in prescribed length.

retention Requiring a student to repeat a year of schooling at the same grade level due to a lack of academic progress and hence lack of preparation for the next grade. Colloquially termed "flunking."

rote learning Learning by memorization.

safety/health education Instruction including such topics as personal hygiene, nutrition, traffic awareness, bicycle safety, fire safety and escape, drug and poison awareness.

SAT Scholastic Aptitude Test — A verbal and mathematical aptitude test given to pre-college students to determine their potential for college success.

satellite school A school which enrolls home students as satellite students. Satellite school services may be minimal and primarily provide a legal option for otherwise illegal home schoolers or cover for home schoolers who want to avoid standardized achievement tests. On the other hand, the services may be many and perhaps include correspondence courses, record-keeping services, consultations, materials, testing, and others.

school board Elected, non-paid officials who are responsible for the overall operation of a school district. May also be referred to as a board of directors or board of trustees. A school board's main responsibilities include the establishment of general policies, the hiring of a district superintendent, and budgetary decisions. School district employees then implement school board policies in the day-to-day operation of the schools within the district.

school counselor A certified school employee with special training who provides professional counseling services to students. Such services can range from giving students guidance regarding vocational choices to assisting them with both short-term and long-term emotional problems.

school officials Local and state school board members, state department of education administrative personnel, local school district superintendents, assistant superintendents, principals, vice principals. Some states also have county level school officials, such as a county superintendent.

school psychologist A certified educational specialist with concentrated training in the field of psychology. The individual most responsible for a student's evaluation for special education through the use of I.Q. and other tests.

school suppliers Companies that sell textbooks and workbooks, record forms, subject specific equipment and materials, and other school products. These companies vary in size and may support one or more curricular areas. Some cater exclusively to the needs of home-schooling parents.

school year The period between the first and last days of a designated block of instructional time. During this time period a student supposedly learns the outlined content of a particular curriculum. For example, third grade reading, third grade math, etc., are covered during the third grade school year. Each state has designated a minimum number of days that comprises a full school year.

sciences Biology, physics, chemistry, astronomy, geology, earth science and other common science courses at levels of difficulty appropriate to the ages/grades of the students being taught.

scope and sequence chart A chart accompanying a curriculum or a textbook series which shows the sequence of learning goals and skills that are covered in the curriculum or series.

secondary (high school) Grades nine, ten, eleven, and twelve. In some school districts grades seven and eight are also designated as *secondary.*

semester One-half of a school year. In high school, some courses of study last just one semester.

sequential curriculum (or sustained curriculum) A curriculum listing learning goals and objectives in order of increasing difficulty.

sight word approach (see Appendix A)

slow learner A student whose academic progress is slower than that of his peers. Such a designation may be appropriate in only one subject, such as arithmetic, or in all subjects. A student may make slow progress for a number of reasons besides ability, reasons such as language barriers, lack of background information, or inexperience, or poor prior instruction.

social behavior A student's interactions with his peers and with school personnel in the normal routine of a school day. In the case of home-schooled children, peers would include other children with whom a child interacted, and school personnel would include the general adult community that comprises the child's extended learning community.

social progress The development of age-appropriate individual and group interaction skills.

social promotion The passing of a student from one grade to another even though the student has not mastered the year's curriculum. This action is frequently taken due to a student's chronological age and sometimes physical size, limited probability of academic success through retention, or the potential emotional damage resulting from retention.

social studies Courses involving history, government, current events, sociology, world cultures, citizenship, and so on.

socialization Development of social characteristics such as cooperation, participation, a sense of brotherhood, and interpersonal behavior.

special education A program in each public school of legally-mandated educational services for students who are defined as mentally-retarded, emotionally disturbed, learning disabled, etc. Special education also includes special services for gifted and talented students when such services are provided. (see also *Public Law 94-142*)

special services Education-related services provided to children in addition to the regular curricular and extra-curricular instructional program. These services are often designed to enable a student to participate successfully in the regular program, often encompass what is otherwise referred to as special education, and may include additional services such as counseling, physical therapy, and speech therapy.

speech therapist School or other professional personnel who treat children with speech defects or provide other special education programs for them.

standard error of measurement (see "Annual Evaluation" in Section Three)

standardized achievement test A test which measures academic achievement, is given under the same conditions in each testing (hence is *standardized*), and which has *norms* which enable a student's test results to be compared with those of other children.

standards Content standards define what students should know and be able to do as a result of a series of learning experiences in a given content or discipline area; e.g. science. Performance standards, sometimes referred to as performance expectations, define the level at which students are expected to demonstrate such knowledge and skills.

state board of education A group of citizens usually appointed by a governor which provides policy direction for a state's commissioner of education (or similar administrator) and hence a state's department of education in implementing the educational program of a state government.

state commissioner of education The executive officer of a state's department of education responsible to a state board of education. May be referred to as state superintendent of schools.

state department of education The division of state government that administers public education in a given state. Responsibilities typically include the licensing (certification) of all professional education personnel, managing the state's funding of school districts, serving as a flow-through agency for federal funds, establishing recommended state curricula, and providing technical assistance to school district personnel.

statement of intent Also called *declaration of intent, notice of intent,* and *home-school proposal.* A statement of intent is in effect an enrollment document, enrollment, that is, in a home school. It also often includes a home-school program plan and other requirements. Statement of intent and home-school proposal formats and contents vary from state to state.

student placement Placement of a student in a particular classroom, with a particular teacher, or at a given grade level.

student rights Legal and other rights guaranteed to all students by the Constitution and federal statutes, by state laws governing public education, and sometimes by school district policies.

success/failure ratio The percent of problems or questions which a student completes successfully while engaging in guided practice or independent work. If lessons are at appropriate levels, a student will experience at least 75% success during guided practice and close to 100% success during independent work.

superintendent The executive officer of a school district, responsible for the administration of the district's education program, fiscal and facilities management, etc. The superintendent is hired by and responsible to the district school board.

support group A group of parents who home school their own children or are otherwise involved in the home-schooling movement and who provide encouragement and assistance to each other and to newcomers interested in learning more about home schooling. (see also *networking*)

sustained silent reading (see Appendix A)

syllabus A description of a course of instruction that includes a statement of the course goals, learning objectives, the general topics covered, materials to be used, teacher expectations with respect to assignments, grading procedures, assignment due dates and test dates, and time periods for various other instructional activities.

teacher competency test A standardized test administered to a teacher or potential teacher to determine whether or not the individual in question possesses skills and knowledge thought essential to successful teaching. Many present teacher competency tests are nothing more than basic skills tests at approximately an eighth to tenth grade level. (see also *National Teacher Exam*)

teacher expectation (see Appendix B)

teacher qualifications The requirements in a particular state for the issuance by the state's department of education of a certificate (or license) to teach in a public school. Teacher qualifications usually include at a minimum the possession of a bachelor's degree and the completion of a teacher training program at a college or university. Teacher qualifications for home schoolers vary greatly and in most states do not mandate teacher certification.

teacher's manual/guide A book that accompanies student textbooks and which shows or suggests how to teach the material in the textbook, and which sometimes suggests supplementary activities.

teacher-student interaction (see Appendix B)

test format The manner in which the questions on a test are presented. Examples: essay questions, multiple choice, true or false, select the one answer that is not correct, etc. The manner in which a student indicates an answer is also part of the test format. For example, completing an answer may involve circling a number or letter, checking a box, filling in a space. Students familiar with a test's format prior to taking the test tend to achieve higher scores than students with equal knowledge of the test's content but who are unfamiliar with the test format.

testing service An organization or individual authorized to administer certain tests. Some states require home schoolers to have their children take an annual achievement test, administered by an authorized party such as someone from a testing service.

test management guide A handbook test publishers make available to schools who use their tests. Includes information regarding testing environments, test readiness activities, test item formats, and outlines of test content.

textbook series A series of books in one subject area, one text for each ability level or grade level, published by a single publishing company. Students progress from text to text as they move from grade to grade.

thematic lessons (see Appendix A)

traditional instruction (see Appendix A)

transcript A record of classes completed, credits earned, grades achieved and diplomas or degrees awarded to an individual by an educational institution such as a high school or college.

transition time The time required in a classroom to move from one learning activity to another. A part of noninstructional time.

umbrella school (see *satellite school*)

unit study (see Appendix A)

unofficial policy Customary practices established informally by school personnel and carried on as tradition.

vocational education Courses intended to prepare students to enter vocations. Often include business courses and industrial arts courses.

waived regulation The exempting of an individual from the requirements of a regulation. For instance, in the case of home schoolers, sometimes teacher certification requirements can be waived.

whole-language approach (see Appendix A)

WISC The Wechsler Intelligence Scale for Children. The most commonly used intelligence test in public schools.

word attack (see Appendix A)

writing process (see Appendix A)

❊❊❊❊❊❊❊❊❊❊❊❊❊❊❊❊❊❊❊❊❊❊❊❊❊❊❊❊❊❊❊❊❊❊❊❊❊❊

Index of Checklists, Worksheets and Samples

State Index

General Index

ORDER FORM

Your name and address:

_____

_____

_____

Qty.	Title	Price
_____	Home School: Taking the First Step	$14.95
_____	How to Write...a Curriculum ...	$12.95
	Add $2.00 shipping for the first book & 50¢ for each additional book:	$ _____
	TOTAL	$ _____

☐   Check enclosed.

☐   VISA   Expiration Date:_____

☐   MasterCard Expiration Date:_____

Card Number:_____

Signature:_____

**Mail to
Mountain Meadow Press
P.O. Box 318
Sitka AK 99835-0318**